"Engaging and compelling…. A fierce and often very funny guide to the distaff side of geekdom."

—*LOS ANGELES TIMES*

"Part biography, part memoir, part detective story and part #MeToo pushback again~~st th~~ ~~fi~~ deep-rooted patri

—*THE WASHI*

"If you loved *Hidden Figures*, ~~y~~ biography of Disney's first female ~~…~~ Hollywood's only woman (still) to design a monster for a major motion picture."

—*TOWN AND COUNTRY*

"*The Lady from the Black Lagoon* is a marvel."

—*TOR.COM*

"An incisive criticism of the erasure of women in Hollywood through the lens of the life and legacy of Milicent Patrick."

—*BUSTLE*

"O'Meara's investigative skills match her crackling, engaging prose. Even her footnotes are hilarious. This is a wonderful, enlightening mixture of film history, memoir and love letter to the horror movie genre."

—*SHELF AWARENESS*

"A long-overdue tribute to Milicent Patrick, who made her way in Hollywood when women were never given equal standing."

—**CHARLAINE HARRIS, #1** *New York Times* **bestselling author**

"*The Lady from the Black Lagoon* is not just a story that needed to be told; the exact right person told it…. Profound."

—**JOSH MALERMAN, author of** *Bird Box*

MALLORY O'MEARA

THE LADY FROM THE BLACK LAGOON

HOLLYWOOD MONSTERS AND THE LOST LEGACY OF MILICENT PATRICK

Published 2021 by Rebellion Publishing Ltd,
Riverside House, Osney Mead, Oxford, OX2 0ES, UK

ISBN: 978-1-78108-902-6

First published by Hanover Square Press, 2019

10 9 8 7 6 5 4 3 2 1

A CIP catalogue record for this book is available from the British
Library.

Printed in Denmark

To all the monster girls.
Show them your teeth.

TABLE OF CONTENTS

*In a low-cut, tight-fitting black crepe dress, worn under a
white lace coat, with flashing necklace, earrings and bracelets,
Miss Patrick, who is of Italian German descent, looked a lot more
like a fashion illustration herself than a creator of bizarre monsters.
Unmarried, she admits to no current romance.*

*"Why should I bother with the Hollywood wolves?" she murmured.
"I'm happy with my monsters."*

—Milicent Patrick in an interview with journalist Jane Corby for the
Brooklyn Daily Eagle, Valentine's Day, 1954

AUTHOR'S NOTE

During the course of Milicent Patrick's life, she went by many names. To keep things straight for me as a writer and you as a reader, I'm going to refer to her as Milicent throughout the book, even during the early days of her life, long before she decided to call herself Milicent Patrick. Milicent was the name that she chose for herself. It's the name I'll use to tell her story.

INTRODUCTION

In 1954, Milicent Patrick was an artist working for the world-renowned special effects shop at Universal Studios in California, the movie company famous for its monsters. Dracula, the Mummy, the Wolfman and Frankenstein's monster all had leaped from the studio there onto the silver screen and eventually, into the pantheon of film legends. That year, Universal was gearing up to unleash their latest horror creation upon the world, *Creature from the Black Lagoon*, and Milicent Patrick had just made history by designing it. No woman had ever designed a monster for a major motion picture before.

Universal sent Milicent on a press tour across the country to promote the film. During the months she was away, a storm of resentment and jealousy raged back at the studio. The head of the makeup shop, a man named Bud Westmore, wanted the recognition Milicent was getting. Even though he received sole on-screen credit for the Creature, he couldn't stand seeing Milicent in the spotlight while he stayed behind at Universal. By the time she returned to Hollywood, she no longer had a job. He pulled her from the film projects she had already started working on and refused to hire her for future work.

After that, Milicent never designed another monster. She never designed anything for film ever again. Her name faded into obscurity while the Creature went on to become one of the most iconic movie creations of all time.

On-screen credits in the 1950s were not as comprehensive as they are today; her name does not appear anywhere in the film. Her contribution to cinematic history soon sank into a black lagoon of its own. The only people who remembered her were dedicated monster fans. Even they were in the dark as to where she went, what happened to her.

That's where I come in.

Until I started writing this book, the previous few paragraphs were all I, or any of my horror film colleagues, knew about Milicent Patrick. She is, at the time that I write this in 2018, still the only woman to have designed an iconic movie monster. Her rise, fall and disappearance behind-the-scenes in Hollywood is the type of story films are made of, the type of story that needs to be told.

This book started as a straightforward biography, the fascinating story of a fascinating person. But the more people I told about the project, the more I was asked why I was doing it. She was some woman who designed a monster for an old black-and-white movie. Why was that important?

It was a good question to think about as I began to spend all my savings and all my spare time investigating what happened to this woman who I didn't know and wasn't related to. Why *was* I doing this? Why did it matter so much?

When I first heard Milicent's story, my heart lurched with a terribly familiar ache. Hearing about a career beset by sexism, I could easily put myself in her shoes. I have the same pair—every woman in film has them. They're standard issue and they're uncomfortable as hell. Almost every day of my life as a filmmaker, I face the same kind of infuriating, misogynistic bullshit that

Milicent faced in 1954. I didn't have to imagine what it felt like for her because I constantly feel it myself.

So many women share this experience, women in every profession. We're ignored, sexually harassed, talked down to, plagiarized and insulted in and out of the workplace. It's worse if you're a woman of color, a queer woman, a disabled woman, a transwoman and worse still if you're a combination of any of these. I don't know a single woman working in my field, or any creative field, or any field at all, who cannot relate to Milicent Patrick. It's not just her story. It's mine, too.

This toxic environment made it difficult to uncover much of Milicent's history. The sad truth is that many of the male collectors and historians I spoke to who had pictures or information about her were only interested because she was gorgeous, not because of her artistic talent. Some openly scoffed at the project and doubted her contribution to film history. But I never doubted Milicent. From the first time I saw a picture of her, I knew she was exceptional.

I was seventeen years old when I found out about Milicent Patrick.

I had just finished watching *Creature from the Black Lagoon* for the first time. Like millions of viewers before me, I was completely entranced. The film is a masterpiece. Over sixty years have passed since it was released and it's still stunning. The story, about a group of archaeologists who travel to South America to investigate the mysterious fossil of a fish-man hybrid, is compelling. For an old monster movie, it holds up. The cast is a pleasure to watch, with lead Julie Adams lighting up the screen.

As with all great monster movies though, the true star is the Creature himself. He is still one of the best designed and recognizable movie monsters in Hollywood history. The pairing of grace and primal power as he moves through the murky depths of the lagoon is astounding. You can't tear your eyes away from the horror and beauty of his longing as he swims beneath the heroine. The Creature is absolute movie magic.

Like all the best magic tricks, I needed to know how it was done.

This is a normal thing for me. I see a great movie, look up everything about it online and learn about all the people and processes involved in creating it. That's just what nerds do. But this time was different.

All of the well-known special effects artists are men. The Wolfman, Frankenstein's[1] monster, Dracula, King Kong, Godzilla—the artists who created all of them were male. Even the most devoted monster geek—which, at seventeen, I already was—would have a hard time naming a woman in the field.

This didn't seem strange to me. It was status quo. All of my monster-making heroes—Rick Baker (*American Werewolf in London*), Tom Savini (*Dawn of the Dead*), Dick Smith (*The Exorcist*), Jack Pierce (*The Wolfman, Frankenstein*)—were guys. I had never seen myself reflected in the world of horror filmmaking. The possibility of it never crossed my mind.

So, I sat at my computer and read about *Creature from the Black Lagoon*. I happily stuffed new movie facts into my brain. Directed by notable 1950s science fiction director Jack Arnold, shot in 3D, inspired by *Beauty and the Beast*; cool, cool, cool. I scrolled down and studied the black-and-white behind-the-scenes photos.

Then, there she was.

A beautiful, statuesque woman leaning over the Creature with a paint brush. *Milicent Patrick, animator and creature designer*, the photo caption said. She worked on the monster suit with an easy confidence and a broad smile. This woman would have turned

---

1 One of the most iconic monsters of all time, created by Mary Shelley, the woman who invented the science fiction genre by publishing *Frankenstein: or The Modern Prometheus* in 1818. She started writing the book in 1816 when she was only nineteen years old, making her the ultimate goth badass.

heads in any room she walked in. But standing on a film set, working on amazing special effects, she was galvanizing to me.

She clearly didn't fetch coffee for anyone. She wasn't someone's assistant. She wasn't being helplessly carried away in the arms of the monster. She was creating it. Looking at this picture was like being struck by lightning. It was the first time in my life I had ever seen a picture of a woman like that.

Milicent was holding a door open for me that I never realized I had considered closed. Come on, she said. We belong here, too.

I accepted her invitation. I make monster movies for a living. I produce them, I write them. Over the years, I searched for information, for anything that could tell me more about her. For all of my adult life and film career, Milicent Patrick has been a guiding light, a silent friend, a beacon reminding me that I belonged.

But while Milicent opened the door to horror filmmaking for me, the door to her own story was closed. Information on her life was scarce and often contradictory. Some claimed that she didn't design the Creature at all.

As I worked my way into the business, I thought of all the girls in the world, girls who love monsters, girls who love film. These girls are sitting on the sidelines, not content to watch, but filled with a frustrated desire for momentum and creation. All these girls are potential artists, designers and filmmakers. It's so difficult to be something if you cannot envision it. To see no way in, to see the world that you love populated exclusively with those who are not like you is devastating.

I wanted to whisper in all those thousands and thousands of ears that yes, you belong. Yes, you can do it. Look, look at this woman, she did it, and she did it way back in the 1950s. Seeing Milicent Patrick work on the Creature blasted open my mind and I wanted to amplify that force, immortalize it. Because the hard truth is that yes, Milicent did it over sixty years ago, but not many women have done it since. As a woman currently working in the same field she did, I can see some improvements, but not many. Certainly not enough for how many decades have passed. Every female filmmaker I know has struggled and continues to struggle against the same hardships that Milicent faced. Looking at the statistics, it is easy to see why someone would be surprised to discover that a woman was involved in designing one of the most famous movie monsters of all time.

In 1981, the Academy of Motion Picture Arts and Sciences finally created an Oscar category for Best Makeup and Hairstyling. Rick Baker won the inaugural award for his legendary special effect creations in *An American Werewolf in London*. Since then, men have been given roughly twice as many Oscars as women have in that category, and have been nominated three times as often. This is actually a very impressive ratio, considering that in the category of Best Visual Effects (digital effects integrated with live action), women have been nominated only three times since 1939, and only won once (Sara Bennett for the film *Ex-Machina*). Those women are also, by and large, white. The two Special Achievement Awards in this category have both been given to men.

I would cite sources for the stats here, but I could find none. I had to go through lists of all the nominees and winners of both categories, count them and do the math myself. These depressing statistics do not just affect women in the special effects world, either. Fortunately for my math skills, and the wallet of my local bartender, the miserable facts about women in other parts of the film industry are well documented, thanks to the Center for the Study of Women in Television and Film.

One hundred percent of the top American films of 1954, the year *Creature from the Black Lagoon* was released, were directed by men. Ninety-six percent of the top American films for 2016, the year I started writing this book, were directed by men. In sixty-two years, we have improved gender equality in American film directing by four percent. At this rate, we'll be colonizing

Mars before we see an equal number of female directors.[2] It's terrible all the way down the line of the film crew, too. There has been only one female cinematographer even nominated for an Oscar. Eighty-one percent of films do not have female production designers. Ninety-nine percent of films do not have any female gaffers or key grips.[3]

All of this…and women account for fifty-one percent of movie goers. We see more movies, but see less of ourselves reflected in those who make them. This is why Milicent was such a miracle to me.

Women have always been the most important part of monster movies. As I walked home one night, I realized why. Making my way down dark city streets to my apartment in Brooklyn, I was alert and on edge. I was looking for suspicious figures, men that could be rapists, muggers or killers. I felt like Laurie Strode in *Halloween*.

Horror is a pressure valve for society's fears and worries: monsters seeking to control our bodies, villains trying to assail us in the darkness, disease and terror resulting from the consequences of active sexuality, death. These themes are the staple of horror films.

There are people who witness these problems only in scary movies. But for much of the population, what is on the screen is merely an exaggerated version of their everyday lives. These are forces that women grapple with daily. Watching Nancy Thompson escape Freddy Krueger's perverted attacks reminds me of how I daily fend off creeps asking me to smile for them on the subway. Women are the most important part of horror because,

---

2   This is not an exaggeration. Sally Ride became the first American woman in space in 1983. Kathryn Bigelow became the first woman to win an Oscar for Best Director in 2010, the first and only. Sixty women have been to space. It's harder for women to get into Hollywood than it is for us to get to *space*.

3   Production designers are in charge of the art department and work closely with the cinematographer and costume designer to create the overall look of the film. Key grips oversee the other grips, the rigging technicians on a set. Gaffers head up the electrical department on films.

by and large, women are the ones the horror happens to. Women have to endure it, fight it, survive it—in the movies and in real life. They are at risk of attack from real-life monsters. In America, a woman is assaulted every nine seconds.

Horror films help explore these fears and imagine what it would be like to conquer them. Women need to see themselves fighting monsters. That's part of how we figure out our stories. But we also need to see ourselves behind-the-scenes, creating and writing and directing. We need to tell our stories, too.

Unfortunately, just like in the rest of the film world, the statistics of women working in the horror genre are abysmal. In 2016, of all the film genres, women were least likely to work in horror. In the face of these odds, Milicent should have been hailed as a hero. She's not just the queen of monsters, she's the goddamn Joan of Arc. When I drive down Hollywood Boulevard, I should have to honk at a group of incorrigible drunken tourists as they take selfies with a statue of her. Milicent's incredible life should have earned her an honored place in film history. But few even recognize her name.

There's still time to change that.

1

Establishing Shot

Having a new tattoo really sucks.

Getting one isn't a total picnic either, unless you're into being stabbed repeatedly with ink-covered needles. Hey, I'm not one to judge. But I've always found the aftermath to be the toughest part. Over a few weeks, your tattoo undergoes a transformation from raw, open wound, to itchy, flakey mess. Eventually, the swelling goes down and you stop wanting to scratch it. The irritation fades. It's a part of you now, in your skin. All that suffering and you can't even feel it there. Those weeks of discomfort are worth it, though. You get to dedicate a place on your body to an idea you believe in, a piece of art you think is beautiful, to something beloved.

The tattoo I walked into that party trying not to itch was all three.

It was a portrait of Milicent Patrick being embraced by the Creature from the Black Lagoon. I had had it for a couple of weeks and there was still some residual discomfort. The tattoo wraps around the underside of my left forearm and I was holding it at the awkward angle you usually reserve for holding other people's babies.

The party took place at the Manhattan headquarters of The Society of Illustrators, blocks away from Central Park on the Upper East Side. It was a long haul on the subway from where I lived in Brooklyn and by the time I arrived, I was thrilled to step out of the biting December air. New York City can be beautiful in the winter, but that doesn't make it any less miserably cold.

Milicent was my eighteenth tattoo and not one that I expected. It wasn't that I planned on stopping at number seventeen. I was twenty-five years old and had been steadily accumulating tattoos since being legally able to at age eighteen. Thanks to my full-time job as a genre film producer, I didn't have to stop accumulating them. There's a different definition of "looking professional" when you make horror and science fiction movies for a living. That said, I didn't expect to get this particular tattoo because I had always shied away from portraits of real people. It's difficult to find an artist talented enough to put one to flesh that doesn't end up looking like some child's nightmarish drawing.

The suggestion came while I was getting tattooed by my regular artist, Matt Buck, a few months before. Matt and I have similar tastes and over the many uncomfortable hours we spent together while I paid him to stab me, we talked about the things we love: horror and monsters. During this particular session, *Creature from the Black Lagoon* was mentioned. Like a nerdy Old Faithful, I began my usual gushing about Milicent. I never missed a chance to tell people what little I knew of her story. Matt had heard of the Creature, but never of Milicent. By now, I was used to people exclaiming, "Wow, I never knew it was designed by a woman!"

Ever the artist, Matt wanted to see a picture of her. I pulled one up on my iPhone and he whistled.

"Man, I'd love to tattoo her on you. She looks incredible."

"I don't know, dude. I'm not into portraits."

"Let me draw something up. I promise, it'll be amazing."

"Okay...but you've got to incorporate the Creature into it, too."

Holiday parties always make me uncomfortable. I don't really celebrate any holiday that isn't Halloween. I wear only black, so it's difficult to pick out festive holiday wear from my regular wardrobe. Everyone wants to air kiss and I never figured out how to do that without looking like I'm trying to eat someone's ear. All of this makes me want to find an air vent to crawl into.[4] As far as holiday parties go though, this one was fine. Since it was in The Society of Illustrators building, there was a lot of gorgeous art to look at. Many of my friends were there. Also, free food.

It was my second holiday season in New York City. Two years before, I moved from Rhode Island to Brooklyn so I could live with my boyfriend. Said boyfriend was also the reason that I moved from my warm bed and to-be-read book pile to the party that night.

The air in the room was stuffy with conversations, with wine and warm string lights combining to make everybody glow. As I meandered among clusters of increasingly drunk partygoers, Milicent's portrait throbbed on my forearm. Scratching a new tattoo can damage it, so I had to make do with surreptitiously slapping the area around it and trying not to look like a weirdo conga drummer.

The social merry-go-round of the party kept turning and eventually I found myself talking to Sam Morgan, a literary agent friend of mine. Sam is a great person to hang out with at a party because he's extremely funny, but more importantly, extremely tall and easy to find in a crowd. We started talking and he asked about my new tattoo, a picture of which I had recently posted on Facebook. Everyone who had seen the tattoo was wowed by the portrait. It made a lot of people curious, including Sam. He wanted to know more about Milicent.

---

4   If you're into *Die Hard*, this counts as a holiday activity.

When I walked into the tattoo shop for the appointment, I looked on Matt's desk and fell in love. Milicent's face commands attention no matter what medium it's in. Matt kept his word; it was an amazing sketch. He had penciled a stunning portrait of her adorned in pearls with the Creature looking over her shoulder, his long, scaly arm reaching around with a protective hug. I was struck, just like I was the first time I saw her, with how capable and collected she looked.

A few months before, the first monster movie I had ever worked on was released and Milicent Patrick had been an inspiration through the entire process. If I was going to have any face permanently inked into my skin, hers was the one. She was a talisman I always carried. Now it wasn't just metaphorical.

I finished gushing to Sam about Milicent, her work and her mystery, enthusiasm enhanced by my second glass of house white. He looked at the tattoo again.

"Man, that story would make a great book."

"Oh, shit, yeah it would!"

"You should write it."

I laughed.

"No, really. You should. It's a great story."

Thanks to that second glass of house white, I had to make my way to the bathroom. As I walked into the stall, my mind whirled from more than booze. I was stuck on Sam's words. Surrounded by fantastic art by famous illustrators, I thought about how Milicent belonged in there, too.[5] Why shouldn't I tell her story?

The idea was so exciting that I was finally distracted from wanting to scratch the tattoo.

A few days later, I saw Sam again at another event. This time he was accompanied by Brady McReynolds, who worked at the

---

5   Maybe not in the stall. Although, to be fair, there were some amazing pieces in that bathroom.

same literary agency. Brady is one of the friendliest, most equanimous people you'll ever meet. He's the kind of person you hope to consult if you ever have to buy an expensive, confusing appliance. The three of us started talking about the tattoo of Milicent and the concept of a book about her life. Brady was enthusiastic about the idea. He encouraged me to think about writing it and offered to send some information about creating a nonfiction project.

I wanted to tell Milicent's story, of course I did. But first, I had to find it. I'm not a detective. I had no clue where to start tracking her down. Most of the time, I can barely keep track of my sunglasses. Milicent lived in a time before the miraculous internet. How do you find people without Facebook?

Getting tattooed requires some serious dedication. Hours and hours of being stabbed with tiny needles as something hopefully beautiful and maybe meaningful is driven into you. It's the reverse of writing. If I could get tattooed for Milicent, I could write for her, too.

Milicent Patrick was born Mildred Elisabeth Fulvia Rossi on November 11, 1915. I found her birth certificate listed in genealogical records as Mildred Elisabeth Tuloia Rossi, which is the government equivalent of a mistake on your Starbucks cup. This name confusion was the perfect way to start a life made up of a multitude of identity changes. Milicent's propensity for shifting personas made sense once I discovered where she came from. Her life was in constant flux from the beginning.

She was born the second of three children to Camille Charles Rossi and Elise Albertina Bill. The couple met in San Francisco, California, in the early 1900s, where Elise was raised.

Elise was born in San Francisco, the blonde, blue-eyed daughter of German immigrants. Her parents, Conrad Bill and Elisabeth Krausgill, had both been born in Nieder-Weisel, Germany. They immigrated to America separately, met in San Francisco and were married in 1872, thirteen years before Elisabeth gave birth to Elise in 1885.

Elise was a society girl who loved the arts, especially theater and performance. Her family considered her unhappy, a description that would follow her into adulthood. She had what her family called a "nervous breakdown" when she was eleven years old, a term that today could mean any number of different types of mental affliction: depression, anxiety, panic attacks, a whole menagerie of illnesses. The vagueness of the term makes it impossible to say what specifically Elise was struggling with, besides some form of inner turmoil. Milicent would describe her mother as a "frustrated woman." This unhappiness and frustration was passed down to Milicent, along with her love of art in all forms.

But it was Camille who would ultimately be the force that shaped Milicent's life. And force he was. His dealings with his employees and with the women in his life deeply affected the way that Milicent interacted with the world, for better and for worse. They cast a long shadow that she was never quite able to escape.

Camille started life in Naples, Italy, in 1885. He was born Camillo John Chris Vincent Chas Rossi to Mario Rossi and Anna Lauria de Palombara. When Camille was eleven, the family immigrated to New York City, where his parents stayed for the rest of their lives. Camille was tall, with dark hair and hazel eyes. He had a sculpted face: a strong, straight nose with prominent cheekbones and heavy brows that are echoed in Milicent. From a young age, he wanted more out of life, but not just excitement. Milicent described her father as a power-hungry man. Camille wanted influence and authority. Along with a strong work ethic, Camille had a wild, ambitious streak that he rode all the way to the West Coast. Although primarily self-taught, he studied architecture at the Mark Hopkins School of Design in San Francisco, California.

At the time, San Francisco was the dominant city of the far side of the country. Its population had swelled after the Gold Rush of 1849 and it joined the forefront of urban America. Architecture was a booming industry here, and Camille, a young structural engineer, found this to be the perfect place to start his life. Mansions and hotels rivaling that of Manhattan were popping up all over the city.

More than the attraction of industry, Camille must have felt pulled toward San Francisco because of its culture. As a newer city—it was only established in 1847—traditions were not as strong here. The social climate was a little more ethnically and religiously diverse.[6] It was a hotbed of social movements and political reform. This was where the first state organization dedicated to the furtherance of women's suffrage was created, in 1869. Status and prestige could be based on individual achievement, rather than group identity. It wasn't all Yosemite-Sam-looking dudes hunting for fame and fortune, but there was an air of tradition-flouting, adventurous individualism that San Francisco's Gold Rush roots inspired. Lots of young, experimental thinkers and writers—like Mark Twain—flocked to the city. It was a place for reinvention. California has always been the place to change who you are, something Camille wanted desperately to do.

He arrived in California and started passing as a natural-born American citizen. He claimed on official documents that he had been born in 1886 in San Francisco to Andrew and Anna Rossi and that his name was Camille Charles Rossi. San Francisco had more relaxed views on immigration; at this time it was over 90 percent European American immigrants and their descendants. But Camille was an intelligent, ambitious man. It wouldn't have been difficult for him to figure out that he would have an easier shot at success in this country as an American than as an Ital-

---

6   It still wasn't great. Racism and discrimination were still widely accepted.

ian immigrant. Beautiful high-society, American Elise would have seemed like a perfect match for him. The two fell in love.

In 1906, when Elise was nineteen and Camille was twenty, a disaster halted the boom of San Francisco. On April 18, the great San Francisco earthquake hit. Over three thousand people died; the city was devastated. Buildings, infrastructure, dreams. There was a mass exodus from the city, including vast numbers of writers and artists. The roaring arts culture of San Francisco never fully recovered from this blow and the creative torch of the West was ultimately passed down to Los Angeles, a city not on a fault line. Los Angeles still has never been devastated by a major earthquake.[7]

Elise stayed in the city with her family but by 1907, Camille had left San Francisco to make his fortune. His school was one of the buildings destroyed in the earthquake. A shrewd man, it must have seemed fruitless for Camille to try to make his way in the devastated city. He headed to Mexico City and planned to return to San Francisco to marry Elise when he was financially secure. There, he was hired as a junior engineer by Adamo Boari, an Italian architect tasked with creating the Palace of Fine Arts.

Mexico City was also a city prone to earthquakes and Camille's talents were sorely needed. As a structural engineer, rather than an architect, he did not design; his job was to make sure the designs were functional. Structural engineers work as partners to architects, applying engineering principles to the construction, planning and design of a building.

It was a relatively new profession, emerging in the twentieth century as a result of the rapid technological advancements of the industrial revolution. As skyscrapers began to rise in the city, along with the use of reinforced concrete and the demand for plumbing, structural engineers were sorely needed. There were not a lot of official certification processes and it would

---

7   I'm nervous even typing that.

have been easy for Camille, with his talent and ambition, to advance in the field.

Mexico City was also an opportunity to explore his adventurous side. Camille spent his off-hours indulging in bullfighting, motorcycle and sports car racing, fencing and mountain climbing. Yes, they had sports cars back then and they weren't lumbering Model Ts. Some of them went over one hundred twenty miles an hour. They just didn't have a lot of important safety features yet, like windshields. So this was a little extra badass and also a little extra crazy. Camille sought acclaim even in his leisure activities. An expedition he was part of, up Mount Popocatépetl, was written up in the September 1910 issue of *National Geographic*.[8]

While Camille was having a blast during his recreational time, his work hours were filled with frustration. Mexico City is built on top of an underground lake and the soft subsoil the palace was being constructed on was a nightmare for the project. Camille was vocal about his dissent on the structural integrity of the building. He insisted that the soil underneath wouldn't support the palace, but he was overruled by senior engineers. The heavy building began to sink even before it was finished.

Between the structural issues and political instability—the Mexican Revolution was on its way—construction on the Palace of Fine Arts stopped in 1913 and it sat untouched for twenty years. Much like the Monty Python sketch about building a castle on top of a swamp, the palace and its sinking base became a classic symbol of things to avoid in structural engineering, something I'm sure gave Camille some satisfaction.

In 1910, Camille left the project and relocated to La Boquilla, where he took a job helping to build a dam in the region of Chi-

---

8   Overjoyed that I was finally able to justify having a subscription to *National Geographic*, I combed through their digital archives for days, looking through century-old issue after century-old issue until I found the article. There are many photos, one which supposedly includes Camille, but it is so blurry that I initially thought it was just a bad painting.

huahua. Nearly three thousand miles north of Mexico City on the Rio Conchos, La Boquilla Dam provided hydroelectricity, flood control and irrigation, and created Toronto Lake in the process. It was, at the time, slated to be one of the largest dams in the world. Nearly all of the projects Camille worked on carried some element of prestige and history.

Elise, meanwhile, was still waiting back in California with her family. After two years working on the dam, in 1912 Camille took leave and traveled back to marry her. He returned to find that the city was rapidly on the mend from the earthquake. San Francisco was being built and rebuilt in a grand way. But La Boquilla Dam was nowhere near completion and Camille wanted to continue his work down south. Together, he and Elise traveled to Mexico. This wasn't a great idea. In 1912, the Mexican Revolution was in full swing. Armed rebellions were breaking out all over the country. It wasn't a safe place to travel. Camille left Elise at the home of his friend Juan Brittingham, who lived close to the Texas border, and continued south to the dam construction site in Chihuahua.

Elise spent most of the next year with Juan's family. Juan was a pioneer in the decorative tile industry, the son of a prominent family of soap and cement magnates, which unfortunately for Juan, is one of the least impressive types of magnates. A dual citizen of Mexico and the United States, he was born in Los Angeles. In 1910, with the Border War on between the countries, those with dual citizenship were forced to declare sides. Juan declared Mexican citizenship and traveled there to build his tile business. The business did well, which meant Elise had a very comfortable home to stay in while she waited for her husband.

It's a treasured family story that while en route to the dam, Camille was captured by Pancho Villa, the infamous Mexican revolutionary. Villa originally only wanted to commandeer Camille's automobile, but once he found out that he had captured an engineer, he detained him for a while so he could also commandeer his professional skills. Pancho apparently had the idea that an engineer would be an expert on artillery. Once he realized that was not the case, he let Camille go.[9]

For the next year, Camille worked on the dam with periodic visits up north to visit Elise. In September of 1913, she discovered that she was pregnant. When he got the news, Camille decided that they should return to the United States. Widespread violence and worker strikes made Mexico an unstable work environment for anyone in construction and there was no end in sight for the roiling revolution. The dam was incomplete (it would not be finished until 1915) but he now had a pregnant wife to worry about and family on the horizon. The couple left Mexico and arrived back in San Francisco just before the birth of their first child, Ulrich Conrad Marion Rossi, on May 30, 1914.

But Camille was soon itching to get back to work, back to adventure. Within a year, in 1915, the family moved to El Paso, Texas. Camille had friends and business associates in this part of the continent and he headed as close to Mexico as he could get without actually entering the country. It was here, on November 11, 1915, that the family celebrated the birth of their second child, Mildred Elisabeth Fulvia Rossi. A few days later, on the afternoon of the seventeenth, was the biggest celebration the Southwest had ever seen. Twenty-five thousand people thronged the streets to get a glimpse of the Liberty Bell on its tour home to Philadelphia from the Panama-Pacific International Exposition, a world's fair in San Francisco. The timing was a coincidence, but I hope that little Milicent thought the excitement was for her.

In 1917, Camille took a job as a mining engineer for the Cerro de Pasco Copper Corporation and the entire family moved down to South America, to Oroya, Peru. At the time, Cerro de Pasco was the largest copper mining company in the world. It seems as if every job Camille took had to have some sort of superla-

---

9 I have been unable to confirm this, but it is a pretty cool story.

tive. Oroya is in the center of Peru, on a plateau in the Andes Mountains. Milicent, not even two years old yet, and the rest of the family had to adapt to the high, dry air and cold climate. The family stayed there for three years.

Moving from the warmth of Texas to an average temperature of forty-five degrees must have been a shock, but Elise was devoted to Camille and followed him anywhere. If she was unhappy in their new home, she wouldn't have said anything. All her husband's brilliance and ambition and work ethic came with a dark side. Camille was power hungry, both at work and at home. His will was law in the Rossi household. Later in life, Milicent would describe how strict her father was with Elise. He wouldn't tolerate being told no and had a reputation of expecting submission from all women, not just his wife and children. This came back to bite him. Unfortunately, it eventually bit Milicent, too.

In Oroya, Camille was in charge of the mining operations, a position that suited his temperament. Elise settled in and cared for Ulrich and Milicent, and in the summer of 1919, she was pregnant again. Camille stayed busy at work and applied his talents elsewhere in the town. Along with overseeing the building of the mines, Camille helped build the first modern hospital in Oroya. It was completed, conveniently, just in time for Ruth Rose to be born there on February 8, 1920. This was the last baby for Camille and Elise. At four years old, Milicent became a middle child.

Oroya did not leave much of a mark on Milicent's life. She didn't pick up a fluency in or understanding of the Spanish language. She never publicly spoke in detail about this period of her life besides occasionally mentioning that she grew up "briefly" in Peru. My guess is that she just didn't remember much and fair enough, I don't have a lot of memories from when I was a toddler, either.

A few months after Ruth was born, news reached Elise that her mother had died. She wanted to be with her family, so Camille decided that it was time to say goodbye to Peru and head back to California. Milicent was only four years old and already embarking on her second continent hop.

Camille, Elise, Ulrich, Milicent and Ruth had a lengthy trip to San Francisco. They traveled through Argentina before sailing out of Chile's Valparaíso seaport on June 12, 1920. After two and a half weeks at sea, they arrived in the sweltering New York City summer heat.

The family likely visited Camille's mother, Anna, who was living in Brooklyn. Camille's father, Mario—or Andrew, depending on who you were and when you asked—had died a couple of years earlier, in 1918. Camille did not visit his family often, so Anna would have been delighted to see her grandchildren.

With Elise anxious to return to her grieving family, the Rossis didn't stay for more than a week before embarking on the final leg of the trip. A cross-country train sounds glamorous, but this was before many of the transit luxuries we now take for granted. If you have ever looked with pity at a mother consoling a crying baby on a flight, imagine Elise traveling by car, train and ship through four countries with a baby, two small children and no disposable diapers or air conditioning.

After several days, the family finally arrived in San Francisco. The mild weather of northern California in July must have been a welcome relief. Elise's family was thrilled to have her back after so many years away. With the loss of his wife weighing on his mind, Elise's father, Conrad, pleaded with Camille to take a job closer to home. The Bills—Elise's extended family—were prosperous and deeply entrenched in San Francisco. Conrad wanted his daughter near this affluent support system. Camille agreed and began to look for work in the area. Conrad got his wish when Camille was offered the job of a lifetime.

So I wanted to learn more about Milicent. Where to begin? I didn't think I could afford a private investigator, but it couldn't hurt to check. I had fantasies of strolling into some grungy New York City office to talk to a worn-down guy wearing a fedora. He'd be smoking a cigarette and would refer to me as a dame. After some wisecracks and banter, he'd take my money and go off on a quest to find Milicent while I leaned against his desk, wearing a really nice pair of heels.[10]

Feeling a little silly but unsure where else to start, I simply Googled "NYC private investigators." The first page of results dashed all of my film-noir-inspired hopes. The companies that popped up were run by guys who looked like suburban dads. My fantasy couldn't take place on a well-manicured lawn with a guy wearing khaki shorts and flipping burgers on a grill. On a more practical note, they were also expensive. Making independent genre movies isn't like making blockbuster Hollywood movies. I was on my own.

The only publicized part of Milicent's life was her work on *Creature from the Black Lagoon*, so this was my starting block. There had to be some clues as to where she came from and where she went after the film. Sitting at my desk in Brooklyn, I started scouring the internet.

There were a handful of blogs featuring posts about her, but they were all without sources and had wildly differing claims. Some said that she had nothing to do with design of the Creature, some said that she did everything herself. None of them had any new information for me.

There was a single article about her from a notable speculative fiction website, but it was incredibly long-winded and ended up being more about the sci-fi films from the era in which she worked in Hollywood. The parts of the piece that were actually about her had no sources and the few facts of her life it presented were disputed in the comments section. Even the queen

---

10 My standing for any length of time in heels is the most unlikely part of this fantasy.

bee of unsubstantiated information, Wikipedia, had no article on her.[11] The internet failed me. I needed help.

Luckily, I had an ace up my sleeve. Many aces, actually.

There are no private investigators in my contact list, but I sure know lots of monster nerds. One of the greatest things about making horror movies is the people you meet. I'd been working in the industry for several years at that point and had an excellent network of friends and colleagues that adore monsters as much as I. My unabashed enthusiasm for the Creature was shared by many. I sent a flurry of emails out to writers and historians and filmmakers. *Of course they're going to want to help me find Milicent Patrick*, I thought.

I had no idea what I was in for.

I was so thrilled about finding people to help with this project and the prospect of bringing Milicent's story to the world that it was all the more disappointing when I began to get emails back. That disappointment quickly shifted into frustration, which shifted into rage. Most people were tentative. Several expressed doubt that her story could be more than an article, let alone fill an entire book. Some said that she didn't seem interesting enough to merit examination and implied that was why no one had looked into her story before. I don't need to tell you that every single one of these infuriating responses was from a man. These casual dismissals made me want to fling furniture through windows. Fancy, heavy furniture through large, expensive windows. One guy suggested that I not waste my time, since he thought that the only reason she was seen on the set of *Creature from the Black Lagoon* was because she was someone's girlfriend.

Molten anger bubbled inside my chest. If hate-lasers could shoot out of my eyes, I would have melted my glasses. I immediately began to craft a response to him that justified Milicent's

---

11   While I was writing this book, someone created a Wikipedia page for Milicent, but it doesn't have a lot of information and some of what is there is incorrect.

work and contribution to the film. I got about halfway through this scathing email before I realized why I was so upset.[12] It wasn't just because some crusty old dude insulted my hero. It was because having to justify and validate a female presence in a male-dominated space was a reflex.

Two years before, I helped produce a feature film called *Kids vs Monsters*, a cheesy, special effects–laden romp filled with— you guessed it—monsters. None of the crew was under the illusion that the film would be in the running for an Oscar, but I was over the moon with joy. I was making a monster movie! In Los Angeles! All around me, there were men and women in monster suits, monster puppets and artists applying amazing special effects makeup. If you stuck me with a pin, all the happiness leaking out would have made me sail around the room.

I was twenty-three years old and just an associate producer on the film. I was clinging precariously to the bottom rung of the producer hierarchy ladder. The production company, Dark Dunes Productions, had hired me only seven months before. *Kids vs Monsters* wasn't the first film I was a producer on for this company, but it was the first to go into production and would end up being my first completed film. I knew this was my foot in the door to the horror film industry and I wasn't going to take it for granted. I would sometimes work over sixty hours a week, sitting in front of my computer and monitoring my email inboxes like a hawk.

A film producer is the person who oversees the creation of the film, from its start in development as an idea or a screenplay, all the way to marketing and distributing the finished movie. There are many types of film producer: executive producer, line producer, supervising producer, etc. But a plain old producer is the one involved in every single aspect of the film at every stage of the process. You're a project manager, businessperson, people wrangler, problem solver, salesperson, logistical wizard, creative

---

12   I never sent that email. I deleted it before it set my computer on fire.

guide, financial coordinator and a supervisor. You become a producer because you adore cinema, you're great with organization and you're able to stifle the constant urge to scream. An associate producer is essentially an assistant producer. My tasks included all manner of things, from picking up a fake hand from the special effects studio, to weighing in on wardrobe choices, to running the social media pages, to hiring a sales agent. My main job, just like any producer, was to be stressed out all the time. But I loved it. I woke up for every early call time with unbridled glee.

My boss at Dark Dunes Productions, Sultan Saeed al Darmaki, was also the director of the movie. He was and is like my big brother. At the time, I lived in New England. Sultan had flown me out to Los Angeles so I could help with both the preparation and the shooting of *Kids vs Monsters*. Feeling unbelievably lucky and desperate to earn my place, I threw myself into every task assigned to me with the charged determination of a seagull on a fallen bag of Cheetos.

While running around the set, making sure nothing was literally or metaphorically on fire, I was constantly aware of the fact that I was the youngest, least experienced producer. Everyone suffers from imposter syndrome sometimes. It's the feeling that you aren't qualified and that you have no idea what you are doing. It's the feeling that you are an impostor and soon, someone will discover that fact and kick you out. I wanted to buy a hat that declared IT'S OKAY I BELONG HERE mostly so that I would believe it myself.

Toward the end of the month-long shoot, I drove over to the production office to pick up the T-shirts we had custom made for the project. Every member of the cast and crew was getting one. I rifled happily through the boxes full of black shirts, each emblazoned with the electric green words KIDS VS MONSTERS. I did it! I survived my first film shoot! I literally had the T-shirt to prove it!

One of the production managers in the office came over to see the shirts.

"Hey, Mallory, there's something I've been meaning to ask you."

I looked up.

"How often do you have to sleep with Sultan to keep your job?"

I stared at him for a moment. I wish I could tell you that a vicious, brilliant barb shot out of me. Instead, I sputtered. The joy in my chest popped like a balloon.

"Oh. I, uh, don't."

That's all I could manage.

"Really? Huh."

He shrugged and walked away. I was too stunned to be angry, too stunned to say anything further. I immediately welled up with a hundred reasons why I belonged there, a hundred things I had done in the past months to help this movie get made, a hundred justifications for my presence there in that office.

They didn't fly out of my mouth. They congealed in my stomach as I carried the shirts out to my rental car, wondering if I could fit inside one of the boxes and seal it up. A male producer, even one that was only twenty-three, would not have been asked that question. He would not have been asked to justify his presence. Because I was the only female producer and I was young, the immediate assumption was that I must be earning my place with sex. "She must be fucking her boss" instead of "Wow, she must be really good at her job."

Now, years later, I was reacting to this same assumption, except it wasn't about me.

This was it. This is what was being said between the lines in the emails I was getting back about Milicent Patrick. No one had looked into Milicent's story because she was a woman. Historians had dismissed her because she was a woman. Milicent was the only female in a male-dominated space. Instead of assuming that she was there for work because she was talented, these troglodytes assumed she was there for the only thing many men assume women are there for: male pleasure. In order to invalidate that assumption, they needed her artistic contributions to be proved beyond all doubt.

There was another artist who worked on the Creature, a man named Chris Mueller. He was a sculptor. Like Milicent, there were photos of him working on the monster suit even though his name was also left out of the credits for the film. Individual credits for those working in special effects were not usually included in movies during this period; the only name that appeared was the head of the makeup department. But Chris Mueller was included in nearly every article on *Creature from the Black Lagoon*. No one doubted his work on the monster. It wasn't even a question.[13]

It was becoming clearer with every email I received about the project that I needed to go to Los Angeles. I wasn't getting anywhere with correspondence. Nearly every film historian I spoke to was located there, along with most film archives and studios. I firmly believed there was evidence that Milicent designed the Creature and somewhere there was a clue to where she had gone. I needed to find it myself.

I was always happy to go to Los Angeles. Years of traveling there for work with Dark Dunes Productions had turned it into my second home. It could be the constant sun and warmth. It could be the omnipresent hustle of creativity. It could be the tacos. Whatever the cause, I was deeply enamored with California. Living in Brooklyn didn't agree with me. I couldn't figure out why people love New York City so much. Everything is expensive and everyone is in a rush and everything is crowded. Los Angeles was my escape.

My plan was to spend two weeks staying with friends while

---

13   I've made sure of this. I cannot find a single instance where Mueller's contributions were doubted.

I interviewed historians and investigated archives. I booked a flight, rented a car and stocked up on sunscreen.

A week before I was set to leave, however, the boyfriend I had moved to Brooklyn for dumped me. I felt like a rug had been pulled out from under me. But in the midst of a drunken cry that night, I realized that my life was much better without that rug. I didn't have to live in Brooklyn anymore! I could move to California! I already had a plane ticket!

The gracious friends who had originally offered their guest room told me that I could stay with them while I looked for a place to live. I didn't have an apartment set up. I didn't even know how I was getting all my stuff out of my now ex-boyfriend's tiny studio. My search for Milicent was the only certain thing. In the midst of all the upheaval and packing and sadness, I was reassured by how committed I was to this project, to finding Milicent.

Just like before, she was reaching out her hand to me. She belonged in Los Angeles, working on movies. I belonged there, too. I followed her to find my career, so following her to my new home felt right. Turns out she was leading me exactly where I needed to go.

2

Fade In

In 1921, when Milicent was six years old, a wonder was being built.

World War I had ended, the 1920s were starting to roar and San Francisco was enjoying its rebirth. Fifteen years had passed since the earthquake and it was a beautiful city that the Rossi family returned to.

While Camille was looking for local work, he came across an advertisement from a San Francisco architecture firm looking for a structural engineer and superintendent of construction needed in San Simeon, California. San Simeon was a day's train ride south from San Francisco, but that's not what attracted Camille. The ad was being run by Julia Morgan, the star architect in charge of creating a new summer home for William Randolph Hearst, America's first media mogul. You might not recognize Hearst's name, but you've probably seen the film loosely based on his life, Orson Welles's mighty classic *Citizen Kane*. Hearst was one of the most wealthy and influential men of his day, so this wasn't going to be any old summer home. The plans were for an opulent, over-the-top 127-acre estate known as La

Cuesta Encantada (The Enchanted Hill) that was in keeping
with his opulent, over-the-top lifestyle. Camille, always drawn
to prestige, was attracted to this project like a moth to a flame.
He applied and got the job. Hearst, his colossal and extravagant
home, and Milicent's experience growing up there would become some of the forces that shaped her life.

Hearst was born in 1863 in San Francisco, the only son of
Gold Rush millionaire[14] George Hearst.[15] After being expelled
from Harvard for misconduct—Hearst was always a partier—
he returned to San Francisco. While he was away at college, his
father had acquired the newspaper the San Francisco *Examiner*
in a bet. When Hearst arrived back on the West Coast in 1887,
he begged his father for permission to take it over. George said
yes and Hearst immediately went to work.

Right away, Hearst invested a lot of money in the *Examiner*
and upgraded all the equipment. He also wisely invested in the
best equipment of all: his writers. He hired great writers, many
of whom would go on to become American literary legends,
like Mark Twain, Ambrose Bierce and Jack London.

Along with quality writing, as the editor, Hearst encouraged
a sensational brand of reporting. The *Examiner* had a lot of old-
timey clickbait: lurid headlines, wild stories, overblown writing. Despite being booted from Harvard, Hearst was a smart
businessman. He didn't beg for the *Examiner* from his father as a
hobby; he wanted money and influence. He knew that the more
sensational his headlines, the more the papers sold.

The *Examiner* became a success and Hearst set his sights on
the East Coast. He used his profits to buy the *New York Morning*

---

14 Remember, this is an 1860s millionaire. This is I-can-pee-in-a-golden-
    chamber-pot money.

15 George owned lots of property, including, for a time, the Cerro de Pasco
    mine that Camille oversaw in Peru. Whether Camille knew this, and knew
    George, is cause for speculation. I can find no evidence that says either way.
    Small world!

Journal, and a year later started publishing the *Evening Journal.* Both papers featured his sensational reporting style. Hearst soon entered into a fierce competition with Joseph Pulitzer, the then-king of New York newspapers, who ran the *New York World.*

Hearst wanted to be the top in circulation and used his vast amounts of money to raid the staff of the *New York World,* offering them better positions at higher salaries. The term *yellow journalism* comes from this battle. The *New York World* ran a very popular cartoon, drawn by a man named George Luks, called *The Yellow Kid.* When Hearst lured Luks over to his paper with an insane sum of money,[16] Pulitzer was furious. The battle became even more intense after Pulitzer hired another cartoonist to make an unsuccessful knockoff of *The Yellow Kid.* Pulitzer and Hearst became locked in a battle of sensationalism, each trying to outsell the other with more and more eye-catching headlines, and the term *Yellow Kid journalism*—eventually shortened to *yellow journalism*—was born.

By 1897, Hearst had won out. His newspaper circulation numbers were higher than Pulitzer's. He began to buy newspapers in cities all over the country, including Chicago, Boston and Los Angeles. At his peak, he owned more than two dozen; one in four Americans would get their news from him.

He had a brief political career in New York; for four years, he was in the House of Representatives. But it was difficult to handle the responsibilities of being a representative and build his massive media empire at the same time. So in 1907, he returned to publishing.

By the time 1920 rolled around, Hearst was spreading his empire even further. The reach of media was expanding and Hearst was savvy enough to see it. His was one of the first print media companies to enter radio and he became one of the major pro-

---

16 I could not find exactly how much money was offered to Luks, but I like to imagine Hearst opening a door and Luks diving into a room full of money, Scrooge McDuck style.

ducers of movie newsreels and of movies themselves. Over his lifetime, he would produce more than a hundred films.

When he hired Morgan to build his summer home, Hearst was fifty-seven years old and his wealth and influence were enormous. The year previous, Hearst's mother died and bequeathed him the land in San Simeon. George had purchased the land in 1866, originally forty thousand acres of ranchland, a mere sixteen years after California joined the United States. The original plot belonged to a well-known Spanish California family, the Estradas. It was a cattle ranch, called Piedra Blanca Ranch, and the area was called Piedra Blancas.[17] In 1865, after a series of disasters, the family put the land up for sale. There was a massive flood that devastated the crops, followed by a drought, which devastated the cattle.[18] The families in the area were being financially ruined by tax increases and legal bills due to litigation over land grants and rights in the brand-new state of California. Welcome to America!

George purchased more and more land as the years went on, eventually totaling 168,000 acres, or 262.5 square miles. These are miles of picturesque coastal prairie, nestled between the Pacific and the rolling foothills of the Santa Lucia mountain range. The views are dramatic, but the land is difficult to develop. Earthquakes and mudslides are common and water is not in abundance. The surrounding countryside is still largely undeveloped. It has Mediterranean weather—cool wet winters and hot dry summers. Isolation, if you're a working-class rancher. Peace, if you're a rich businessman.

Being a rich businessman, George fell in love with the area. He built a beautiful redwood ranch house that would become the

---

17 Translated as "White Rock Ranch." Some books, usually the pro-Hearst ones, cite the beautiful white ocean waves breaking on the seaside rocks as reason for the name. It's actually because those lovely rocks were white from all the seabird poop. Marketing!

18 As in, lots of cattle died. Not that the cattle were like, so devastated about it being dry.

base of operations for the ranch farms. He wanted to maintain the land as a working ranch and hired a member of the Estrada family, the son of the former owner, to help run it and serve as the majordomo for the cowboys there. It would also serve as the home base when he took his son camping in the hills.

Hearst quickly adopted his father's love for the place and continued to travel to San Simeon into adulthood for camping trips. It was his escape from the stress of his life in New York City. The East Coast never grew on him and as his media empire expanded, the peaceful California hills became more and more alluring. When he and his wife, Millicent Hearst, began to have children, he would continue his father's tradition and take them camping in San Simeon.

So when the land was left to him in 1919, Hearst got the idea of building a house up in those beloved hills. He wrote to Julia Morgan. He had worked with her several years before on the headquarters for his newspaper in Los Angeles (also called the *Examiner*). "I would like to build a little something," he said. That little something ended up becoming what is now known as Hearst Castle.

Morgan accepted the project and started plans in her San Francisco office, beginning a collaboration that would last for twenty-eight years. Hearst almost immediately expanded the scope of his original idea, and the blueprints quickly started to show a massive estate. Organizing a project of that magnitude took a lot of time and a lot of money, and Hearst was willing to spend both in abundance.

In 1921, Morgan ran an ad for a structural engineer and Camille answered. He started that same year in her office, working on the rapidly multiplying plans. Morgan's office was on the thirteenth floor of the Merchant Exchange building, a fifteen-story skyscraper in the financial district near the waterside. In 1906, the building had been heavily damaged in the earthquake and Morgan had helped design the repairs. Her own small office at her parents' home was also destroyed in the earthquake, so she moved her operations into the newly repaired Merchant Exchange, where she stayed for the rest of her career. It was a beautiful office, with carved wood ceilings, marble columns, six-by-eight-foot oil paintings of ships and a library containing over five hundred books on architecture. After years of working in a remote mining town in Peru, I imagine that walking into this stately space every day would have been thrilling for Camille.

Hearst was a man who liked to do things big, a trait that jibed right away with Camille's ambitious personality. Eventually, the two men would become lifelong friends. But at the start of the project, Camille wasn't working with Hearst every day. He was working with Morgan. It was the first time in his career he had to answer to a woman.

Morgan was California's first licensed female architect. Over the course of her life, she would design almost eight hundred buildings in the state. Born in San Francisco in 1872, she studied civil engineering at the University of California at Berkeley and then went on to attend the École des Beaux Arts, one of France's most influential art schools.

The school initially refused Morgan admission because she was a woman. After two years and multiple applications, she was finally accepted. But it wasn't because all those snooty French dudes suddenly realized that sexism was bad, it was because Morgan was that talented. Even though the school eventually allowed her to attend, the administration continued to make things hard for her. Her first attempts to receive her certificate were all denied without reason. Finally, in 1902, after five years of kicking ass, she became the first woman to receive an École des Beaux Arts certification in architecture.

She returned to America and began to work for an architecture firm in San Francisco. It was very important to her to design buildings in her hometown and the use of materials that were from the surrounding area of a building project became part of her signature. Unfortunately, Morgan didn't leave the misogynistic hardships behind in France. Her first employer, John Green Howard, liked to brag to colleagues that he didn't have to pay Morgan as much because she was a woman.

Luckily, this was the firm that was hired for several projects by Phoebe Hearst, William Randolph Hearst's mother. Morgan worked on these projects and the Hearsts were impressed with her work. They became clients that she would take with her when she opened her own office in 1904. Suck it, John Green Howard.

Her first big job on her own was the post-earthquake reconstruction of the Fairmont Hotel in San Francisco. At the opening, while everyone was commenting on the beauty of the new building's design, a reporter approached her. He asked her about being the decorator of the place, assuming that was her contribution. She was furious. From that point forward, Morgan shunned the press and never gave another interview.

Needless to say, by this time, Morgan was an old hand at dealing with men who looked down on women, a skill that would prove problematic for Camille.

The San Simeon buildings were to be designed in a combination of European and Spanish Colonial Revival styles. Hearst's taste was inspired by tours of Europe he took when he was young. He was filled with a desire to recreate the majesty he witnessed in European castles and cathedrals, a desire that would last his entire life. The main house on the estate, in fact, was modeled after a Spanish cathedral.

Hearst had also amassed a vast and rather motley art collection. After WWI, import duties on European art and antiquities were reduced. This, combined with rising estate taxes in Europe, made it a perfect time for American buyers. Hearst bought the vast majority of his collection at auctions and galleries in New York City. He had an incredible array of paintings, statues and furniture from all over Europe. One of Morgan's tasks was to integrate these pieces in the design, no small feat. She had to mix, match and blend art and architecture that spanned a thousand years. Hearst was the extremely wealthy version of the aunt that wants her leopard print armchair to match all her Precious Moments figurines.

The designs were created by Morgan and her team in her San Francisco office. There were over nine thousand architectural drawings by the end of the project. At the end of every Friday, Morgan would take the train down to San Luis Obispo, the nearest town to the building site, and a man named Steve Zegar would drive her in his taxi all the way to the Castle.[19] Every Sunday night, she would reverse the trip and head back to San Francisco so she could be in her office Monday morning.

The monthly allowance Hearst sent to Morgan started at $500 and grew to $60,000 during heavy construction periods (about $837,000 in 2017 American dollars). This may seem like a lot of money, but the amount constantly proved insufficient for the massive project and caused Morgan a lot of frustration. These were the funds she had to use for everything: workers' salaries, materials, equipment, transportation, landscaping and her own salary. Over the twenty-eight years she worked on Hearst Castle, her salary varied between 6 percent and 8 percent, which many felt at the time was low, especially considering the scope of her work.

Morgan's duties were far more extensive than most architects back then, and even most architects now. Through her firm, she hired all the employees, handled the payrolls, ordered and oversaw the shipments of art and materials, even supervised the details of landscaping and housekeeping. She was doing all this in her late forties and at the peak of her impressive career. I think

---

19   Steve would eventually be able to buy a fleet of taxis with all the money he made hauling visitors to the Hilltop, since presumably, his was the only taxi service around. Even now, it's not a place you can call an Uber. Over the almost thirty years he ferried her to and from Hearst Castle, Julia Morgan got close to Steve and she designed a playhouse for his daughter.

that having to constantly ask for more money from one of the most wealthy men in the country must have been irritating.

But make no mistake, Morgan loved working with Hearst, especially on this fantastic house. They were both workaholic dreamers with a deep passion for architecture and the two really understood each other.

Julia Morgan was a practical workaholic with no artistic ego. A small woman, she subsisted mostly off black coffee and candy bars. She always wore glasses and eschewed makeup. Morgan refused to carry a purse, but as far as I can tell from photos, had an impressive collection of shapeless felt hats. She cared about her work first and foremost and expected everyone else in her employ to do the same. Most of her time was spent at the office and her staff became a kind of extended family. She made a point of hiring women, both as artists and for drafting. In other words, she was a badass.

The roads between San Simeon and San Francisco were poorly maintained and indirect, making it costly and difficult to ship materials over land. Construction supplies were sent to San Simeon by sea. William Randolph Hearst's father had a wharf built in San Simeon Bay in 1878 and when construction on the Castle hit its stride, Hearst decided to enlarge upon the idea. He had Julia Morgan design bayside warehouses for whatever needed to be stored, whether it was construction materials or priceless pieces of art.

Ground had been broken up on the Hilltop in 1920, the year before Camille joined Morgan's team. Construction started on the three guest cottages before the main house was built. Hearst loved to entertain in a grand fashion, so these were less cottage and more sumptuous villa. The first cottage, the Casa del Mar, faced the sea, while the Casa del Monte faced the mountains and the Casa del Sol faced the setting sun.

In early 1922, Camille was asked to take over as on-site superintendent of construction. The Rossis packed up and headed to

San Simeon that June. Sadly, Elise's father did not get to enjoy having his daughter close to San Francisco for very long; he passed away shortly after the family settled in San Simeon. Camille, Elise, Ulrich, Milicent and Ruth would spend the next ten years of their lives living on the Hearst estate.

Milicent would spend her formative years as Alice in Wonderland.

Before I had recovered from jet lag or adjusted to my new time zone, I threw myself into the search for Milicent. All the meetings I had set up and inquiries I made before flying out from New York turned out to be dead ends. Few film historians had heard of her and the ones who had didn't care much or have any information to share. It was as if she vanished after *Creature from the Black Lagoon*.

I would've been frustrated if I wasn't buzzing with the low-grade high that East Coast natives feel in Southern California. Your body simply isn't used to so much vitamin D. That, combined with the fact that I could see the ocean from where I was staying, made living out of suitcases while trying to get my life back together bearable.

The stress of uprooting myself was eased by the support of Chuck and Belinda, the friends whose guestroom was now crammed with all the stuff I could take with me on the plane to Los Angeles. Not only did they kindly take me on as a temporary house guest, but Chuck and Belinda both lent their prodigious smarts to my search. They're best friends and business partners and after decades of working in the entertainment industry as producers, they know everyone. Both of them had been racking their brains for names of people that might be able to help me.

One morning over a meal that probably involved avocados—that California stereotype is absolutely true—I was talking about the project with Belinda. Belinda is the kind of sunny and sage woman who belongs in an enchanted forest drinking dew and having birds braid her long, blond hair. Lucky for us, she spends her time developing creative projects and making pie instead.

Belinda suggested looking through the *Los Angeles Times* archives for articles mentioning Milicent, so we both got our laptops out. If any newspaper in the country had some missing pieces of Milicent's life, this would be the one.

"Hey, look at this!" she gasped.

I leaned over and read the headline on her screen.

"'Daughter Traces Builder's Role at Hearst Castle,' holy shit!"

It was an article from 1986, an interview with a Milicent Patrick *Trent*. I almost jumped out of my chair. That's why I was having such a hard time finding her; she must have gotten married and gone by a different name later in life! I read her father's name, Camille Rossi. Rossi. So she began life under yet another name and Patrick must have been a business pseudonym. That brought the count of names to search for up to three. I was starting to see why Milicent was a difficult woman to track down.

The interview was not actually about Milicent herself. It was all about her father and his role as the superintendent of construction of Hearst Castle. It was also about Milicent's frustration that Camille wasn't mentioned in the histories written about the Castle. She was on a mission to get him more recognition.

"Hearst Castle, that's amazing!" Belinda exclaimed.

I had never even heard of the place. Belinda explained that it was a famous California landmark and that because of her father's professional connections, she had visited it as a child and gotten special tours of the estate. She spoke of it with wonder while I scrutinized the years that Milicent said her father worked at Hearst Castle.

"This must have been where she grew up!"

"Mallory, you have to go!"

When I sat down to book the trip, I didn't realize the vastness of Hearst Castle. You can't just buy a ticket there. The estate is so large that there are multiple guided tours, each one to three hours in length; I wouldn't be able to see all of Hearst Castle in one trip. I picked two: a tour of all the main rooms and a tour of the architectural highlights. I hoped that if I was going to find out something about Milicent's father, those would be the ones to mention him. I rented a car for the four-hour drive north from Los Angeles to San Simeon. (My driving style is best described as "cautious geriatric," so with me behind the wheel it was going to be a five-hour trip.)

As a woman who watches lots of horror movies, I hate embarking on overnight trips by myself. I know the hills probably aren't filled with bloodthirsty cannibals, but I don't like taking chances. Luckily, I wasn't the only friend that Chuck and Belinda were hosting. The woman staying in the guestroom across from mine, Kate, agreed to accompany me. Along with being a talented actor and director, Kate is a very practical person. She is blessed with the sort of common sense and moxie usually only seen in film noir detectives. Being that my plan was mostly to show up at Hearst Castle and ask people if they had heard of Milicent Patrick or Camille Rossi, I was happy to have Kate with me.

The "little something" that William Randolph Hearst told Julia Morgan he wanted to build would end up sprawling across 128 acres. To put it in perspective, Disneyland is only 85 acres and it takes most visitors several days to see the entire theme park, although the Hearst Castle[20] estate has significantly less traffic.

Hearst Castle itself crowns a hilltop overlooking the San Simeon Bay. At the bottom of the hill is where the original Hearst Ranch once stood. If you stand there on the grassy plain,

---

20 No one actually called it Hearst Castle. At least the Hearsts and the people who worked there didn't. The official name of the home was "La Cuesta Encantada." The staff would refer to it as "the Hilltop" and William Randolph Hearst called it "the Ranch" or just "San Simeon." It's called Hearst Castle now because that became the official name when the house and land were donated to the State of California.

you can just make out the white buildings of Hearst Castle shrouded in mist. It's like looking up at a fairy tale.

But that is not where the Rossi family took up residence during their time in San Simeon. Camille was hired to oversee the construction of this incredible house; he didn't get to live in it. The household staff stayed in the south wing of the house and the construction crew were put up in wooden barracks on the south side of the hilltop. The support staff, which meant Camille, lived in San Simeon or the nearby town of Cambria.

By 1922, the town of San Simeon had become a thriving estate village of nearly a thousand residents. Located a mile south of the Hearst Ranch, it was populated by families of ranch employees and the support staff of the Castle. If this puts in your mind the vision of a pseudo-European town from a 1950s film, where all the villagers sing a cheerful song every morning and work for the lord who lives in the big castle, well, you're not far off.

Moving to San Simeon would be another drastic life shift for Milicent and probably the first one she could remember. The Rossi family moved from their life in bustling San Francisco with the prosperous Bill family into a quaint, isolated village near a working ranch. Streetcars were replaced by cowboys who would regularly drive herds of cattle through San Simeon.

To make an even starker contrast, they moved into an old two-bedroom house that was initially inadequate to serve the family. There was running water and hot water, but no indoor toilet. A bathroom (just for baths), kitchen, additional bedroom and enclosed porch were added to make it more livable. The house was heated by a living room fireplace and a wood and coal cooking stove in the kitchen.

If you've got to use an outhouse, this is the place that you want to do it. Whenever the Rossis stepped out of their house, they were treated to truly stunning views. Soft, low clouds hang over the coast in the morning until the sun dissolves them. The hilltops are often varnished in golden California sun while the prairie below is cloaked in grey fog. In abundance are live oaks,[21] their gnarled limbs blocking out that sun and creating welcome shade. Hearst loved these trees and had strict rules against harming them or cutting them down.

The Rossis' arrival was greeted by the other families who had already moved into San Simeon: the wife and children of the head gardener, head electrician, head carpenter and other staff and Ranch workers. It was a quaint living situation. There was a general store and a little one-room schoolhouse, the Pacific Grammar School where all eight grades were taught in one room. Milicent would attend for five years, until she was eleven and moved to Cambria Union High School nearby. Along with the other students, she took a bus to the school every day, driven by the student with a license who lived farthest from the school.

Milicent was a good student, getting As and Bs on her report cards in nearly every class. She took chorus and orchestra, excelling at both. Elise was a skilled piano player when she was young and passed that enthusiasm on to her daughter. Milicent showed that she had talent as well, performing a duet with her brother, Ulrich, at her graduation ceremony. In addition, Milicent performed a skit. Acting was another interest from a young age. Both passions she would maintain until nearly the end of her life, but she never played piano professionally.

Camille ran a strict household. He had stringent rules about behavior and appearance, and the Rossi children were forced to dress in severe, formal clothes. Milicent would climb onto the school bus every morning wearing a heavy dress that looked very much like she was slowly being swallowed by a pile of funeral drapery. Not even drapes could cover the fact that Milicent was growing up to be an eye-catching person, though. She inherited Camille's strong features and they became more noticeable

---

21   This is actually a type of oak, and does not imply that all the other oaks you have seen are dead.

as she approached her teenage years. Her full lips, straight nose and strong brow made her striking, even as a child. She was interested in boys, but her parents forbade her from dating. When she reached high school, the rules stayed the same. Milicent had a crush on one of her classmates—a boy named Billy Lyons—and she was unhappy about her parents' rule. I'm willing to bet that Billy was, too. There were only sixteen students in their graduating class and only five of them were girls.

Every day, a bus would arrive in San Simeon from nearby Cambria to bring mail and supplies, and to fill orders from the butcher shop. Camille had a personal secretary, a man named Ray, who would make daily deliveries to the Rossi house of mail and ice. Life in San Simeon was quaint, but Hearst made sure it was as comfortable as possible.

While construction buzzed up on the Hilltop, San Simeon was also in a state of constant growth. It was in such isolation that to support Hearst's grandiose vision, much needed to be built. He didn't need just a summer home; he needed an entire town to go along with it. Julia Morgan designed dairies, stables, hay barns, orchards, bridges, reservoirs, rock walls, airplane hangars, landing strips, garages, warehouses and hundreds of miles of backcountry roads. New houses were designed for the staff and the Rossis soon moved into a larger, beautiful Spanish-style home near the coast.[22]

In addition to work on the three guest cottages, construction finally began on the main house, called La Casa Grande, shortly after Camille arrived. Cement and steel were shipped by boat to the wharfs in San Simeon and would then be taken up to the Castle by horse-drawn wagons. Water was piped in from nearby natural springs. Rossi's crew began to pour concrete in the summer of 1922 and poured continuously throughout the rest of the year to finish not just the foundation but also the first two stories.

---

22 No update on the toilet situation, though.

The massive scope of the project and the constant lack of funds did not foster a calm environment for Julia Morgan and Camille. As the project progressed, tensions between the two began to rise. Morgan would usually stop at the Rossi house on her way up to the Hilltop, bringing along an issue of *Cosmopolitan* that she had read on the train. She knew Elise enjoyed the magazine. Camille started resenting these visits, since Morgan usually brought along challenging new plans for current or future projects up at the Hilltop. Hearst's architectural desires were always impressive, but difficult from an engineering perspective. Hearst was, for an amateur, well versed in architecture and would often bring specific examples of things for Morgan to create at the Castle. If he found something he admired in an architecture book, he would buy two copies, one for him and one for Morgan.

Camille was frustrated by these challenges. But he wasn't frustrated with Hearst, he was frustrated with Morgan. More specifically, he chafed at having to answer to her. With Hearst, he was always agreeable, even though Hearst was the one asking for these over-the-top designs. With Morgan, he was obstinate. Instead of Camille confronting her directly about the engineering issues he saw in the plans and offering his solutions to her, he would often go over her head by writing directly to Hearst to tell him instead. It did the double duty of disrespecting Morgan while showing off his ingenuity to Hearst. Camille was ruthlessly ambitious. This behavior infuriated Morgan. She would regularly reprimand Camille, to no effect. But because Morgan was not one to complain, Hearst seemed mostly oblivious to the growing contention.

Camille would explain to his family that he was simply refusing to compromise his structural engineering principles and that when a decision went his way, it was because of the inarguable facts of physics that he would present to Hearst. Camille was just trying to ensure Hearst's approval, even against Morgan's wishes and directives. He truly was a brilliant structural engineer, but instead of working as part of Morgan's team, he leveraged his skills against her.

To be fair, many of the things Hearst wanted were outlandish, difficult to create, or both. He would bring antiques he loved and ask for them to be in very specific places. A four-foot Italian wood door for an eight-foot frame, a thirty-foot-long antique carved ceiling for a forty-five-foot-long room. Hearst always said that he liked antiques that were useful, not considering the incredible amount of work it would take to make them so.

Adding to the frustration was Hearst himself. He would change his mind regularly, sometimes even after something was built. When the Neptune Pool—a massive outdoor swimming pool—was finished, Hearst surveyed the work and asked Camille if they could make it a little bigger. Construction began again.[23] Workers would consistently walk off the project, despite being paid and treated very well by Morgan. It was too disheartening to see their work demolished over and over.

Camille took pride in his ability to accommodate Hearst's outlandish requests. "Father enjoyed pleasing him to the minutest detail and was often called upon to prove it," Milicent said in that 1986 interview with the *Los Angeles Times*. One of the most famous stories of the construction of the Castle is that one day, Hearst and Cecil B. DeMille, one of history's most famous and successful filmmakers, were walking through the gardens. DeMille, not paying attention and lost in conversation, scratched his head on the low-hanging limb of a four-hundred-year-old live oak tree. Hearst was dismayed; the scratch was deep enough to bleed. He asked Camille if something could be done about the tree. Camille said absolutely, assuming Hearst meant remov-

---

23 The second pool was also ultimately too small for Hearst and yet another, bigger pool was built. The final pool is 104 feet long, 58 feet wide and holds 345,000 gallons of water. Or would, if California wasn't in a terrible drought.

ing the limb. Instead, Hearst asked if the tree could be moved—actually turned around.[24]

No live oak had ever been successfully moved and replanted, but Camille agreed to try. It worked! He became the first man to move an ancient live oak, all six tons of it. The tree was humongous, covering about an acre of land with shade. Camille got a lot of acclaim in the press and in newsreels for the feat. He would go on to move other oaks on the Hearst property.[25] The tree is still there, alive and well to this day.

The wild requests and elaborate plans were not the problem for Camille, at least if they were coming straight from Hearst. He had an innovative and sharp mind. If Camille didn't welcome the challenges, he certainly welcomed the acclaim he received for completing them. The problem was being subordinate to Morgan.

Morgan could have been a role model to Milicent in her early life. Could have been, but was not because Camille villainized Morgan behind closed doors. Milicent idolized her father. What girl would want to be like the woman her father was constantly railing against? Morgan was an artistic genius, but she was what Camille disapproved of in a woman: she was independent and strong willed. She was also unmarried and unglamorous, not especially dazzling in her frumpy hats.

Once, sometime during this period,[26] Milicent was struck with appendicitis. The local doctor in San Simeon misdiagnosed

---

24 To make sense of this bizarre request, you have to understand that Hearst had a thing about life and death and injury. No one at the Castle was allowed to even talk about death. Guests were forbidden to mention it. He refused to have any animal killed, even mice. Groundskeepers had to covertly remove dead flowers and leaves from the garden at night with flashlights because Hearst didn't want to see them doing it during the day and be reminded of death or disease.

25 Those trees wouldn't make it into the headlines. I guess once you've moved one giant ancient tree, you've moved them all. Old news, Rossi. Call us when you move a mountain or something.

26 I have been unable to narrow down exactly how old Milicent was when this story happened, probably between ages seven and ten.

it as intestinal flu and soon, the appendix ruptured. After three weeks of life-threatening misery, Milicent was finally transported to a nearby hospital, likely in Cambria, where she was treated for peritonitis for the next three months. Elise rented an apartment by the hospital to stay close to her daughter, who was given poor odds to live. Milicent pulled through, but the battle with peritonitis had lifelong effects, including thin hair. It also rendered her infertile.

During this time, Julia Morgan would come and visit Milicent every single day. She'd send big boxes of gifts, one for Milicent to open every day she was in the hospital. They contained things like German Kewpie dolls, which Milicent loved.[27] Morgan was known for this sort of caring behavior with her staff's families. She was even the godmother of her secretary's child.

Despite all of this, Morgan didn't leave much of a mark on Milicent's life. Milicent never spoke publicly about Morgan's personal acts of kindness or praised her work. When Milicent did mention Morgan, it was only in passing when speaking about her father's work on Hearst Castle. Morgan's generosity and care toward Milicent seems to have been overshadowed by Camille's anger at Morgan.

But there was a woman at Hearst Castle that Milicent did admire. When she left behind the name Mildred as an adult, she renamed herself Milicent[28] after Hearst's wife.

Millicent Hearst was adored by Milicent, who would describe her as "tiny, dainty and lovely." By comparison, William Randolph Hearst frightened Milicent as a child. He was a huge man, tall and heavyset, but he had a small, thin voice that would disconcert people. Milicent thought he sounded "like a little boy." But Millicent Hearst was the other way around: small but

---

27   I'm very sorry that you are now imagining a room filled with ninety Kewpie dolls.

28   One *L* instead of the traditional two. I believe this is a nod to the name Mildred, but I have no proof of this.

with a deep, rich voice. The pairing struck Milicent and when she became an actress, she intensified the already low pitch of her natural speaking voice to be deeper and richer.

More interesting than the fact that Julia Morgan didn't seem to have much of an influence on Milicent is the fact that Millicent Hearst did. Millicent Hearst was William Randolph's wife, but she was not the queen in Hearst Castle. That crown was worn by an actress named Marion Davies.

Marion Davies met William Randolph Hearst in 1915 when he saw her performing onstage in New York City in the musical *Stop! Look! Listen!* He was fifty-two, she was eighteen. After years of discreet and persistent courting, Hearst finally won her over and they began to secretly date. She became his mistress. He still lived with Millicent in their home in Manhattan, but moved Marion, her mother and her sisters into their own Manhattan apartment.

His marriage to Millicent was an unhappy one and as it declined, Marion began accompanying Hearst to more and more public events. She also started making trips with him to Hearst Castle. Millicent's visits to the Hilltop became seldom, usually only so she could be there to welcome royal guests or foreign dignitaries. Hearst knew that it presented a better picture to have political visitors greeted by his wife rather than his mistress. But as soon as they left, so did Millicent. When Hearst hosted friends from the entertainment industry, he brought Marion to be the woman of the house.

By 1919, the year that William Randolph's mother died and he inherited San Simeon, Hearst and Marion were openly together, on the West Coast, at least. It was part of California's appeal for him. He had always felt calmer there. Then it became a place of respite from the stresses of New York City. Ultimately, it became an escape from his failed marriage and a place to be with the person who he thought was the true love of his life.

Hearst Castle became his fantasyland, the place where life was as he wanted it to be.

In 1925, William and Millicent formally separated. He and Marion began to live openly together on both coasts and Millicent moved into her own home in New York City. This was an incredibly scandalous arrangement for the time. William and Millicent's five sons—ages twenty-one, seventeen, fifteen, and twins at ten—were fairly accepting of Marion, but were much closer to their mother and usually took her side. William and Marion never had children. They stayed together until his death in 1951.[29]

Marion Davies had always been at Hearst Castle more often than Millicent was, but after 1925, Marion was the official hostess of San Simeon. This was not something to be taken lightly, considering the guests that stayed in Hearst Castle over the years. Celebrities, business colleagues, millionaires, artists, filmmakers all visited. An invitation from Hearst and Marion to come stay at "the Ranch" was a coveted thing. People like Charlie Chaplin, Winston Churchill, Aldous Huxley, P. G. Wodehouse and George Bernard Shaw had all been guests.

Those were never the most exciting residents, however. Hearst loved animals and was adamant about having a private zoo up on the Hilltop. He set about collecting animals with the same enthusiasm he collected art. Two thousand acres were set aside, enclosed within ten miles of wire fencing. At its height, the Hearst zoo was the world's largest privately owned zoo, with almost a hundred different species.

Penguins, polar bears, kangaroos, antelope, elephants, giraffes, zebras, Indian spotted deer, camels, yak, musk oxen, cheetahs,

---

29 It's easy to read this situation as a gold digger-type scenario, but that wasn't the case. In fact, toward the end of his life, Marion Davies would be the one to financially support him; she loaned him large sums of money. He was jealous and possessive and controlled her career, but she always insisted to friends that she loved him. It still doesn't absolve him of being sort of creepy, though! Fun fact—double footnote! Julia Morgan also designed the Beverly Hills house that Hearst and Davies lived in late in their life together.

cockatoos, eagles, monkeys, primates, leopards, panthers and mountain lions all roamed the hillside. There were over three hundred different animals, with zookeepers and staff to take care of them.[30]

Just like Hearst loved to mix and match artistic styles for his enjoyment, he wanted the same thing in his zoo. He often attempted to place species together in the same enclosure to make them more visually interesting and to increase, as he said, their dramatic effect. Oh, to be so rich that a bunch of leopards isn't dramatic enough for you.

It might come as a surprise, but these misguided arrangements usually failed. Don't worry, not failed in the gruesome way you might be imagining. Like awkward roommates, the animals just sort of avoided each other and did their best to stay hidden, much to Hearst's chagrin. Not to be outsmarted, he had the enclosures moved right next to the roads so the animals could not dash out of sight. The animals had the last word, however. Because Hearst insisted the animals had the right of way on all roads, there were regular traffic conflicts. Guests were often exasperated when their trip to the Hilltop was held up by an unhurried herd crossing the road.

Camille Rossi took a particular liking to the zoo. Building the enclosures and fields and bear grottos was part of the construction he oversaw, so he was around the animals frequently. He had no previous experience with animals, either caring for or training them, but having unlimited access to a private zoo would pique anyone's interest. When Hearst acquired lions, Camille would go into the enclosure with a chair and a whip to try to tame them. Try, because generations of circus performers have

---

30 In the late 1930s, when Hearst's fortune declined and the magic of Hearst Castle was coming to an end, the zoo was abandoned and many of the animals were sold to zoos on the West Coast. Left behind were the zebras, hopefully not because they were at the end of some alphabetically sorted list. They adapted so well to the environment in San Simeon that they were able to wander off into the backcountry, where they multiplied. The herd is still there today, which you can see if you visit the Castle.

proved that the old-timey chair-whip combination certainly distracts lions from eating you, but it doesn't actually tame them.

He formed a particular bond with a leopard cub, who he would lead around on a chain. He named it Lepsy.[31] Camille once took Milicent's little sister, Ruth, up to the hilltop to see some of the animals and surprised her by having Lepsy jump down upon her from a tree "just to see what she would do." This is not the type of surprise a ten-year-old child expects from the zoo. Camille had some rather curious ideas about parenting along with all his strict rules.

Eventually, Hearst had to put a stop to Camille's zoological antics. One day, one of the workers witnessed Camille feeding the lions by hand. The man, thinking the lions were tame, stuck his arm into the enclosure and one of the lions took the man's arm right off. Again, those chairs do not make the lions more tame. Hearst was outraged and Camille was no longer involved with the zoo. The Rossi children were likely relieved.

Sadly, it seems like they were used to this sort of behavior from their father. Irrational strictness pervaded the household. He liked to get Milicent, Ulrich and Ruth up first thing in the morning for an icy swim in the nearby ocean. But it wasn't just Camille enforcing the rules. Elise supported his demands. Both of them discouraged Milicent from socializing. She said that they "wouldn't even let me have a girlfriend or boyfriend... and I wore heavy skirts because my mother wouldn't want me to look sexy. It was a horrible situation. I was never allowed to date...and no social life." She and poor Billy Lyons couldn't even platonically hang out.

Even though her parents were intensely controlling, there was happiness inside the Hearst estate for the Rossi children. They would often accompany their father on weekend trips up

---

31   Nice. Very creative, Camille. Lepsy ended up at the Lincoln Zoo in Chicago, where I hope they graced him with something even slightly more dignified, like Fluffy.

to the Hilltop, where they would play tennis, have the run of the grounds and even enjoy gourmet food in the giant dining hall. According to Milicent, the children "ate wherever my father dictated us to eat," but when they were allowed to eat up at the Castle, "everything was so fancy all the time. They always had frogs' legs and French sauce of some sort and all of the different side dishes…it was really rich living."

Movies were shown once a week for the workers and their families, often before they were released in theaters. Milicent developed her early love of film at these screenings. These nights only took place when Hearst was away from the Castle. There were frequent movie screenings for his guests while he was there, but those weren't for the workers to attend.

Over the years, Hearst purchased more and more of the land surrounding San Simeon. By 1927, he owned the entire view from the Hilltop. As far as the eye could see in any direction, every acre of shaggy golden grass and rolling hills was his. Milicent was quite literally living inside someone else's dreamland.

It's important to remember that there were constant reminders to the Rossis that this opulent life was not theirs. Milicent did not get to feast on frogs' legs alongside the visiting movie stars and politicians. Most of the time, she and her family had to stay in the mist down at the bottom of the hill, looking up at Hearst Castle shining in the sun. It is surreal to grow up in a literal wonderland, but I imagine it would have been even more surreal to grow up in a wonderland that was not your own.

After the long drive, a slightly cramped Kate and I finally arrived at the Hearst Castle visitor center. The drive north was gorgeous. For hours, we cruised along the coast across vast stretches of foggy plains, misty beaches and farms full of bored, robust cows.

Just like Milicent wasn't allowed, you're not allowed to go straight to Hearst Castle whenever you want. Today, you must go through the very modern visitor center. Hearst Castle itself is five miles up the hill behind the center. I was expecting a single grumpy employee guarding a turnstile, but the visitor center turned out to be about the size and frustration level of a small airport. Kate and I hurried through several different lines and information booths, and had to acquire multiple color-coded wristbands. It didn't help that we were slightly late (thanks to my glacial driving habits) and had to miss the introductory film being shown to the swarms of arriving tourists.

As our group was called and we were loaded onto a lumbering tour bus, I was happy that we had missed the film. Kate and I were getting an experience more like one of Hearst's guests, except instead of famous actors and business moguls, we were surrounded by vacationing families, foreign tourists and couples weighed down with gigantic cameras and bulging fanny packs.

With the sea fading behind us to a twinkling backdrop, the bus plodded its way up the hill. The ride to Hearst Castle isn't a straight shot. Our bus took nearly twenty minutes to make it up the winding road. I felt a lot of sympathy for the horses pulling those wagons full of supplies and construction materials under the hot California sun.

Finally, we rounded a bend and there it was. A great white stone crown perched on top of the hill. We stepped off the bus and stepped into a fairy tale. Blooming gardens and lush greenery were nestled in between regal cottages, sweeping marble staircases and the main house itself, posed proudly at the center. There was Hearst's disparate collection of art: Egyptian sculptures, Italian marble busts, Spanish architecture. Julia Morgan's genius was on full display. The collection did not seem hodgepodge. Certainly nothing matched, but it looked right together, as if they were all just more guests for the party. There was a cohesiveness to it; it made a sort of dream sense. This must have been what walking around inside Hearst's brain looked like. I expected to see men dressed as cards, painting all the bright colors on the roses.

As Kate put it, "Damn!"

Unfortunately, the breathlessness and wonder we felt getting off the tour bus dwindled slightly once the guides started looking at the color of our wristbands and herding us into groups. It is such a surreal place that seeing it with a crowd of Nikon-laden tourists and "Do not touch!" signs seemed right. I felt like Milicent probably felt; you can look and appreciate, but remember, none of this is yours.

We were brought through the three guest cottages first. The furnishings in each one were unique and equally lavish: silk tapestries, oil paintings, antique European furniture. To my American mind, inexperienced with a sense of what royalty looks like, it didn't seem like the estate of a media mogul, it felt like the estate of a prince.

I was distracted during the first part of the tour, overwhelmed by the beauty of the place. Once we got inside the main house, I started paying attention to all the historical and architectural details coming out of the mouth of the guide: all the statistics of the construction, all the time and money that went into it all, some stories about Julia Morgan and Hearst. It was all fascinating, and of course the main house was even more extravagant and fantastic than the cottages. It was filled with arts and antiques and even the vaulted ceilings were skillfully carved wonders.

Soon, over an hour had passed and our first tour was nearly up. Camille's name had not been mentioned, not once. When the guide pointed out that we were passing the infamous live oak that had been moved, Camille was referred to as a "construction engineer." If Milicent had worked in the 1980s to get recognition for her father, what happened? Why was his mark on Hearst Castle erased? I raised my hand.

"Hi! What can you tell me about Camille Rossi?"

The guide frowned. "I don't know who that is."

My stomach dropped. "He was the superintendent of construction here for a decade."

"Oh, huh. I have no clue. I've never heard of him."

Kate and I exchanged glances. This place was great and all, but I really hoped it wasn't a gigantic and beautiful dead end.

The guide brought us all to stand on a sunny plaza to wait for another guide to come and bring us to our next tour. I was starting to panic. Kate sidled up to me and nodded toward a group of tour guides.

"Let's go question them. Someone has to know who he is. Grab your recorder!"

"Kate, there's no recording of sound or video here!" I hissed. If speeding while driving gives me hives, breaking the rules of a historical landmark was going to send me into a panic attack.

She reached into my purse, snatched my recorder, turned it on and then stuck it discreetly inside one of the pockets.

"There! No one will know. Let's go."

Actually sweating because I was convinced someone, perhaps with X-ray vision, would see the recorder in my purse and immediately tackle me and haul me off to jail, we walked over. Kate marched right up to the group and asked, "Hey, anyone know who Camille Rossi is?"

Most of the group shook their heads, but an older gentleman grinned.

"I know who he is, that rascal."

"Rascal?"

"Oh, yes he was."

Kate and I listened with rapt attention while he regaled us about Camille's infamous reputation at Hearst Castle and how he was fired.

"Fired?"

"Absolutely!"

As I started to tell him all about my project, our next tour guide had arrived and we needed to leave. Our storyteller gave me some resources about Hearst Castle history and promised to ask around to see if anyone could help me. I didn't realize how quickly.

Thirty minutes later, while getting a tour of the elegant game room inside the main house, a small woman stepped out of a side passageway and put her hand on my arm.

"Are you Mallory O'Meara?"[32]

As the tour continued without me, this woman quietly explained that she was one of the Hearst Castle librarians and had just heard about my project. There was a recording related to Milicent Patrick I could listen to that might be useful.

"That's awesome! Thank you so much. I'd love to hear a recording about her."

"Not about her. *By* her. We recorded an interview with her in the late 80s."

The librarians charged with preserving the history at Hearst Castle began a project in the 1980s, locating surviving workers (or their families) who were involved with the construction and interviewing them about their memories of the Castle. I could finally hear her speak to me. It's easy to find DVDs and online clips of movies and television shows that Milicent acted in. Some of these parts were speaking roles and you can hear her sonorous professional voice. But I had never heard her speak conversationally or privately. She could tell me herself about growing up here in this fantastical place.

The grandeur of Hearst Castle set me up for disappointment when I was invited to come to the nearby Hearst Research Library, situated between two maintenance buildings on the Castle grounds. Instead of a grand building, it was a group of cramped trailers off to the side of one of the staff parking lots. Inside one of the trailers filled with modern office equipment and shelves

---

32   It sounds impressive that she found me, but I am covered in tattoos and have a lot of long, blue hair. I'm incredibly easy to spot in a crowd. Not to take away from the fact that a librarian popping out of a secret passageway to give me research help is one of the coolest things that's ever happened to me.

crammed with books and binders, I sat at a desk. Giddy with anticipation, I slid the CD-ROM the librarians had given me into an ancient desktop computer. The media player popped up, but I couldn't hear anything. I had to crank the volume up all the way and press the cheap headset to my ears.

Milicent Patrick's sonorous voice filled my head. She spoke with a kindly old woman who asked her questions about her father and their life at Hearst Castle. It felt so intimate, like I was sitting there with her in the living room. Here was a relic of her life, a very personal piece of her puzzle. I finally believed that I could find her.

Seeing Hearst Castle helped me understand why Camille worked so hard to ingratiate himself with William Randolph Hearst. He wanted to get as close as possible to the source of that wonderful dream. Being on Hearst's good side could only help him so much, however. Camille was often the source of conflict both up at the Hilltop and down on the ranch. Workers saw him as productive and talented, but also difficult to work with. One of them described Camille: "He seems satisfactory on construction matters but I think he is more of a hindrance than a help in other matters… I don't think he gets along with people."

An inability to get along with people certainly was a hindrance for someone so involved with the daily construction of the Castle and the ranch. Besides all the extravagance being built on the hilltop, Camille oversaw construction of ranch staples like barns, animal shelters, poultry ranches, warehouses, stables and employee residences. He was even involved in the landscaping. During the work day, dozens and dozens of artisans, laborers and tradesmen had to interact with Camille and endure his tyrannical behavior, his powerful desire to always be in charge and his need to always be right.

That he spent ten years in the employ of Hearst Castle is a testament to his talent and intellect. His innovative methods saved time, an invaluable resource to such a drawn-out and expensive endeavor. Morgan praised Camille's leadership skills when he first arrived in San Simeon, but as the years went by, these skills were eclipsed by a personality that his workers and Morgan eventually found intolerable. By intolerable, I mean that the superintendent of the ranch, Arch Parks, said that Camille "seemed to glory in human misery," a description usually reserved for villains who live high in mountain caves. According to one of the plumbers working on the hilltop, Camille started carrying a gun to work because the men of his crew were ready to "wrap a two by four around his head." He was an expert engineer, but the persistence of his dictatorial attitude eventually caused the situation to come to a head.

In early 1932, Morgan gave orders that no work was to be done on the indoor pool without her permission. Camille ignored her wishes and brought his crew in to start pouring concrete anyway. When Morgan next visited and saw the work, she was so furious that she had workers chop out all of the concrete and do it all over again to her specifications. Livid, she hung a sign on the doors to the pool that read "Mr. Rossi, under no circumstances are you to enter this pool." He never went in again.

Morgan finally had enough. She wrote to Hearst, calling for Camille's removal. She kept her anger restrained in her letter, but privately wrote in her diary that Camille was "so unduly revengeful, he finds so many ingenious ways for indirect expression of his sentiments." After ten years of quietly dealing with Camille without complaint, this statement speaks volumes of all the injustices she must have suffered and never reported to Hearst.

Hearst instructed her to fire Camille. Keeping with his usual behavior, Camille went over Morgan's head and appealed to Hearst directly, insisting that his fights with Morgan were his attempts to keep the project efficient and save Hearst money. Hearst, not one for conflict, relented and asked Morgan if she could keep dealing with him. She calmly wrote back, hinting that if Camille stayed on the project, she might not. Hearst got the hint. He liked Camille, but Morgan was invaluable to him as a friend and collaborator. Camille was finished at San Simeon.

It was not a happy time in the Rossi household. Elise's melancholy saturated the atmosphere of the home.[33] Teenage Milicent was straining against the strict rules of the household and taking after her father in one important aspect: she wanted more. She was intelligent and ambitious and desperate to get out of the tiny social bubble of San Simeon.

Morgan replaced Camille with engineer George Loorz, who proved to be a worthy and well-loved replacement. It wasn't a bad time for Camille to leave the project. At that point, the Hearst estate was already in a decline. Three years earlier in 1929, the Depression hit and Hearst began selling off land. He whittled down the estate slowly for the next decade. When the Second World War broke out in 1939, construction had slowed. Hearst sold one hundred forty thousand acres of ranch land to the United States government as military training ground to help his suffering finances. The zoo was closed and the animals sold off to public zoos all over California.

In 1946, Hearst suffered a heart attack and was advised by his doctors to live somewhere less isolated. He reluctantly followed the advice, and moved with Marion Davies to a home in Beverly Hills. He never returned to San Simeon, and died in 1951 at the age of eighty-eight.

Julia Morgan went on to lots of other architectural projects, plenty of which are still standing today, like the Berkeley Playhouse in Berkeley, California. She was passionate about advancing opportunities for women and made many contributions to Mills College, a women's college in Oakland, and YWCAs up

---

33 Both Ruth and Milicent described their mother as unhappy and frustrated, but whether that's because of some unnamed mental health issue mentioned earlier or her marriage to Camille, I don't know.

and down the California coast. In 1951 (the year Hearst died), when she was seventy-nine, she closed her office. She never married, had no children and spent her last five years in content, modest seclusion. In 2008, governor Arnold Schwarzenegger announced that Morgan was to be inducted into the California Hall of Fame.

For a long time after Hearst's death, the Hilltop was unoccupied, save for the caretakers and groundskeepers. During his lifetime, Hearst specified that he wanted the estate to be given to the state of California after his passing, to become a cultural center. Many years of legal fiddling ensued before it was finally open to the public for tours in 1958.

When remembering their time at Hearst Castle, the Rossi children gave a very different account of their reason for leaving rather than what you've just read. Ruth's version was that because of financial troubles, Hearst could no longer afford expansion on the hilltop, so he and Camille decided together that it was the best time for him to leave. Milicent said in interviews that it was because all major construction was completed. Neither of these stories is true, but they could be what Camille told his family. These women could also have been trying to protect their father's reputation. He became estranged from both Ruth and Milicent later in life,[34] yet they still furthered this misinformation about his time at Hearst Castle. They might have said this because they still loved him or to protect their own family pride. Perhaps they truly did not know the reality of the situation. I will probably never know.

I originally felt conflicted about including the unvarnished truth of Camille's temper and lust for power in this book, especially considering the fact that my first big break in finding Milicent was that *Los Angeles Times* article detailing her mission to restore her father's legacy. I felt guilty exposing something that she tried to bury. She spoke highly of her father's accomplish-

---

34 I have no evidence of an estrangement between Ulrich and Camille.

ments and it was clear that she was proud of growing up around the glamour of the Hearsts and in San Simeon.

Milicent was right; her father did deserve remembrance for a decade's worth of hard work and creative problem solving at one of the most famous and beautiful estates in the country. If he is going into the history books, all of him needs to go in, not just the talent but also the darkness. Because the truth is, that's why he was left out in the first place. His time at Hearst Castle was so fraught and his exit so tense that it overshadowed his many contributions to the estate. You cannot find anything about Camille on the official website for Hearst Castle. It was only through many hours at the library, searching through piles of books and collecting scant information from each one and combining it with family history that I was able to put this chapter together.

Despite her dislike of Camille, Morgan did decide to help him find a new job in Southern California as a state engineer. It was time for the Rossis to leave San Simeon and return to the real world.

Well, not quite.

At age seventeen, Milicent and her family moved south to Glendale, a suburb of Los Angeles. Milicent was going to trade one dreamland for another—Hollywood.

3

Smash Cut

It was a sunny day in Southern California when I drove to visit the small house in Glendale that the Rossi family moved into. It's always a sunny day in Southern California. *Saved by the Bell* did not lie to you. Palm trees, blue skies, warm weather, lots of men in cutoff T-shirts—Southern California delivers on it all.

The house Milicent lived in sits on a wide street in a quiet, unremarkable residential area. It's part of a row with other similar two-story homes, all with identical short flights of red brick stairs leading into the arch of the front door. This was about as far away from Hearst Castle as you could get. Marble was replaced by stucco, ornate architecture was replaced by plain buildings, lush gardens were replaced by plain, trimmed hedges. No more sweeping seaside vistas, no miles of rolling coastland, no enveloping fog.

No more movie stars and glamour, either. Glendale is in Los Angeles County, but it is not actually Los Angeles. It's the neighbor with the well-kept lawn, peering over the fence at the craziness of Hollywood. For a conservative man looking to relocate his family, it was a good spot for Camille.

In the 1930s, Los Angeles had already grown into one of the biggest—geographically speaking—cities in the world, as anyone who has had to drive during rush hour[35] can attest. The city is a sprawl. Aside from the cluster of skyscrapers downtown, construction in LA happens outward, not upward. There were no freeways yet, but there was an efficient and inexpensive streetcar system, which might seem laughable to today's Uber-dependent residents. LA's current public transit system is most kindly described as inconvenient. But back then, many people used the streetcars to get around town.

Camille started his job as an engineer for the State of California and the rest of the family settled into their new, quieter lives. The days were frustratingly quiet for Milicent; her parents still had a strict hold on her social life. The rules about her appearance had not shifted, either. Milicent was strolling around in the Southern California sunshine in heavy, dowdy dresses, with unstyled hair and no makeup. That's a fine look if it's what you like, but Milicent loved glamour and fashion.

The next year, in 1933, when Milicent was eighteen years old, she got to experience a little more social freedom and enroll in Glendale Junior College.[36] Ulrich joined her there, participating in the Engineers' Club both years, something I'd bet Camille was pleased about.[37]

Glendale Junior College was a small, fairly new school. There were fewer than five hundred students and it had been open for only six years. The attractive grounds were (and still are) filled with wide green lawns and long two-story buildings. Five hundred students probably felt like a massive crowd to Milicent and Ulrich, who were used to the tiny Cambria high school and the quaint life in San Simeon. Unlike her big brother, Milicent was

---

35   Rush hour is a filthy lie told by Southern Californians who want you to believe that traffic gets less abysmal at other times of the day.

36   What community colleges were called during this time.

37   There was an Engineers' Club but sadly, no art club for Milicent.

not a part of any clubs or sports teams here. She did not show up in any of the society pages, either. The only thing she seemed focused on was art.

Milicent was still an active pianist, but now that she was an adult, she shifted gears to make visual art her focus, instead of music or theater. This was something purely hers, without the history of either of her parents attached. The small schools she attended in San Simeon did not seem to have had any sort of art curriculum to encourage and grow her talent. Now she was in a school near a big city where she could explore her passions. With the stifling atmosphere in the Rossi household, art was a place for her to express herself.

Milicent's Glendale Junior College photo. (*Glendale Community College Archives*)

The only extracurricular activity she was involved in at Glendale Junior College was art for the school yearbook. The first year she was the assistant art editor working on other students' pieces and the second year, for the 1935 yearbook, she created pieces of her own. Milicent produced six beautiful illustrations and a page full of simple ink drawings of various student activities: the campus, school dances, sports games. Already she was honing the unique soft pastel style that she would use in future design work.

Milicent did not graduate from Glendale Junior College. She was focused, not on getting a degree, but on moving forward in a specific direction. Art was her calling and she wanted to continue her education at an art school.

She applied for three scholarships to Chouinard Art Institute, a college dedicated to visual arts. It was a smart choice for Milicent. Founded in 1921, Chouinard was one of the leading art schools in Southern California. Both fine artists and commercial artists alike trained there and it would give her a wide variety of art classes to explore exactly what she wanted to do.

Milicent won every single scholarship.

After leaving Glendale Junior College in 1935, still living at home in Glendale, she enrolled for classes at Chouinard. There she would encounter the second bespectacled female genius in her life—Madam Nelbert Chouinard.

There are few women with as great an influence on Southern California's reputation as a hub of twentieth-century American art than Nelbert Chouinard. She was, as they say, one bad motherfucker. Only a year after women were allowed to vote, she opened her own art school in Southern California and soon transformed it into an institute with an international reputation for producing quality artists.

Born in rural Montevideo, Montana, in 1879, as a child she had wanted to follow in her father's footsteps and be a doctor. Her father did not approve. He proclaimed that "there will be no woman doctor in this family!" She acquiesced and gave up her medical ambitions. Luckily for the creative world, she decided to pursue her other dream of being an artist. Her father wasn't happy about that choice, either, but she managed to win that battle. Apparently being a woman artist wasn't as appalling to him as being a woman doctor.

Nelbert attended art school in Brooklyn, New York, where she had to lie about her age to get in. She was a naturally talented artist from childhood. Born Nellie Murphy, she always hated her name. While in college, her brother wrote to her from dentistry school in Chicago to warn her that there was a dancer named Nellie Murphy who was gaining a sordid reputation from her saucy exploits. A family friend jokingly renamed her Nelbert after hearing the contents of the letter and she liked it. The name stuck and when she married a man named Burt Chouinard, she took his last name and became Nelbert Chouinard.

She received her teaching certificate in 1904 and soon after, headed west to California, where she got a job at a school in Pasadena. Nelbert taught art at several schools in Southern California over the next few years. She developed a devoted following of students who eventually convinced her to open her own school, a place that would set scores of successful artists on the right path, including Milicent.

After a few months living with Chuck and Belinda, I found a studio apartment right on the edge of the very hip neighborhood of Echo Park. I was just close enough to be able to walk to all the very hip things there, like fancy coffee shops and restaurants selling ten-dollar shots of wheatgrass juice. It was a tiny space, but the rent fit my "single, working creative who just paid an astronomical amount of money to ship all her books from Brooklyn to Los Angeles" budget. When my research turned up that Milicent attended Chouinard, I was thrilled to discover it was a mere mile from my new place. If it wasn't so hazy all the time, I could probably have seen it from the roof of my building.

All of my stuff barely fit in the apartment, but I loved it. Living in California was just as fantastic as I thought it would be. I was on my own in my favorite city, writing, working on movies, eating a lot of tacos and rarely having to wear pants. This was the neighborhood where Milicent went to school as a young artist and I imagined that some of the joy and freedom I was feeling was what she felt here, too.

Walking around the building now, you would never know it used to be a thriving scene for budding artists. What was once the Chouinard building is still a school, but all the artsy coolness has been eradicated. It is now an elementary school in a part of town known for its abundant homeless population. Barbed wire tips the high fence surrounding the building, looming over the groups of children and their brightly colored playground.

But when twenty-year-old Milicent was here in 1935, it was a handsome building that housed a cutting-edge art school. Chouinard was poised to become one of California's most important creative institutions. The wide variety of visual art disciplines offered at Chouinard was very progressive for the time. Fashion design, magazine illustration, industrial design, set design, graphic design and lettering were all taught alongside more traditional disciplines like painting, sculpting and drawing.

In addition to being the founder of the school, Nelbert was also the school's director and one of the teachers. She encouraged a spirit of freedom and adventure and it made her beloved by students and staff. Other schools in the area—such as the ArtCenter College of Design—had strict dress codes, but the atmosphere at Chouinard was relaxed. The art you created there was more important than whether or not your shirt was tucked in while you created it.

This was probably Milicent's first taste of freedom as an adult and I imagine that she was all too happy to get up and go to class. It wasn't a totally wild and uninhibited freedom like many college students experience today. There were no dorms here, so she had to return home to the Rossi household every night. Milicent wasn't doing keg stands at frat parties and experimenting with nose piercings and slam poetry. But for the first time, she was spending her days in an environment that was filled with hundreds of fellow artists, an environment that actively encouraged self-exploration and personal expression. For a woman who grew up in the shadow of Camille's strict rules, Chouinard was an illumination.

Undated sketch done by Milicent of an unknown woman. (*Author collection*)

Philosophy aside, Nelbert worked hard to make Chouinard an enriching environment for her students. There was an influx of European artists into Los Angeles at this time and she took advantage of it. The school featured a constant rotation of guest teachers from all over the world and from different creative backgrounds. Donald Graham, Doris Kouyias, Charles Swenson, Llyn Foulkes—all taught at Chouinard at some point in their careers.

Both the staff and student body were fairly gender balanced. It was a wonderful environment for Milicent to join, not just to meet new people and socialize, but to see working female artists. She was exposed to a wide variety of people and new ideas, all under the caring tutelage of Nelbert Chouinard.

Said Madeline Ellis, a student in 1931, about their school's founder:

> She usually wore a long green smock, and often a small black hat, about an inch and a half high. I don't remember what she looked like without a hat, but she was a tall, rather large woman then, and as I remember, her manner and way of speaking, were "no nonsense and definite" but she was always pleasant and had a twinkle in her eye. She wore glasses with narrow rims. Every Thanksgiving she invited all the students who were away from home to her home for dinner—I always wished I could go.

Nelbert was remembered for being tough and for being a fighter. Other schools tried to poach her students and teachers, but she would recruit new artists herself, calling up the parents of potential students to pitch her institute and promote her methods. At Chouinard, there was a focus not on natural talent, but on work ethic. Nelbert believed in the idea that good art could be taught, that it was not something inherent and that drive and determination were just as important. From the pamphlet advertising the school the first year Milicent was a student:

> If your son or daughter shows an inclination towards art have him study to become a proficient artist. Then success will take care of itself—the success of his own spiritual happiness—and the success of being able to interpret and express his artistry with skill and ease. One must be

more than a dreamer and poet to be an artist—he must learn and expertly handle the fundamental rules and use of tools of his art.

Chouinard School of Art has assisted many students to become nationally successful artists—because it claims no short-cuts over the fundamentals of art training.

In other words, get the fuck to work.

The school's methods were effective; many influential and important artists were Chouinard graduates. Mary Blair, Chuck Jones, Ed Ruscha, and Edith Head—who went on to win a stunning eight Oscars for costume design and receive thirty-five nominations—are all alumni.

Nelbert was usually willing to make financial accommodations to further the artistic reputation of the school. She'd ask the staff to take pay cuts so the school could afford to hire new teachers with exciting ideas and constantly gave scholarships to students in need. In 1929, this tactic caused Nelbert to make a decision that would change the course of both her life and Milicent's. The reason was a request from Walt Disney.

This was in the early days of Disney. In 1928, Walt Disney brought the popular character of Mickey Mouse to the world. The cartoon mouse appeared as a character in several short films, most notably in the short *Steamboat Willie*, codirected by Walt Disney and Ub Iwerks. Mickey Mouse was a hit and Disney wanted to make feature-length animated films. He knew what he needed to make his visions come to life—incredibly talented artists and lots of them. The artists couldn't just be talented, they needed to be trained in a particular way to produce the illusion of movement that Disney wanted to convey. The problem was, he didn't have the money to fund the classes to teach all these artists he was hiring.

He approached art schools all over Southern California but because he couldn't pay, they all turned him down. When he met Nelbert and told her that he didn't have the money now, but that he'd like to send his artists down and have them be taught how to draw, she surprised him by saying yes. "Mr. Disney, I admire very much what you're doing: just send your boys down and we'll worry about the price later." A lifelong, mutually beneficial friendship was formed.

In the beginning, years before Milicent attended, Disney would drive the artists down to the Chouinard school himself, pick them up after the class had ended and then drive them all home. He felt that the right schooling was one of the top priorities to the success of his early movies and wanted to do anything he could to facilitate that.

By 1930, the school had grown enough to move into a new building built especially for Nelbert. An elegant art deco facade led into a simple box of a building filled with open spaces and light. In the center of the school was a courtyard complete with a fish pond, where classes were often held. Milicent would have walked through wide airy hallways and attended classes in bright rooms filled with students.

The Chouinard Institute was in Western Central Los Angeles at a time when there was a lot of commercial and residential growth in the area. The neighborhood bustled with commerce and an influx of people. Easy access to public transportation made it a perfect location, since many students rode on the inexpensive streetcar system to school. (Milicent's home in Glendale was only about a twenty-minute drive away.) Disney Studios, at their own location on Hyperion Avenue in Hollywood (before their move to their current location of Burbank), was just a short drive north and the movie studios of young Hollywood were developing to the west, less than five miles away. The school sat at the center of a hub of creativity in a growing metropolis.

Eventually, the instructors at Chouinard started going up to the studios at Disney to see what the artists were working on and what issues the artists were facing while trying to create the illusion of movement. According to Walt Disney:

> I made a deal with some of the teachers at Chouinard to come out and work with me, to sit with me by the day and know my problems. That, in turn, gave them the chance to know what we had to work on. They sat right in the room with me...fifty percent of my time was spent in the sweatbox going over every scene with every animator.

The sweatbox was a projection room where animators would sit with Walt Disney and "sweat out" his acceptance of their latest animation work. It wasn't just a mental sweatbox, either. It was uninsulated and Walt Disney said it was as "hot as the dickens." Chouinard teachers would sit in there with him, analyzing why the animation did and didn't work, taking these issues and solutions back to the classroom. There was a lot of artistic cross-pollination, which became key to the successful growth of animated movies.

Disney explained the way animators were taught to draw at Chouinard:

> We think of action, we think of drawing for action. We call it action analysis. You draw from a static figure when you're in Life class...so we have a model go through actions, she goes through it and then sits over in a corner... and they sketch what they saw.

In 1935, when Milicent arrived at Chouinard, serious training of animators had been going on for only a few years. With Disney animators being taught at the institute, other students there were beginning to learn how to animate, as well. While the Disney artists were in class, Walt would get a look at the other students working at the institute, and soon a pipeline formed between Chouinard and Disney. Many students would go on to work at the animation studio in a variety of jobs.

These drawings show Milicent's skill in "drawing for action," which drew the attention of Walt Disney. (*Author collection*)

Both Nelbert and the institute were at their peak during the years that Milicent attended. In spite of the Depression, the school was doing well. European journalists were beginning to travel there and wrote rave reviews of both the teaching methods used and the art being created there. Milicent stayed at the Chouinard Institute for three years, concentrating on illustration and drawing. The three scholarships that Nelbert awarded to her were not misplaced; Milicent's talents blossomed. In 1938, she experienced a major achievement in her artistic career: her work caught the eye of Walt Disney.

He asked her to come work for him.

4

Dissolve

Disney: the biggest name in animation and one of the biggest names in film. They own Star Wars, your childhood emotions and by the time this book is published, probably several planets. Disney is arguably the most prominent name in entertainment. It is such a powerful name that it overshadows almost everyone who works under it. The average person would have a difficult time naming anyone involved with the production of Disney animated films, be it director or animator. They know only the name of Walt Disney. You may have heard of the guy. His brilliance wasn't even in directing or animating, though. It was in producing, for which he won more Oscars than anyone else, ever.[38]

In the late 1920s, Mickey Mouse put Disney on the map. After that success, Disney Brothers Studio, which Walt formed in the early 1920s with his brother Roy, became more ambitious with their movies. By 1937, Disney had created *Snow White and the*

---

38   Twenty-two, out of fifty-nine nominations.

Seven Dwarfs, the first full-length cel-animated film.[39] This was during the time that Walt Disney joined forces with Nelbert Chouinard to properly train the massive number of artists that he needed to produce more feature-length movies.[40]

When I started my research, I knew Milicent had animated for Disney, but that was all. In interviews, she sometimes said that she was the first woman animator for them, but never mentioned specifics. I had no idea what projects she was on or what exactly she did. Milicent worked in a time when film credits did not list individuals like they do now. If you go see a movie today and stay through the end credits, it can take up to ten minutes (especially if it's a big budget movie) for a list of everyone in the film crew to slowly scroll up the screen, from the director all the way down to the production assistants.[41]

Research at my branch of the Los Angeles Public Library gave me plenty of information about animation and Disney film history, but not detailed information about the hundreds and hundreds of artists and technicians who worked on these 1930s-era films. (Most feature-length animated movies hire that many people, even today.) To get specifics about who worked on these movies and what exactly they did, I needed to talk to someone in—or with access to—the Disney archives. In case you were wondering, you can't call up Disney and ask to chat. Their Animation Research Library has no contact information listed besides an address. At one point, I got desperate enough to consider showing up, possibly holding a boombox over my head.

---

39 Obviously there is a lot more history in between here. But if there is one man on this planet that doesn't need any more coverage of his life and work, Walt Disney is it. Aliens in other solar systems know who Walt Disney is.

40 Feature length is, according to the Academy of Motion Picture Arts and Sciences, aka the Oscar People, forty minutes or more. The Screen Actors Guild–American Federation of Television and Radio Artists says eighty. Feature-length films nowadays are usually ninety to one hundred fifty minutes. You know how new parents refuse to refer to their children as a year, or two years old, and say only how many months they are? That's how filmmakers are with films and minutes.

41 As they should! Movies are hard to make! People deserve credit!

Like most people, my first exposure to animation came when I was a kid. In fact, my first memory of seeing any sort of animation is also my first memory of seeing any sort of film and also seeing something that made me feel fear. That's a lot of pressure to lay on one film. Luckily for me, it was one that could hold that burden: *Fantasia*. Tiny toes curled deep into the carpeting in my grandparents' living room, I remember looking up at the screen in wonder as the symphony of sound and light played across the screen.

Fantasia is a 1941 anthology film[42] comprised of different animated shorts set to pieces of classical music. The shorts are all of a fantastical nature, as you might expect. Waltzing flowers, dancing hippos, galloping centaurs, roaring dinosaurs, all those magical brooms. I was entranced. What kid doesn't want to watch a bunch of animals twirling around in tutus? Plus, with all that classical music, it's a great watch-with-grandparents movie.

As the last segment of the film began, my little brain sensed something was different. Everything was darker, more sinister. The brightly colored fantasy landscapes of the previous segments were replaced with a midnight mountaintop that loomed over a small town while *Night on Bald Mountain* played. If you haven't heard it, it's the sort of string-heavy piece of music that makes you feel as if you are about to get murdered. A great black demon unfurled his wings, stood on top of the mountain and spread his shadow fingers across the village. They reached out of the television screen and squeezed my hammering heart. I was utterly absorbed and could not look away, but I was terrified. This is my first clear memory of any sort of art deeply affecting me. The animation is spectacular, somehow dreamy and nightmarish at the same time.

---

42 Anthology films are made up of several short films, like a party mix of movies. Sometimes, the films can be centered around a theme or idea. They can be made by one director, or a different one for each film short. If you want to be fancy, next time you eat a bag of Chex Mix, you can call it an anthology snack.

The segment is the most beautiful in the entire film. A demon, the size of the mountaintop, pierces the indigo sky behind him with the inky points of his fingers and the sharp tips of his Stygian wings. Skeletons and witches swirl through the air as ghouls dance through the fire conjured from the demon's fingertips. That is, until the pure, holy sounds of a church bell ring throughout the land, putting an end to the macabre party.

It wasn't until I was an adult that I found out the demon is Chernabog, an evil Slavic deity, and in the film, he raises unhappy souls and wicked entities so he can transform them into demons.[43] As scared as I was of Chernabog, I couldn't help but feel disappointed when the church bells started, banishing him back inside the darkness of the mountain. I didn't want to watch the scene that followed with the boring procession of candle-bearing people walking through the forest. Bring back those dancing demons and flying skeletons! Those guys made me feel something. They affected me.

I wasn't old enough to articulate it at the time, but that sequence and the fear it evoked moved me. I pestered my grandfather to crack open that clamshell VHS tape case and play *Fantasia* again and again and again. It was my first taste of film and my first taste of fear and I was hooked. As a very anxious child, being afraid of something that wasn't real was actually a pretty nice change of pace. Chernabog became—and is to this day—my favorite animated monster. It seems impossible that something so ghoulish can be so graceful. I get it, people are really into Mickey Mouse and Tinkerbell. But ever since I can remember, Chernabog has always been the most magical Disney character for me.

I'm not the only one that *Fantasia* affected so deeply. The movie remains critically acclaimed, nearly eight decades later. It is widely regarded as one of the greatest American films and

---

43   My childhood fascination with this film probably explains why I grew up to be a goth.

is the twenty-second-highest grossing of all time. This is especially impressive, considering that anthology films are generally not as commercially successful. Not bad for a bunch of hippos dancing to classical music!

Fantasia is probably not a movie that a big studio would make today. A producer with very expensive shoes would scoff and say that it wouldn't make any money. He would probably be right. It consists of animated segments, eight in total. Each segment is a family-friendly cartoon set to a famous piece of music. The pitch sounds like a snore. But it is a compelling piece of cinema, with sound, color and motion working together to create a magnificent tapestry of sensory experience. It was Walt Disney's grand effort to elevate animation to an art form and I would say that it worked.

It all started as a comeback vehicle for Mickey Mouse,[44] who was falling behind his pals Donald Duck and Goofy in popularity. Walt Disney began to work on a short film based on composer Paul Dukas's *The Sorcerer's Apprentice*. It was intended to be another "Silly Symphony," one of the many animated shorts set to pieces of music that originally helped Disney rise to fame. Walt wanted to step up his game. The production on *The Sorcerer's Apprentice* was more elaborate and pushed the budget of the film to $125,000,[45] three or four times as much as a "Silly Symphony" cost. Walt realized there was no way he was going to earn back the money he was putting into it.[46] Leopold Stokowski, the conductor of the music for the film, had originally suggested an entire feature film made of animated segments set to pieces of classical music, an idea Disney laughed off. But after sinking so much time and effort into *The Sorcerer's Appren-*

---

44 By comeback vehicle, I mean a blood-drenched, Mad Max-style war machine that Mickey revved up and rode to become one of the most recognizable characters in the world.

45 Which is still a lot of money for a short film *today*.

46 Alas, something still true of short films.

tice, creating an entire feature didn't seem so crazy anymore. In early 1938, a year before Milicent arrived at Disney, they began to develop the feature film.

I needed another research breakthrough, so I worked diligently on the most important part of the creative process that nobody tells you about: networking. Filmmaking is generally not a journey you embark on alone. Besides a lot of smarts and a generous local bartender, the best thing you can have as a producer is a long list of contacts. You never know when you'll need a puppet maker, a skilled cinematographer or an actress who has a great scream. I went to lots of industry events and sidled up to friends I knew who worked in the animation industry. Getting an in at Disney was like going on a diet; everyone seemed to know how to do it and none of their advice seemed to work. Everyone knew someone who worked there, everyone would ask around for me and none of it came through. I asked, pleaded and coaxed people for nearly a year.

Finally, at a completely un-film-industry-related brunch with friends, I met Michele Wells. Michele is a whip-smart businesswoman, the kind of intensely capable person the hero in a film calls on to make important decisions about bombs. Someone at the table asked me about the book I was working on and I vented my frustrations with trying to get access to Disney information. A golden ray of sunshine shot out of the sky and haloed Michele's brunette locks, causing everyone's mimosas to sparkle.[47]

"Disney? Ha, I work there!"

I couldn't believe my luck. This was my first direct contact with someone who worked at Disney. We exchanged contact information and she agreed to find someone for me to talk to. Soon she emailed me, letting me know that she had set up a meeting with a Disney historian. It felt like a miracle.

---

47   This is a dramatic reenactment.

A month later, I was getting out of an Uber in front of the massive complex of Disney offices in Burbank. Everything at Disney looks picturesque and well, Disney-like. Even the tops of the wrought iron fence posts are shaped like Mickey Mouse heads. I tentatively poked one of the hedges before I started walking toward the entrance, half hoping that the hedge would start singing a song about me that all the surrounding greenery would join in to, while a passing bluebird dusted off my jacket and a friendly rabbit led me toward the gate.

There was a line of people I presumed to be employees—judging by how unimpressed they were by their surroundings—and I joined them, still not quite believing that after all this time, I was being allowed in. But as I gave my name, no swarm of men in Mickey Mouse-print uniforms swept in to carry me off. The security guard handed me a temporary visitor pass and I was directed toward Michele's office. She found me in the lobby and we walked through hallways adorned with a treasure trove of memorabilia from Disney, Marvel and Star Wars movies. I did my best not to stare. It's hard to stay professional when you're a nerd.

After looking in awe at a display of Walt Disney's personal writing desk protected behind glass, Michele led me to the office of Ken Shue, a kindly, bespectacled older man. Ken is the vice president of Global Art for Disney. He's been with the company for over twenty years and is one of the best people to talk to when it comes to anything related to Disney art. His office is covered, floor to ceiling, in books on Disney artistry and original framed art from various Disney animated films. This room hummed with a love for beauty and stories and I was humming with excitement. This had to be a man who could help me. Finally! I was in!

Michele and I sat down across from his desk. I was practically levitating above my chair. After pleasant introductions, I could barely contain myself. I half expected Milicent herself to leap out from under his desk with a full marching band. I would at last be able to learn about the work she did for Disney.

"So, tell me about your project, Mallory."

"Well, I'm writing a biography about Milicent Patrick, or, as you would know her, Mildred Rossi."

This was it. I prepared for all the confetti.

He stared at me.

"Hmm. I don't recognize the name."

My heart was a popped balloon. I explained to him how Milicent claimed that she was the first female animator at Disney, but because I did not know what she worked on, I could not give him any more information. He explained that because he didn't know who she was, there wasn't much he could do to help.

"Wait. You know who you should talk to? Mindy Johnson. She's writing a book on female animators right now. If anyone will know anything about her, it's Mindy. Let me call her right now."

He dialed on his office phone and put the call on speaker. After a few rings, a cheerful female voice answered and Ken introduced me to Mindy.

"Hey, Mindy, do you know anything about a Milicent Patrick?"

"You mean Mildred Rossi? Of course I do! She worked on *Fantasia*!"

My jaw actually dropped open. Mindy went on to talk about the book she was working on, a history book detailing all the female artists and animators who had worked at Disney.[48]

"So, Milicent was an animator?"

"Oh, yeah. She animated on the Chernabog sequence!"

I cannot accurately tell you how the rest of the conversation went. I know that Mindy told me more about what Milicent did for Disney, but said that she didn't know much about the rest of

---

48   It's called *Ink & Paint: The Women of Walt Disney's Animation* and it's absolutely fabulous.

Milicent's life, before or after. I vaguely remember saying that I was happy to tell her all about Milicent's life if she could tell me about Milicent's work for Disney. It was a true "You got your peanut butter in my chocolate! You got your chocolate in my peanut butter!" moment. I know that Mindy and I exchanged contact information and agreed to meet up very soon.

The only thing that I accurately remember from this conversation is thinking, over and over again, "Chernabog. Chernabog. Chernabog." The strings of *Night on Bald Mountain* surged in my ears. I saw that colossal monster as he raised his sinister wings and struck terror and love and instant devotion deep into my young heart. Chernabog. She worked on Chernabog. Of course she did.

Mindy and I had lunch on a cold rainy afternoon in Burbank.[49] A radiant blonde woman, Mindy sat down and after introductions, poured out a queen's hoard of information on women in animation and what Milicent Patrick was up to at Disney. We ended up talking for over five hours, until we looked around and realized that the café workers were shooting hateful looks at us because they were trying to close.

An animator is defined as someone who makes animated films. But making an animated film usually involves much more work than drawing a picture and waving it around in front of a camera.

First, there's an idea for a story and a script is written. Next, a storyboard, which is a sequence of drawings representing planned scenes, is put together. Then, the sound and dialogue for those scenes is recorded. The background artists get started on the, you guessed it, backgrounds of the scenes, and the animators work on the characters. After the animators complete these drawings, they get inked onto clear sheets of celluloid acetate, called cels. The painting department applies colors to the reverse side of

---

49 I'm kidding! It was beautiful and sunny. It's California.

the cel. Tens of thousands of cels are needed for a feature film. These go to the camera department, where camera operators photograph the cels frame by frame over the background. Finally, the soundtrack is added.

Disney's pool of animators at this time consisted entirely of men. But those tens of thousands of tiny cels made from the animators' drawings, those sprang out of the Ink and Paint department, staffed entirely by women. This was a department where hundreds of women worked to, well, ink and paint these minuscule pieces of art. It was a rare place in the 1930s, a company where female artists could make a living.

It was here that Milicent started work in early January 1939. The fifteen-minute drive from her home in Glendale, where she still lived with her family, to the Disney studios on Hyperion Avenue in Silver Lake, an East Los Angeles neighborhood, would have been a breeze. An easy commute, even by today's standards.

The Ink and Paint building was kept meticulously clean and quiet to ensure a dustless environment for the intricate art being created by the many women inside. Milicent and her colleagues worked at tables that Disney had custom built for the purpose, in a room filled with large windows to let in as much natural light as possible.

Non-Ink-and-Paint-workers (men) were discouraged from entering, both to keep their filthy shoes and more importantly their filthy minds out of the clean rooms. Many of them weren't thinking that it was a department full of talented artists trying to get some goddamn work done, they were thinking that it was a convenient place to look for dates. (Even without getting into the building, male artists and technicians sought to interact with the Ink and Paint women. It was at Disney that Milicent would meet her first husband, animator Paul Fitzpatrick, but more on that later.) If a guy made it into the building, he would have been disappointed anyway. The Inkers and Painters wore shapeless smocks over their clothes to cut down on dust, visors to keep their hair away from the cels, and gloves to keep their hands clean. There wasn't a lot of skin being shown off.

The way Ink and Paint work was regarded didn't do much to disabuse male employees of this notion. Because it was a tedious and delicate process, cel inking and painting wasn't thought of as artistry. It was merely women's work, like stitching and sewing.[50] The level of artistic skill required to translate animators' drawings onto the tiny cels—without erasers!—was extraordinary. The reason that Disney was specially training his artists, including Inkers and Painters, at Chouinard was that he didn't just need artists who could draw, he needed artists who could draw motion. Each piece of art needed to be imbued with a dramatic flair, a kinetic energy. Yet at the time, journalists would come in and talk about the beautiful girls "tracing" in the Ink and Paint department, which is a gross oversimplification of what the actual work was. They were not taken seriously as artists, not remotely as seriously as the male animators were taken.

Milicent was originally hired for the paint department, but her flair for line work soon led her to be switched over to Ink. Inkers required a delicate skill. The artists here needed to be loose and relaxed. Remember, this wasn't on paper. This ink was applied to pieces of slippery celluloid, the link between the animators' paper drawings and seeing the image on the silver screen. Drawing the characters on these clear sheets made it possible to create a scene without drawing a new background for each frame.

The work needed to be perfectly accurate to the original drawings, with all lines at the correct width and with exactly tapered ends. The lines ran in thickness from fine to heavy, something difficult (for the untrained eye) to discern on a drawing

---

50 The problem here is considering disciplines that are generally thought of as "women's work" as lesser than other forms of art. At best, this thinking is stupid and at worst, it's misogynistic.

the size of a quarter. Even mixing the ink was an art, since the lines couldn't be made with ink that was too watery or it would become translucent. This work required nearly surgical precision for hours and hours on end, staring in one spot that was lit underneath by a light box.[51]

For work that was looked down on, it was physically demanding. Sore shoulders, headaches, eye strain were all a regular part of the job for the women of Ink and Paint. There were morning and afternoon breaks, with lunch at noon, but inking was a strenuous job. These morning and afternoon breaks were fifteen minutes long and called, in an adorably Disney way, Teatime. Teatime was available only for the women. Painters could have coffee, but Inkers could have only tea, in case caffeine jitters screwed up those perfect lines.

Once the cels were finished, they needed to be dried, stacked and passed on to a supervisor to be checked for accuracy and of course, to make sure they were in the correct order. Next, they would be checked against the background drawing. Then they went off to the painting department, where a group of women armed with an array of brushes and an extensive variety of colors (that they mixed themselves) painted the underneath of the inked cels.

When the paint was dried, the cels were sent to shadow painters,[52] airbrushers if airbrushing was needed for effects on images like clouds or glass, and then got one last check from a final supervisor. If they passed, they were ready for their close-ups, literally! They were ready to be filmed.

As far as first jobs go, working as an artist at Disney Studios might be one of the best. Milicent was working in film, helping

---

51   Literally a box, usually topped with glass, that contains an electric light. Often used in art and animation, it lights up a drawing from underneath, ensuring the most detailed view of lines and paint possible.

52   Which sounds like a group of ghosts or maybe demons that lived in the studio and wielded bloody brushes. These artists specialized in painting shadows, if needed, onto the cels with a transparent grey solution. They might have also been ghosts or demons, but I think there is a separate union for that.

to make movies alongside hundreds of other artists. She woke up in the morning and headed to a bustling studio where she was surrounded by fellow creative women. These were happy times for Milicent. Even though she was still living with her family, being a gainfully employed adult afforded her a little more personal freedom. Milicent was finally able to express herself with fashion. She started wearing makeup, stylish heels and more form-fitting dresses. The dresses were hidden under her big white smock, but I bet it was wonderful for her to have a choice about how she looked.

Milicent Patrick and Retta Scott, two of Disney's first female animators. They're ready to kick ass, take names and not drink any caffeine. (*Family collection*)

In early 1940, after a year of working in the world of Ink and Paint, a twenty-four-year-old Milicent was transferred into Animation and Effects alongside another female artist named Marcia James. Marcia and Milicent were not the first two women in animation at Disney; a few women had already been training in the department to be assistant animators and inbetweeners. Being an inbetweener is exactly what it sounds like. After the key animators[53] draw the key frames (the main poses in a scene), inbetweeners draw the frames in between them, usually the frames that give the illusion of motion. Despite her claims later in life, Milicent was *one of* the first female animators at Disney, but not the first. At this point, though, no one had seen their work on the big screen yet. That was about to change. The animation studio was working on its most ambitious project yet—*Fantasia*.

Milicent was promoted to Animation during the time Disney was moving shop from the older, smaller offices on Hyperion Avenue to a new studio in Burbank. The company was doing well and it was time to expand to a bigger, better space. Like a college campus, there were on-site restaurants and cafés, gymnasium—men's only—and masseurs, dry cleaners, even a barber. The Ink and Paint women got to eat in their own cafeteria.

Walt helped design the buildings himself; he wanted the space to achieve as much creative flow as possible. The complex was revolutionary in design—a studio built to fit the needs of artists. The buildings were laid out in the succession of the animated film process and all the workspaces were situated to get the best possible light, especially for the animators. The twenty-five buildings were crossed with spacious hallways and large, air-conditioned rooms. It was a beautiful place to work.

Not only was Milicent adjusting to a new job, she was doing it in a brand-new environment that was three times the size of her old work space. She went from being in a women-only building to being among the mostly male employees in the animation and special effects departments. Of the hundreds of artists working there, only a handful were women. Disney had

---

53   These were the senior animators, or main animators. In the film industry, the word *key* before any job title usually means that that person is the head of whatever they are doing.

released a memo reminding all the male employees to act appropriately and politely to make sure the environment was one where women could be comfortable. But this was still the 1940s. It was a time when a prime question of etiquette when a man hit on you was how to let him down gently.

At this point in animation history, every film Disney Studios released was groundbreaking in some way. In order to achieve Walt's new visions for his artistic masterpieces, new techniques needed to be invented and employed, especially in regard to color. Each segment in *Fantasia* is a smorgasbord of color in every possible shade, from the fiery hues in the *Rite of Spring* segment, where you see the primordial earth heaving and breaking and forming a land where dinosaurs roam, all the way to the deep darkness of shadows and stark white of bones and ghosts in the *Night on Bald Mountain* segment.

Not only did the range of hues need to be revolutionized, but so did the way that the colors were used. Some of the scenes in *Fantasia* required such delicacy and intricacy that they couldn't be done with the usual pens and ink. For them, the special effects department developed something called the Pastel Effect. Pastel itself was useless for animation: it was too smeary compared to paint. Disney wanted the style of pastel, the softness and subtlety of it. The Pastel Effect was a way of using brushes and diluting the paint to make the piece look like it was done with a chunk of chalky pastel. This look was something never seen in film before and part of what made *Fantasia* so striking.

By creating sequential color drawings with this technique, Milicent and Marcia were animating with just color. Neither of them—nor any of the other women in the department— were key animators. (Women in the department worked only as inbetweeners and assistant animators on *Fantasia*.) They *were* color animators. The term *color animating* is confusing because on *Fantasia*, it was considered a special effects technique. But it *was* animation, doing the work of key animators, only using color instead of pencil drawings.

Milicent and Marcia's color animation was used in four of the eight segments of the film, including creating Chernabog[54] in the *Night on Bald Mountain* sequence[55] in the final segment. Milicent helped bring what is arguably the most famous animated monster in all of cinema history to the screen.

By the end of the year, more women had been promoted to the animation team. Walt Disney started a program to train artists from the Ink and Paint department as animators so they could make the same jump that Milicent had. She went from working on effects to working fully on animating as an inbetweener. Now a third of the company's employees were female. No other animation company had anything close to that number. No other production company did, for that matter. If you were a female artist, Disney was probably one of the best places that you could work.

Fantasia was released to critical acclaim and the animation team went back to work. Disney was bustling. There were various short films being made, *Bambi* was in development and a strange movie called *The Reluctant Dragon* was in the works. It was a live-action anthology film, in which Robert Benchley, a famous humorist and Hollywood personality of the day, stars as himself wandering around the Disney studio lot, trying to find Walt Disney so he can pitch him an idea for a project. It brought audiences on a behind-the-scenes tour of how animated films were made and the live-action scenes were intercut with animated shorts.

The film wasn't shot in the actual animation department or

---

54 Fun monster nerd fact—one of the models used by concept artists for Chernabog was horror king Bela Lugosi!

55 It was used to create the creatures in the opening *Rite of Spring*, clouds in *The Pastoral Symphony*, and those gorgeous, dancing colored forms in *Toccata and Fugue in D Minor*. If you know what you're looking for, even for a visual art imbecile like myself, it's easy to recognize the Pastel Effect while watching the film.

the Ink and Paint building—that would have stopped the work-flow there. The crew created a set version of the studio rooms and cast actual Disney artists as background characters. Early on in the film, Robert Benchley stumbles into a sketching class as a bunch of artists (male and female) draw an elephant[56] and Milicent, in her first on-screen role, is one of them.

The Reluctant Dragon released later that summer in 1941 and didn't do very well at the box office. This was the same month that Hitler invaded the Soviet Union, so there were a lot of people who understandably weren't in the mood to go to the movies. Plus, a lot of moviegoers and critics were hoping for a full-length animated feature and were disappointed by the mish-mash of short animated films with what was essentially a giant live-action commercial for Disney animation studios.

It didn't help that *The Reluctant Dragon* was released at the height of a massive animators' strike. Throughout the film in-dustry, workers had been trying to unionize for the past year. Employees at other studios began to strike. They argued for better wages, hours and working conditions. Disney executives started to feel the pressure.

Before the strike hit, while the momentum and frustration was building, Disney was working on their fourth animated feature, *Dumbo*, a story about a young circus elephant who is ridiculed for his extremely large ears, and eventually figures out that he can use them to fly.

Milicent was an inbetweener on the *Dumbo* animation team. All those flying elephants and gallivanting circus animals— Milicent helped bring that fantastical movement to the big screen. This was the kind of work where that special training from Chouinard made you shine.

Between the ongoing tensions and World War II, it was not an easy time to be making films. Finances, supplies and work

---

56   By this I mean an actual elephant that's standing in the room as a model for the artists. Is it called a figure model if it's an animal?

forces were low. *Dumbo* had to be produced quickly, cheaply and efficiently, three words that an artist never wants to hear. These challenging working conditions made it so *Dumbo* didn't look as lush and detailed as the Disney movies that were released before it. The atmosphere in the studio during this time was tense and stressful, overshadowing some of the joy Milicent might have been feeling.

On top of that, because *Fantasia* was such an expensive, intensive film to make, there was pressure on *Dumbo* to be financially successful. The combined effect of all these pressures probably explains why *Dumbo* is one of Disney's shortest animated movies, coming in at only an hour and four minutes long.

It wasn't all stress, though. Just like in *The Reluctant Dragon*, to get the look of the circus animals right, the animation supervisors would bring in real animals for the artists to sketch. It's hard to have a bad day when you're hanging out with an elephant. Milicent, having grown up around the zoo at Hearst Castle, was probably far less impressed than her colleagues.

On May 29, 1941, union tensions came to a head at the studio and more than two hundred Disney staff members walked out on strike right in the middle of production. Many female artists walked out, but Milicent was not among the striking animators. She never liked to get involved in anything political and was intensely averse to conflict. Milicent always wanted everyone to get along. She stayed on at the studio to help finish *Dumbo*. Paul Fitzpatrick, the man Milicent would marry in a few years, was one of the strikers.

The strike lasted for only five weeks,[57] ending in July after much negotiation. Walt Disney signed the contract making it a union studio. This sounds like it would be good news for the artists and technicians employed by Disney, but the cost of paying union rates threw a wrench into the studio finances over

---

57   Although I'm sure that everyone working on *Dumbo* felt those five weeks keenly.

the following months. There was a massive restructuring of jobs and countless layoffs, right in the middle of production of the studio's fifth feature film, *Bambi*.

Lots of artists left or were forced to leave Disney that fall, including Milicent and the animator she had begun covertly dating, Paul Fitzpatrick. Paul and Milicent ended up leaving Disney on exactly the same day: September 12, 1941. It's impossible for me to say if they both left because of the layoffs, or the fact that someone caught on to their relationship (dating coworkers was frowned upon), or a combination of the two. Some artists returned once things settled down, but not Milicent. While all this outside turmoil was seething around her, Milicent was having her own problems with her work. The antagonist was her own brain.

Milicent suffered from migraines. I don't mean that she was one of those people in migraine pill commercials that put their hands to their heads and look dolefully out the window. I mean the kind of migraines that force the sufferer to be sequestered in a dark bedroom for days at a time. The light boxes Milicent had to stare at for hours on end as part of her job as an animator were wreaking havoc on her physically. Between the migraines and all the other problems at Disney, it was a good time for her to leave. She worked at the studio for only two years. She left a month before *Dumbo* would premiere in the United States.

On résumés and in interviews for the rest of her life, Milicent would sometimes say that she was the first female animator at Disney. This is a claim that has been, strangely, both hard to prove and hard to disprove. Retta Scott is the first woman to ever be credited as an animator at Disney, for her work on *Bambi*,[58] which was released in 1942. Retta Scott was hired during March 1939 in the story department, two months after Mi-

---

58 Retta animated the sequence of the hunting dogs chasing Faline, Bambi's deer girlfriend. I don't think this the zoologically correct term, but it *is* a Disney movie.

licent was hired at the Ink and Paint department. Both women were Chouinard graduates. There is a photo of the two of them, side by side in their Disney artist smocks, both wearing genuine smiles. Retta Scott is also an extra in *The Reluctant Dragon*, sitting right next to Milicent.

Milicent was color animating on *Fantasia* in 1940, but that was alongside Marcia James. Finding individual credits for Disney films back then is hazy at best, impossible at worst. There are so many steps to traditional, hand-drawn animation and when you are creating an animated feature film, steps are happening concurrently. Plus, it sometimes takes years to create a feature and Disney was developing and producing multiple projects at a time. A sequence for one film might be animated before a sequence in another film, but for various reasons, the second film might be released first. What did Milicent mean by first? First hired? First to animate a full sequence? First to see her work on the big screen? There is no definitive moment that I can point to that says that Milicent was the first, nor a definite moment for Marcia James or Retta Scott.

Because color animation was soon phased out after *Fantasia*, the term isn't well understood or widely known. Many claim that it doesn't count as animation at all. I have, on multiple occasions, watched male historians actually roll their eyes when faced with the term. I don't doubt that the fact color animation was done by women has a substantial amount to do with why it isn't considered "real animation" by these guys. There is a history at Disney of the work being done by women not being taken seriously. But by the actual definition of animating—creating successive drawings that give the illusion of movement when shown in sequence—Milicent and Marcia were animating.

Remember, this is animation, not landing on the moon. There were hundreds of artists working at the studio, artists animating and creating multiple versions of drawings that may or may not be used in the final cut of the film. Many sequences were being worked on at the same time. There wasn't a big button labeled "animate" that Milicent was the first woman to walk up to and press.[59]

Was she the first female animator at Disney? I honestly can't tell you. I don't feel comfortable saying either way. She might have been the first woman at Disney to animate. Maybe Marcia was out sick that day. Milicent definitely saw her animation on-screen before Retta—*Bambi* came out a year after *Fantasia* and *Dumbo* did. There's evidence in both directions. After years of research, I will tell you with certainty that Milicent was one of the first female animators at Disney. Retta will be forever the one to hold the title of first credited animator.[60] But it's a nearly impossible task to say who the first uncredited female animator was because, well, they're uncredited. It doesn't help Milicent's Disney legacy that she was there for only two years. Retta was rehired after the layoffs and continued animating for Disney until 1946.

What matters is that Milicent was bringing art and monsters to life on-screen and that she was one of the first women to do so. She was blazing trails in a male-dominated industry, an industry that is still dominated by men. Milicent, Retta, Marcia and many others helped pave the way for more women to enter the animation world. Unfortunately, Walt Disney isn't around anymore to give out stern office memos telling the men to lay off being creeps. Thanks to a work atmosphere rife with sexism, gender equality in the animated film industry has not improved as much as it should have since the 1940s.

In 2017, over two hundred female and gender-nonconforming animation professionals signed an open letter that was sent out to executives at Disney, Paramount, Nickelodeon, DreamWorks,

---

59 To be fair, I still haven't been inside Disney's animation studio. I might be wrong about this.

60 Screen credit. As in, when you see all the credits for the people who worked on a film at the beginning or end of a movie, Retta's name is the first female name ever seen on-screen credited with animation.

Cartoon Network and every other major Los Angeles studio.
The letter was inspired by the #MeToo movement's efforts to
call attention to and wipe out sexual harassment in the film industry. It asked that the studios institute and enforce sexual harassment policies, asked male colleagues to both report sexual
harassment that they witness and start standing up for the victims, and finally asked the union (The Animation Guild) to create new policies so sexual harassers and abusers could be kicked
out. The women and gender-nonconforming people who signed
the letter included showrunners, executives, directors, animators, production designers, producers, writers and artists. Many
of them work at big studios like Disney, Warner Brothers and
Netflix, or on high profile projects like *Adventure Time*, *Steven
Universe* and *Bob's Burgers*.

> We, the women and gender-nonconforming people of the
> animation community, would like to address and highlight
> the pervasive problem of sexism and sexual harassment in
> our business... Sexual harassment and assault are widespread
> issues that primarily affect women, with women of color,
> members of the LGBTQ+ community and other mar-
> ginalized groups affected at an even greater rate. As more
> women have entered the animation workforce, it seems
> that some men have not embraced this change. They still
> frequently make crass sexual remarks that make it clear
> women are not welcome on their crews. Some have pressed
> colleagues for romantic or sexual relationships, despite our
> clear disinterest. And some have seen the entrance of more
> women into the industry as an opportunity to exploit and
> victimize younger workers on their crews who are look-
> ing for mentorship.

Having over 30 percent female employees working at Disney
studios was a progressive number in 1940 and sadly, it would

still be a progressive number today. As of 2017, women make up only 23 percent of union animation jobs. There are many more women working as freelance artists and animators, but for big studio jobs, the numbers are pathetic. It wasn't until 2012 that the first woman (Brenda Chapman) won an Oscar in the Best Animated Feature Film category for the movie *Brave*.

Even in the face of sexism, equality in the animation industry is slowly improving. Numbers of female animators are on the rise and since 2012, at least one woman has been nominated for Best Animated Feature Film Oscar every year, with two wins (Jennifer Lee for *Frozen* in 2013 and Darla K. Anderson for *Coco* in 2017). But we still have a long way to go, especially in regard to women of color. All three of these female Oscar winners are white. (Out of the fourteen women who have been nominated for Best Animated Feature Film, only four are women of color.)

The good news is that we've got more women coming. In 1961, the Chouinard Institute merged with the Los Angeles Conservatory of Music to become California Institute of the Arts, also known as CalArts. At CalArts today, 71 percent of the animation students are women. Many schools across the country are seeing a significant increase in the number of female animation students, like the University of California, Los Angeles's masters program in animation, which is made up of 68 percent women. That's a lot of women getting ready to enter the world of animation, a lot of women whose art I cannot wait to see on the big screen.

Although she left the animation business, Milicent still wanted to work in the film industry. The first (brief) taste of screen acting on *The Reluctant Dragon* agreed with her. She loved being in front of the camera and the camera loved her being there. It was impossible to miss that Milicent was a physically dazzling person.

When she left Disney in 1941, at age twenty-six, Milicent Patrick decided to finally capitalize on that. After years of hiding her figure in heavy, draping clothing, it was time for Milicent to blossom.

5

Wipe

The 1940s were turbulent years for the world, for the country and for Milicent. World War II was raging and the anxiety of technological progress loomed over America. The war cast a dark shadow over everything, even Hollywood and sunny California. Fear and uncertainty were ubiquitous. While the world was swirling in turmoil, Milicent stepped out into it for the first time.

Besides illustration, one of Milicent's great talents was looking beautiful and poised in front of a still or video camera. Believe me, this is a talent. It is not an easy thing to charm a lens. Being aware of every part of your face and body, keeping every muscle posed, tightened and angled *just so* is a sort of creative magic that leaves me in awe.

My partner is a photographer. When I sold this book, the one you hold in your hands, one of the first things I needed was an author portrait.[61] Sadly, none of my carefully snapped Instagram selfies counted, no matter how I adjusted the filter. While

---

61 You can see it yourself somewhere near the back of this book!

I asked around for photographer recommendations, one of my best friends, Lauren Panepinto, insisted that I needed the best. But, she told me, don't worry. A great photographer she knew in Los Angeles would do it as a friend favor.

I had known of Allan Amato's work for a long time. Lots of books on my shelves featured his photography and I was a big fan of writers and filmmakers whose portraits he had taken. Thinking about my own picture being among those illustrious ranks made me nervous. I was so intimidated when I stepped into his Los Angeles studio that my hands were shaking.

On the outside, I was keeping it cool. But on the inside, I was a wreck. I had no idea what I was doing. My last experience being photographed by a professional was at school picture day. Back then, the only thing I worried about was stuff stuck in my braces.

Standing in front of a camera, many people—myself included—freeze. You start to think about all sorts of muscles and body parts you never acknowledge in your everyday life. What do you do with your eyebrows? Where do you point your chin? Why do you have so many facial muscles and why are they all conspiring to make you look stupid?

It was over before I knew it and I was relieved to literally be out of the spotlight. The pictures came out fantastically, but I was stunned to think of the people who do this for a living. There are people who step in front of a lens and wield their physical form with grace and inspiration. I now live with Allan and get to witness professional models executing their craft all the time. It never fails to wow me. Milicent Patrick was one of those people.

Milicent, as with almost every artistic endeavor she put her mind to, excelled at modeling. Over the next decade, from her mid-twenties to early thirties, she worked frequently and made a living as a model. Unfortunately, this was a time before models were credited for their work. Milicent jumped from one industry that was terrible at crediting women right into another.

Before the 1950s, models did not make a name for themselves with their craft. They were essentially anonymous talent. This was before the idea of a "cult of personality" entered the public consciousness. Photography in advertising wasn't widely used in the 1940s. It wasn't until the 1960s that consumers started being able to recognize certain models that were associated with certain brands. There was a lot of work for her, but no real possibility for recognition.

After years of having to hide her figure and being unable to date, having people look at Milicent and gush over her beauty must have been intoxicating for her. Luckily, she was in a city that already had a well-oiled pipeline for tapping the talents of beautiful women. Hollywood was the place you went when you wanted to make a career out of being beautiful, and Milicent was already there.

She quickly learned how to look glamorous: eyebrows shaped, hair styled, ears pierced, lips and nails painted. Milicent absolutely loved getting dolled up and putting on beautiful, showy dresses and high heels. In her late twenties, she developed a personal style that would endure until her death. As far as Milicent was concerned, the fancier and more elegant, the better. For the rest of her life, she was rarely seen without lipstick and high heels on. Glamour brought her a lot of joy.

Milicent worked mainly as a trade show hostess and promotional model in Los Angeles. A modeling agency assigned her to different trade shows and conventions. She modeled jewelry if it was a jewelry convention, standing in a company's booth while wearing jewelry and smiling and talking to people about the products, and modeled housewares if it was a housing convention, candy if it was a candy convention, and so on.[62]

---

62 There are some great photographs of Milicent at a housewares convention where she was promoting a new line of dryers and they just draped her with a pile of laundry line to hold, like a mermaid trying to get out of a net. To her credit, she looks as lovely as you can while smiling and holding an armload of rope.

Even in this world of eye-catching people, Milicent stood out. She was named the "Queen" of some of the jewelry shows she modeled at, which I'm assuming is just a ceremonial title designed to make you wear even more promotional jewelry. She earned many modeling titles like this, such as Miss Rainbow, Miss Complete Petty Girl, Miss Beam, Miss Rehm[63] and the Orchid Girl.

An ultraglamorous modeling headshot. No wonder she was named "Queen of the Jewelry Show." (*Author collection*)

Most of her work was at trade shows, but she did various other kinds of modeling. She was the trophy girl for car races and appeared in television commercials. Again, this was during a time when most advertisements were illustrations or drawings, so consumers didn't see photographs of women showing

---

63 And presumably Miss Kreme, Miss Dream and Miss Gleam if those titles were available.

off products in magazines. Companies needed models for live promotional events. So not only did you have to smile, pose and hold the product, but you had to do it for hours at a time, while talking to strangers about it.

While she was working as a model, she was of course, meeting men. Models holding items for purchase are, by design, there to attract people. It wasn't as provocative as some convention show modeling is today, though. Remember, this was the 1940s. There were no Budweiser booty shorts here. All the women were in dresses that would be considered very classy by today's standards. But make no mistake, they were there mostly to attract men. Especially at trade shows, where the floor was filled with male journalists, businessmen and male company representatives. If you wanted your product to stand out, you made sure a beautiful woman was holding it, preferably being sweet and personable while she was doing so.

This was a thunderous lifestyle switch. Growing up at Hearst Castle, Milicent was discouraged from having friends, let alone dates. Next, she was off to college, where she was living at home under the watchful eye of her father. Then she worked at Disney, where Milicent worked for the first year in a building that men were actively discouraged from entering and she wore a giant frock coat over her clothes. Going from this sheltered existence into Hollywood modeling was a dramatic shift for Milicent.

Camille didn't approve of Milicent's new Hollywood lifestyle. In fact, he hated it. Modeling in Los Angeles was a job that was completely at odds with his conservative beliefs. He worried that the liberal atmosphere of Hollywood encouraged moral decline. This situation became even more aggravated once Milicent began her first romantic relationship. It was her first serious relationship and one that was deeply fraught with moral conflict. This only confirmed Camille's fears. It set a heartrending pattern for nearly every single serious relationship Milicent would have over the course of her lifetime.

While she was working at Disney, Milicent met an animator named Paul Fitzpatrick. (I told you that you'd hear more about him.) I wouldn't call him handsome, but Paul looked like a nice enough man. He was of average build, with brown hair and a pair of round glasses that perched on his long pointed nose. The first film Paul worked on at Disney was *Snow White and the Seven Dwarfs*. He worked on *Fantasia* and *Dumbo* along with Milicent and I'm guessing that they connected there.

The problem with Paul and Milicent wasn't just that they both worked at Disney, which discouraged interoffice relationships.

The problem with Paul was that he was married.

Milicent, just like many people who are prevented from learning how to be in healthy romantic relationships while they are growing up, was about to start a lifetime habit of making poor romantic decisions.

I was unable to find out when it began, but by the time she began modeling, Paul and Milicent were deeply entangled in an affair. It could have started during the years Milicent worked at Disney, or they could have waited until they were no longer working there. I'll probably never know.

What I do know is that some time into the affair, Paul's wife discovered two things. One, that her husband was with another woman. Two, that she was pregnant with her first child.

Paul's wife[64] then went to Camille and begged him to reason with Milicent. She wanted him to convince his daughter to break up with Paul. But Milicent was in her late twenties and having the first serious relationship of her life. I'm in my late twenties and cannot step outside my door without someone inquiring about when I'm going to get married and have kids. I deal with these pressures in 2018, but in the 1940s, most women Milicent's age were already married with several children. Imagine the dizzying intensity of your first relationship, but happening while you were nearly thirty and everyone around you was

---

64 Whose name, regrettably, remains unknown to me.

pressuring you to settle down. Camille didn't have a chance. He couldn't convince Milicent. Milicent refused to leave Paul, and Paul refused to stop seeing Milicent.

Once this was clear to her, Paul's wife took her own life. She was still carrying her child.

Milicent and Paul stayed together after the tragedy and soon got married, around 1945. This was the beginning of Milicent's estrangement from her family, or rather their estrangement from her. To Camille, the tragedy showed him that Milicent was a "black woman," the embodiment of feminine evil. In his mind, it wasn't just Paul's fault for cheating on his wife. It was Milicent's fault for participating in the dreadful situation. Camille discouraged the entire Rossi family, including her mother and siblings, from seeing or talking to her.

Undated sketch for a children's book illustration. (*Author collection*)

During this tumultuous time, Milicent was, in addition to modeling, still creating art both for herself and professionally as a freelancer. Perhaps inspired by her new vocation, she channeled her love of fashion into clothing design. Some pieces she even sewed for herself to wear. Freed from her draping, family-approved dresses and the baggy smocks of Disney, Milicent developed a passion for dramatic clothing that sometimes bordered on the theatrical.

She illustrated, as well. Milicent worked on a strange little book called *Pink and Blue Laughter*, written by Helen Charlot Phillips, published by the now defunct Hollywood House. *Pink and Blue Laughter* at first glance appears to be some sort of light-hearted joke book. Once you crack the spine, however, you see that the first page contains a poem about boobs and is accompanied by a drawing of a well-endowed woman in a very small sweater. It's a stretch to call it a dirty book; nothing goes beyond the suggestive. It's mostly full of off-color jokes about horny widows, nagging wives and cheap businessmen. It doesn't quite reach the point of lewd, but it's rather risqué for 1944.

The poems are forgettable, but the illustrations are incredible. It's impossible to miss the skill in them, even when it's just a caricature of a grumpy housewife. Milicent was able to convey impressive amounts of emotion and movement with only a few confident lines. They are certainly works to be proud of, even if some of them aren't for polite company. This may explain why she published the book under a pseudonym,[65] Paul Fitzpatrick Jr. I can't decide if this is a more or less weird choice because she and Paul Fitzpatrick never had any children. Milicent, due to that childhood peritonitis in San Simeon, was never able to

---

65 This is also why I'm not 100 percent certain that Helen Charlot Phillips is a real person. No other work was ever published under that name. It could also mean that the publishing world did not give a warm reception to *Pink and Blue Laughter* and that Helen turned to another profession. A first edition—there was only one printing—sells on eBay for less than five dollars, which, where I live, isn't even enough to buy yourself a fancy coffee. No biographical information is printed on the book.

conceive. Publishing this indecent little book under that name could only have been some sort of inside joke.[66]

The marriage to Paul lasted only a few years. During this time, she started calling herself Mil Fitzpatrick. Up until this point, she still went by and worked under her given name, Mildred Rossi. This is when her reinvention began. After the divorce, she kept part of Paul's name and became Mil Patrick. She never used the name Mildred again.

Cultivating a new persona to inhabit was not an uncommon thing in Los Angeles. It still isn't. Rita Hayworth, Cary Grant, John Wayne—these were all created for the silver screen. Actors and actresses would arrive in Hollywood and be molded, sometimes by themselves, sometimes by producers or agents, into entirely new people. These new names came with different physical characteristics, different personality traits, sometimes even different ethnicities.

Milicent was alone in an entirely new world and it makes sense that to navigate it, she began to craft an updated version of herself. This was a time when even in liberal Hollywood, a woman entering her thirties divorced and childless was going to be judged by people. She tumbled out of the 1940s without a husband or her family behind her. The only ground she had to stand on was of her own making: her talent, her profession, her contacts, her friends in Los Angeles.

Milicent was crafting her own future and to do so, she started crafting her past. The name Mildred Rossi was left behind like an old coat. In interviews, on résumés, with anything having to do with publicity for the rest of her life, Milicent would say that she was born an Italian baroness, Mildred Elizabeth Fulvia *de* Rossi.

For Americans, who are completely unfamiliar with anything more royal than prom kings, this must have been impressive. In

---

66 My best guess is that Paul Fitzpatrick Jr. has to do with Paul's, well, Paul Jr., and I must posthumously congratulate Milicent on going that far for a dick joke.

the days before fact-checking, the internet and Ancestry.com, these were the kind of claims you could make largely without consequence. She was of Italian descent and certainly looked the part. I'm not sure what a person in the 1940s would think an Italian baroness looked like, but a striking, dark-haired woman in an elegant, sweeping dress was probably it, maybe with a crown made out of uncooked spaghetti and a scepter with a juicy meatball on top. That's probably what most people today would think. Nobody knows what an Italian baroness is. I certainly didn't when I started researching Milicent Patrick.

For a very long time, I believed Milicent's claims, simply because I had no reason to think otherwise. The idea of dramatically casting aside her role as a baroness to plunge into the world of art and film sounded glamorous, fantastic, even heroic. But the truth is, well, it's just not the truth.

First off, barons and baronesses were basically the lowest on the totem pole of Italian nobility. They were usually titles without any land attached to them. Second, they passed down through the male line. You can't be born a baroness, unless the moment you shoot out of the womb, you land on an altar next to a baron waiting with a ring, a very creepy baron that was willing to marry a baby.[67] Third, by 1948, these titles of nobility weren't even officially recognized by Italy anymore.

When I realized this, sitting at a computer terminal in the downtown branch of the Los Angeles Public Library, I was disappointed. I stared at that smudged public computer screen and felt like an idiot, like someone who thought that John Wayne was actually a duke. Milicent, how could you lie? Her being a secret Italian baroness had become part of the mythology surrounding her life. Now she was just a regular person, without a pasta crown! What the hell?

The problem with being the only woman to ever do something is that you have to be perfect. When I found out about

---

67   I'm pretty sure it's illegal to marry babies in Italy.

her as a teenager, I thought that for Milicent to be the first and only woman to ever design a famous monster, to be one of the first female animators, she had to be superhuman. She had to have been better than any other woman who ever wanted to design a monster. She had to have been the only one worthy enough to enter that boys' club. This way of thinking is a mal-adaptation women have developed over the years to be able to deal with the fact that we're getting passed on for jobs because we're female. You force yourself to believe that there just haven't been any women good enough for the job, rather than accept the fact that the entire system just doesn't want you in it. Any-one who flouts that system must be an outlier.

"Ah!" we think when we see a woman who does the thing we want to do. "Of course. She must be perfect. She's got a three hundred-point IQ and can levitate and breathe fire. That's why she got the job. Normal women can't get jobs like that."

Milicent was the only one, so she had to carry the weight of all my hopes and dreams. She had to be perfect, she had to be a ge-nius, she had to be the very, very best. She was more than a hero, she was a goddess, shedding her human form. That's the danger in having so few women acknowledged and hired in the film in-dustry. Instead of looking at these women and thinking "Yes, I can get there, too!" girls can just as easily look at them all alone in a sea of men and think "They must have been perfect to get there. I never will." It's like being a bystander watching Odysseus sending an arrow through all those axe heads. There's no room for faults or flaws. Yes, Milicent was a woman. But she was also a beautiful, able-bodied, straight, white woman who people be-lieved was Italian royalty. You can't blame any girl for looking at that and thinking what she achieved was out of reach.

The grand irony is that Milicent had to create a persona to navigate this world by herself. She created an illusion of perfec-tion because her life was anything but. Her family had abandoned her. The Rossis refused to support her, but she could use what she had left—her family name—to craft a persona that made her feel powerful and confident. Even though she had so many advantages (being white, for example), Milicent had to use everything she could to her advantage. Women looking to get into the film industry are up against a titanic amount of sexism and it was even worse when Milicent was in Hollywood. When you try your very best and it's good, but you know, good *for a girl*, you need to become more than yourself, more than human. Ginger Rogers, doing everything Fred Astaire did, backward and in high heels.

After my initial disappointment, I realized that Milicent being a normal, non-royal was more important to her position as a role model. It was more inspirational. She didn't have superpowers or a magic wand. She was simply intelligent and savvy and good at what she did. We need women to be allowed to be simply good at what they do. We need them on set, in meetings, behind cameras and pens and paintbrushes. We need them to be themselves, to be human: ordinary and flawed. That way, more girls can see them and think "I can do that." That way, no one can look at them and say "She got that job because she's beautiful. She just got that gig because she slept with someone."

Actually, she got hired because she was damn good.

It was difficult for me to reconcile the superhuman Milicent that lived in my mind with the real-life Milicent who made garbage relationship decisions and pretended that she was a baroness. It's always tough to see what your heroes are really like. I was working hard enough to show the world her legacy; I didn't want people to think badly of her. I got defensive, and even briefly considered leaving parts of her life out of this book to make her look like a better person.

But humanizing Milicent made her accomplishments even more important. Thinking about her as an actual human with actual human problems made me feel more capable. I, too, could have success in the film industry, despite my flair for making bad romantic choices! I knew other women would feel the same. Women don't need an idol to worship.[68] We need a beacon to walk toward.

Even though I was enjoying Los Angeles and life in my tiny new apartment, I felt adrift. There were two feature films under my belt, but when you work from home, there's no sign on your door reminding you that you have an actual job. Working as a film producer looks like many other jobs; when the exciting parts (filming) aren't happening, I'm usually just answering a bunch of emails and talking to people on the phone. Most days, if I don't feel like it, I don't have to put on pants. I didn't feel the film-producer-making-it-in-LA part, I felt the woman-who-didn't-know-what-she-was-doing-and-also-wasn't-wearing-pants part. Being a film producer sounded fancy and important. I didn't feel fancy and important. I felt ordinary and flawed. Backward and in heels? I can't even go forward in heels.

I could understand Milicent's desire for a persona. A persona could both dazzle people and shield them from your ordinary and flawed self. I'm not what you picture when you imagine a high-powered producer. As a twenty-five-year-old woman with blue hair and lots of tattoos, I didn't feel impressive. I didn't even own a suit. When I introduced myself to people as a writer and filmmaker, I could almost hear that sad trombone noise play. If I was wearing a fancy dress and said that I was Irish royalty, an O'Meara baroness with a potato fortune, it would certainly help. Maybe then I wouldn't have to try so hard to catch up to the male filmmakers I knew. Maybe then no one would question my abilities.

During the production of one of our films, my boss and I were waiting in a Los Angeles sound studio for an actor to show up.[69] We needed to record his dialogue for the film. Sultan

---

68   There's Beyoncé for that.

69   I'm not yet ready to reveal the name of this actor, for a variety of personal reasons.

and I were thrilled when this man agreed to be in our cast; we thought he was perfect for the role. Sultan was calm as usual, answering emails and looking at pictures of cats on Instagram. I, however, was sitting in a chair in the little lounge next to the glass-walled recording booth and trying not to bite my nails. I still hadn't gotten the hang of meeting celebrities, even ones that I was working with.

I was wearing what I called a "producer outfit," which consisted of anything that was plain black (no skull print) and long enough to cover my arm and leg tattoos.[70] I thought that having my tattoos covered up would help me be taken more seriously. My hair was emerald green at the time, but there wasn't much I could do to cover that up. I definitely looked my age (early twenties), but there was nothing I could do about that, either.

When the actor showed up with his female assistant, everyone introduced themselves. My boss, the director, the sound engineer—each person shook the man's hand. I stepped up and extended my slightly clammy palm.

"Hi! I'm Mallory O'Meara, one of the producers of the project."

He looked at me and gestured at my hair.

"Heh. Is it green everywhere?"

The whole world paused for a horrible second.

I mumbled some sort of noncommittal response, not quite believing that this person would say something so blatantly lascivious and disrespectful to me, right in front of my crew. I helped cast you, you asshole!

"Well, if you need help with that, let me know." He chuckled and walked into the sound booth. Sultan turned to me, stunned. I slowly sank back into the chair.

My first reaction, I'm ashamed to say, wasn't anger. It wasn't fear or sadness. It was confusion. Did this creep just hit on me… by offering to help dye my pubic hair? Seriously? For one thing,

---

70 An outfit that I eventually realized made me look more "cat burglar" than "serious producer."

it takes *six hours* to get my hair this color. Six uncomfortable hours. That's like trying to pick me up by offering me a pap smear. That's the best you can come up with?

Sultan got mad before I did. His anger snapped me out of my disbelief, but neither of us knew how to react. It was the first time Sultan had witnessed a man saying something like this to me. We sat in awkward silence as we watched the actor record his lines. I felt fury spreading through my entire body like a tide.

When the recording session was over, the actor exited the booth and got ready to leave. I'm sorry to write it, but I didn't confront him. In fact, I never said another word to him. I sat frozen in that office chair. I was so upset, so filled with rage and misery, it was as if extra gravity was in the air around my body.

Before the man left, he gestured at his own assistant, a blonde woman a few years younger than myself, and then nodded toward me. He looked at Sultan and said, "If you ever want to swap sometime, let me know. Heh, heh, heh!" Nobody said anything in response. No one knew what to say.

Afterward, we stood in the parking lot and Sultan looked at me with sad eyes.

"I promise, Mallory, we're never working with him again."

Instead of imagining that actor falling into a manhole, all I could think about was whether or not that would have happened if my hair was a natural color. If it would have happened if I was older, or wearing a business suit or looked more "professional."[71] The answer is yes.

Every single woman I know who works in the film industry has not just one story like this, but many. Every single woman, regardless of age, race, body type or whether or not they look "alternative" like I do. No outfit, no dye color, no amount of "proper" looks or behavior shields you. Being a producer or a director or a famous actress doesn't shield you. Nothing shields you.

---

71   Don't worry, *now* I imagine him falling into a manhole. Years later, my hair is still as unnatural as I can make it and I don't hide my tattoos anymore.

Putting all the imperfect parts of Milicent's life into this book is just as important as putting in all the impressive parts. Omitting things to make her look more like a saint would be the same impulse as covering up my tattoos in the hopes that I'll look more respectable. I'd be perpetuating the notion that women need to be a certain way to be accepted in this industry, that women need to change themselves so that men will respect them. I'm worthy of respect, no matter what I look like. Milicent deserves to be known, no matter who she married. No woman deserves the misogyny that we experience and Milicent didn't deserve what ultimately happened to her.

Milicent's flaws started to make me feel more connected to her. They made me feel inspired. Like her, I was also estranged from my family. The only stable ground I had was what she had—talent, friends, contacts, career. Everything keeping me up was what I had built myself. I was very far away from the New England town where I grew up. There wasn't a Dunkin' Donuts in sight.

I didn't go to school for filmmaking. When my boss, Sultan Saeed al Darmaki, hired me, I was putting myself through college for animal science and working as a veterinary technician at a small animal clinic in Massachusetts. But I loved the horror genre—films, comics, books, all of it. In my spare time, I ran multiple chapters of a horror-centric book club[72] and helped with horror-themed events all over New England, including the horror convention in Rhode Island where I met Sultan. His newly formed company, Dark Dunes Productions, was sponsoring the convention. After seeing me working my butt off all weekend, he asked me to come work for him. He wanted me to remotely run the social media and communications for Dark Dunes. I didn't know anything about making movies. During the convention, I ran the volunteer program and Sultan watched me

---

72 One in Salem, Massachusetts, one in Manchester, New Hampshire, and one in Providence, Rhode Island. I did a lot of driving. It was worth it.

direct and solve the issues of hundreds of volunteers, convention goers and guests. I'm good at figuring things out, at handling people, at solving problems creatively and efficiently. I didn't know it just yet, but this is what it takes to be a good producer.

To take the job, I'd have to drop out of college, quit the veterinary clinic and radically redirect the entire direction of my life, which, up until that moment, I had been steering toward animal science and becoming a female Steve Irwin. But how often does a woman get a chance like this? Not very often. I couldn't pass it up, so I didn't. I had to trust that I could be really good at this job, that I could figure out the film industry.

I said yes.

Years later in Los Angeles, surrounded by filmmakers who I automatically assumed had more experience and know-how than I did, I understood the impulse to make myself as strong and impenetrable as possible. But if Milicent Patrick was an ordinary woman who was good at what she did, that meant that it was okay for me to be, too.

I was failing her if I didn't write the truth of her life. Her flaws were a part of the story that needed to be told. It's far more impressive to me that she made her career as a flawed woman instead of as a perfect baroness.[73] Her legacy should be founded on the strength of the art that she created and on the trails that she blazed.

In her early thirties, Milicent's life was almost completely different from what it was when she moved to that suburban street in Glendale. Mildred Rossi was, for all intents and purposes, a new person. She had a new identity as Mil Patrick, a new glamorous look, a new career path as a professional model and freelance artist. She was divorced and on her own, but still standing. It seems appropriate that the next stage of her career would come while she was standing on the street, waiting for the bus.

---

73   Milicent did benefit from a lot of other privileges, like being white and being straight and being able-bodied.

6

Jump Cut

Around 1947, when she was thirty-one, Milicent had just finished a long day of promotional modeling at an event at the Ambassador Hotel. Smiling for hours on end and standing in heels while making small talk with strangers is exhausting[74] even if you aren't doing it for a living.

The Ambassador was not just a fancy hotel, it was a *place* to be. Some of the early Academy Awards ceremonies were held there and it had a reputation for being an establishment where movie stars, prominent politicians and other celebrities hung out.[75] So Milicent must have been a little embarrassed to be leaving for the day, not in a beautiful private car, but waiting for the bus.

It was a good thing that she was standing around in her heels and nice dress. While waiting, she caught the eye of William

---

74 If there was anything superhuman about Milicent, it was her ability to wear heels seemingly all the time. I have seen only one picture of her ever in flat shoes and that is a modeling photograph in which she plays tennis in sneakers.

75 It's been closed since 1988, but it's appeared in a number of well-known movies, including *Forrest Gump*, *Pretty Woman* and *Fear and Loathing in Las Vegas*. You shouldn't film anything there anymore, though, since it's owned by an Orange Monstrosity of a man whose last name rhymes with "dump."

Hawks, brother of Howard Hawks. He was a film producer, but at that point his production company had made only one film, *My Life with Caroline*. He was better known from his days as an agent; he was William Faulkner's. But he wanted to make more films and as both a producer and an agent he was always on the lookout for something new and exciting.

That was Milicent Patrick.

Hawks was walking out of the hotel when he saw her waiting for the bus and he stopped. He approached Milicent and told her that she should work in film as an actress. Looking at her, you can understand why. She was a statuesque, standout beauty. Along with her looks, Hawks was charmed by her warm personality. Milicent was thrilled and interested in the suggestion. Hawks immediately set out to get her up on the big screen. For the rest of her life, she loved to tell the story of how Hawks discovered her, telling her he wanted her "for the pictures."

Milicent, second from left, dazzling in her sideshow girl costume in *Texas, Brooklyn and Heaven*. (*Photofest NYC*)

Soon, Milicent had her first role as Water Nymph in the romantic comedy *Texas, Brooklyn & Heaven*, which was released in 1948. She's seen for a moment in a line of women in a Coney

Island sideshow. That same year, she appeared as Woman in Dorsey Club in the musical *A Song is Born*, directed by William's brother Howard. She was also Lady in Black in *Thunder in the Pines*. Her acting career had begun.

She started, as many actors do, by doing background, aka "extra" work. These are actors who have nonspeaking roles, generally appearing in the background of a scene: Dancer #5, Lady on Bench, Man Eating Ice Cream.[76] The work of a background actor is similar to that of a featured actor. It usually involves getting prepped by the hair and makeup department, and then waiting around for hours on set. Most people don't realize that film sets can be very boring places. It can take a long time for the crew to set up lighting and cameras, so actors have a lot of downtime waiting for everything to be ready.

One of the many portraits Milicent sketched of her costars. (*Author collection*)

Milicent used these filming recesses to draw. She was grateful and enthusiastic about the opportunity to act, but she still

---

76 If you sneer at background actors, go out and try to pretend to do something over and over the exact same way, and do it perfectly each time. After looking like an idiot for a while, you'll realize that it takes a lot of skill to pretend to do things, aka act.

loved being a visual artist. While on set, she would use the time waiting to get in the makeup chair or in between takes to sketch skilled portraits of her costars.

She went under the name Mil Patrick for her first few roles, but eventually decided to change it to Milicent Patrick, after William Randolph Hearst's wife, the woman who had made such an impression on her as a child. She would go through three more name changes during the course of her life, but Milicent Patrick would be the name with which she made the greatest impression on the world.

My search for Milicent hit a wall. I couldn't figure out what she was doing post-Disney-animation work and pre-Universal Studios monster design work. It was time to turn to my strongest resource: monster nerd friends. Never, ever underestimate the power of nerds. Nerds of all shapes and sizes make this world go round. Luckily for me, I'm friends with the biggest *Creature from the Black Lagoon* nerd on the planet.

Most people know David Schow as one of the writers of the popular 1994 film *The Crow*, aka the goth teenage bible. David is a renowned horror writer, for both the page and the screen. We met at Monsterpalooza[77] in 2014. As much as we both love horror, David and I bonded over a more specific love: *Creature from the Black Lagoon*. The first time I visited him at his home in the Hollywood Hills, I gasped. Not over the beautiful panorama of Los Angeles visible off his balcony, but over the life-size Creature sculpture standing in his entryway.

David is an expert on all things Creature-related and was one of the first people I emailed at the start of this project. He was immediately enthusiastic and wanted to help. He didn't doubt Milicent's contributions to the monster. In fact, David was one

---

77 Quite literally a monster-palooza. It's a convention celebrating all things monster related. Films, comics, books, you name it.

of the only film experts early on who encouraged me to write a book about Milicent.

On sight, you can easily guess that David is a horror writer. He wears only black and the dark length of his ponytail is usually hanging over a black leather trench coat. Sometimes I expect a swarm of bats to fly out of his pockets. In other words, he's one of the coolest dudes ever.

When I told him I was hitting a research dead end, he invited me to come over and check out what he had in his files. That sounds like a turn of phrase in this digital age, but for David, it's quite literal. His office looks like something out of an episode of *Tales from the Crypt*. It's filled, floor to ceiling, with shelves of horror novels and boxes of ephemera from the countless projects that he has worked on over the course of his long career.

He pulled up the folder he had for Milicent Patrick on his ancient desktop computer, along with an overflowing three-ring binder. Inside the binder was a collection of pictures: Milicent modeling, newspaper clippings mentioning movies she had been in (unfortunately with the names of the publications missing), promotional materials for said films, and of course, pictures of her with the Creature. We both took a moment to silently appreciate the lovely pair.

The digital folder on his computer contained scans of everything in the binder. David graciously agreed to let me copy everything so I could research each piece further, in exchange for being the first to know about any exciting developments, a bargain I have happily kept up over the course of this project.

After everything was loaded onto my flash drive, he said he had a cool surprise queued up for me on the television upstairs. There was a DVD of *Abbott and Costello Meet Captain Kidd*[78] in the disc player. He pressed play and fast-forwarded to a scene

---

78 For all the young people reading, Bud Abbott and Lou Costello were a comedy duo popular in the 1940s and 1950s. They did quite a few *Abbott and Costello Meet* (insert character here) films. More on these later.

in a tavern. (Of course he would know exactly which moment to fast-forward to. I told you, nerds are the greatest people in the entire world.) He pressed play again and there Milicent was, dressed as a stereotypical tavern wench: low-cut dress, tankard and all. She was sitting at a table next to Captain Kidd himself. It's a short scene, in which she smiles awkwardly and gets smooched against her will by Lou Costello. Not one for the Academy Awards. For me though, it was magic. It was the first time I had gotten to see her on-screen, moving and talking.[79]

Unfortunately, that magic was quickly replaced with a sad realization. The more of her acting work I watched, the more I saw that Milicent's on-screen talent was aesthetic. Her looks were arresting; her dramatic delivery was not. She never progressed beyond background roles and small bit parts during the thirteen years she was a working actress.

I desperately wanted to believe that this was merely a stroke of bad luck, as can happen in the arts. Some happenstance prevented her from getting to an important audition, some film that she had a key role in got canceled, a wonderful scene she appeared in landed on the cutting room floor. But watching some of her films, it's clear: Milicent wasn't a great actress.

It pains me to write this because she loved it so much. Milicent loved films and it brought her a lot of pride and joy to be in them. Even decades after she retired, the first thing she would say when asked about herself was "I've been acting for a number of years." She considered herself an actress first and foremost, and carried her SAG (Screen Actors Guild)[80] member card until she died. Milicent's looks certainly stand out in whatever scene

---

79 Her only lines are "Get me another one! I said, get me another one!" as she tries to get a refill on beer or grog or whatever they pretended was in those pewter tankards in every 1950s pirate movie.

80 This is now known as SAG-AFTRA, aka the Screen Actors Guild–American Federation of Television and Radio Artists. It's a union for media professionals, whether you're an actor, singer, voice artist, etc.

she's in, but her lines aren't natural and smooth. She's always a little stiff and stilted.

But she kept getting background work with the major studios: Warner Brothers, Paramount, Columbia. Milicent was finally part of the Hollywood scene that she watched wining and dining while she modeled at places like the Ambassador Hotel. She continued her modeling work, but from then on, she introduced herself as an actress.

A friendly and warm person, Milicent immediately made friends in the entertainment scene and started getting invited to Hollywood parties. Divorced and without a family, being a part of a community became more important than ever to her. Some of the friendships she made, like with showgirl and actress Mara Corday and with socialite Monique Fischer, lasted for decades. Socializing was easy for Milicent. She loved parties and events, anything where she could dress up and spend time with people.

The good thing about working in Hollywood[81] is that almost everyone is from somewhere else. They move to Los Angeles to try to make it in the entertainment industry, removed from the people and places they grew up with. Many find this to be freeing, being away from family history and expectations. It fosters an environment that is more socially liberal. No one knows you here, so it's easier to be who you want to be.

Even back then, lots of people in Hollywood were divorced or in relationship scenarios that might seem scandalous in other parts of the country. By the 1930s, the term *Hollywood marriage* was already in use to describe glamorous, short-lived marriages that ended in divorce. Milicent's family didn't want to speak to

---

81   When I say Hollywood, I mean the American filmmaking industry. Hollywood also happens to be an actual neighborhood of central Los Angeles. This neighborhood is sort of like the Times Square of Los Angeles; it's the tourist area. Traffic is terrible and parking is worse. It's where the Walk of Fame is, where the Chinese Theatre is, etc. A lot of Hollywood-the-industry events happen in Hollywood-the-neighborhood. But when people say Hollywood, they are usually referring to the industry, unless you live in Los Angeles and are asking for directions.

her, but at least she was surrounded by colleagues who weren't as judgmental of her being a divorced woman. In this industry, there were countless other women like Milicent. It was around this time, right before America launched into the 1950s, that she met Frank L. Graham.

Graham was a talented voice actor who would have been more famous had he lived in a time when voice actors were acknowledged and credited. He was the star of several radio plays and shows, and a couple of live-action projects. But he was most famous for voicing animated characters for cartoons.

His most enduring role was that of the Wolf in a cartoon called *Red Hot Riding Hood*. You might not have seen the cartoon, but you probably know his character from it. There's a good chance you've done an impression of him directed at somebody you think is sexy. In the cartoon, the Wolf, as in the wolf of *Little Red Riding Hood*, is dressed in a tuxedo and sitting at a table in a nightclub. He's looking at the stage, waiting for a show to start, when Little Red walks out as a burlesque dancer. He, you guessed it, wolf whistles[82] at her. As she dances, he starts howling and losing his mind. In the most famous shot, his eyeballs bulge from their sockets so hard that his pupils pop out. This character has become the poster animal for horny people.

Frank was, like Milicent, freshly divorced. He was hustling in the film industry and was at the peak of his career. At thirty-four, Frank was only a year older than her. A small slim man with dark hair, he charmed people with a big smile. He was infatuated with Milicent and they started a relationship.

I have a single photograph of the two of them. It's a group shot of what looks like several couples crowded onto a couch, with Frank and Milicent on the end. Frank leans toward Milicent as she sits smiling on the edge of the couch. They're a handsome couple. Milicent is in an elegant dress, and Frank is

---

82   This is not where the term or the whistle itself originates. Some clever writer just thought it would be perfect to have a wolf be the one wolf whistling.

in a nice suit with his dark hair oiled back. For what it's worth, they certainly look happy enough. Milicent moved in with him in his house in the Hollywood Hills, on the aptly named Wonderland Avenue.

They were together as America entered the next decade, the most significant one of Milicent's life. It got off to a rocky start, though. 1950 was a tough year for her. Milicent didn't get a lot of acting work and she wasn't as professionally creative as she wanted to be. What was worse, she suffered the second in a long line of romantic traumas.

As the year progressed, things weren't going well for Frank and Milicent's relationship. For reasons we'll probably never know, they were unhappy. In August of 1950, she left him.

Several weeks later, on the night of September 2, two of Frank's friends got a call from him telling them that they needed to come to his house to pick up something from the front seat of his car. When they arrived, about an hour later, they found him dead in the front seat of his convertible, which was parked in his garage. The engine was running and a length of vacuum cleaner hose was attached to the car's exhaust pipe and running into the interior.

Near his hand was a photo of Milicent.

The only note that was found that night was one addressed to his friend, radio producer and announcer Van Des Autels.

"Please get keys of the house and car from Mildred. I don't want her to have time to disturb anything here."

Associates and friends of Frank confirmed that until recently, Milicent and Frank were "constant companions," but several weeks earlier, they broke up and were no longer seen together.

An article detailing the tragedy ran in the *Los Angeles Times* and printed photos of both Milicent and Frank.[83] Milicent couldn't be reached for comment. She was probably relieved

---

83   The article also made sure to mention that he died in his "expensive convertible" and that the photo of Milicent was of a "handsome brunette."

that they named her as Mildred Rossi, a name she hadn't worked under for nearly ten years at this point. It must have been deeply traumatic for her. During this horrible time, her family did not welcome her back into the fold.

A follow-up article published a few weeks later by the *Los Angeles Associated Press* made the situation for Milicent worse. Frank's will was found and filed for probate. Part of it was addressed to Milicent personally.

"To Mildred, I leave absolutely nothing except the pleasure she will have knowing that now she won't have to decide whether I am good enough for her or not."

A postscript to the will read "Gee, I wish Mildred had called me back yesterday morning."

The will didn't identify Milicent by her full name. It divided up his estate between his ex-wife, his friends and his family.[84] Milicent would never speak of Frank or his death publicly.

Tragedy and trauma without family support caused Milicent to lean harder than ever on her friends. They would bolster her for nearly the rest of her life. Milicent filled her life with friends, especially her colleagues. Actors, filmmakers, artists— she loved being around creatives like Fred Crane and his wife, Marcelle; Jim Backus; Johnny Carson; Rudy Vallee's wife, Eleanor; and Phyllis Diller. Throwing parties, visiting friends and meeting people was a constant source of joy for her. Her home was absolutely covered in pictures of her with friends and as she became more established in the industry, her with celebrities. Faced with estrangement from her blood family, Milicent decided to craft her own.

Los Angeles is the best place to assemble a chosen family. The same liberal environment that fosters social freedom (the kind that pushed conservatives like Camille into a moral panic) also fosters a powerful camaraderie. When you move to Los Angeles to try to make it in the film industry, even if you're not es-

---

84   He left behind his parents and siblings, a brother and a sister.

tranged from your family like Milicent and me, you're removed from them. You get a fresh start here, but you've got to find new friends and a new community to support you.

By the time I moved to Los Angeles, I had spent so much time here that there already was a wonderful group of people waiting for me: friends I made through my work with Dark Dunes Productions, friends I made on set, friends I made at industry events and through other friends in the horror community. Holidays like Thanksgiving and Christmas always involve multiple invitations to big group dinners with these friends, many of whom don't have family where they're from or can't afford to travel back home. We support each other through stress, creative blocks, moves, losses, breakups, sickness and needing a ride to the airport. Los Angeles is filled with these sorts of friend communities, all functioning as a fully supportive, chosen family. There's a lot of loneliness and frustration here, but there's a lot of love, too.

I know what it must have been like for Milicent to have relatives that didn't support her career. There's no way around it: it sucks. But I also know how amazing it is to be loved by a group of people that understands you and cares for you without having any familial obligation to do so. When I sit down for Thanksgiving dinner with my fellow Dark Dunes producer Adam Cultraro, his wife, Candace, and their children, I don't feel like I'm getting a consolation prize. I feel lucky, unbelievably lucky, that these great people chose to make me a part of their family. When I get good news and immediately call my dear friend and mentor Frank Woodward instead of a mother or a father, I don't feel like I'm settling for something. I feel grateful that I have a warmhearted friend like Frank who wants to be the first one to hear when something exciting happens.

Milicent was divorced, single again and processing the second relationship trauma of her life without the support of Camille, Elise, Ulrich and Ruth. She wasn't isolated, though. Milicent was surrounded by friends who loved her and she used that support to bounce back.

The next two years of her life were extremely productive. She appeared as a background actress in nine different films. For some of them, including *The World in His Arms* (1952), her beautiful face would appear (in the background) on the promotional materials. Her brilliant smile[85] isn't hard to spot alongside the stars of the film on advertisements, posters and press stills.

While I would come to know her as the Queen of the Monsters, Milicent never starred in a horror film. She never shared the screen with any of her creations. She was in comedies, dramas, adventures: what horror nerds call normal movies. Her résumé was certainly nothing to sneeze at. All in the same year, she was in *Limelight*, directed by Charlie Chaplin, *We're Not Married!* with Marilyn Monroe and Ginger Rogers, and *Scarlet Angel* with Rock Hudson, just to name a few. She was even in an episode of *The Roy Rogers Show*.

The most important thing about Milicent's working on films like *The World in His Arms* was that they were made by Universal-International Pictures. This put her on the Universal Studios lot. Being around the studio lot was good for catching the eye of directors and producers and securing more work. But more importantly, it put her in place for another moment that would completely change the trajectory of her career. While Milicent was networking and meeting people on set, she was also diligently drawing.

To find out more about what she did behind the camera as an artist, I needed to talk to more film experts and historians. I knew that David Schow had recently contributed to a book about *Creature from the Black Lagoon* called *The Creature Chronicles*, written by Tom Weaver, with David Schecter and Steve Kronenberg. When I asked, David immediately put me in touch with Tom.

---

85   Milicent had brilliantly white and straight teeth, the kind you can use to sell toothpaste, broken machines, dirt, anything.

Tom responded with hesitant enthusiasm; he was happy to help in any way. He even offered to xerox any materials I wanted and invited me to come visit him at his home in New York. His generosity came with a warning, however. Sorting out the history surrounding the films Milicent worked on as an artist was a confusing endeavor.

I initially accepted the offer to visit Tom in New York and look through whatever materials he had offered to share with me. But as we emailed back and forth, he told me that since I was in Los Angeles, I could go see all the originals myself. I didn't have to fly all the way to New York to check out xeroxed copies. The materials he was talking about were located in the Cinematic Archives at the University of Southern California. The Archives contained a collection from Universal Studios. There were production materials from every film Milicent worked on with them.

That is the magical thing about living in LA. All this amazing film stuff is here, merely a long, frustrating drive in traffic away. After some emailing and scheduling with the wonderful archivists and librarians at the Cinematic Archives, I had a date to come in and look at things Milicent had touched with her own hands.

7

Monster Mash

I don't really believe in good luck, at least not when it comes to professional success. Good luck might come into play for slot machines, or avoiding troglodytes in the algorithms of Tinder, or whether or not your package gets delivered via UPS. When it comes to your career, though, I can guarantee that any moment that people attribute to good luck is at least half you.

People love to tell me how lucky I am that I met Sultan, and I agree with them. It's true. Meeting Sultan was one of the best things that ever happened to me. I love him dearly. Sultan didn't hire me because he just happened to meet me while he was thinking of hiring a social media manager, though. He hired me after watching me work as hard as I possibly could for an entire weekend for no pay, a weekend that I had been planning for and helping to organize for six months. "You make your own luck" can be an overused phrase, but I find it to be accurate. Even in the most extreme cases of good luck, you usually meet that good luck half way.

Every "overnight success" story you hear is likely the result of years and years of hard work and tireless dedication to a craft. Networking and meeting the right people is important, but you have to be the one going out to those events, you have to put yourself there. Those right people aren't going to offer you money on a lark. People like their money. Something has to be there, something worth investing in.

Something was in Milicent when she met a man named Bud Westmore on the Universal Studios lot. She had been working as a background actress for years at this point. On all those sets, and while she was home, she was also working as an artist on portraits, designs and cartoons. Finally, the right person noticed.

In light of how Milicent's story turned out, *right person* is a relative term here. But at the time, it fit. A Westmore noticing you was a big deal, at least professionally.[86] In Hollywood, the Westmores were a dynasty.

It all began with George Westmore, Bud's father. He was a British hairdresser who immigrated to the United States in the early 1900s. He traveled around the country hairdressing for a while before settling in Los Angeles in 1917. George was a savvy man. He talked his way onto the set of a film being made by the Selig Polyscope Company, convincing the director that they needed someone on set to do hair and makeup. It was a bold move, but he was right. The director saw his logic and George was hired on the spot. He established Hollywood's first hair and makeup department. Selig Polyscope ceased making movies the next year in 1918, but George was already on his way to making his mark on the world of film.

George started working freelance after Selig Polyscope closed shop and soon developed a reputation for his high-quality work. This was a time when there wasn't a designated person on set to do makeup. It seems like an obvious thing to need, but Hollywood was still transitioning from silent films, when the stars

---

86   As far as I know, Milicent never dated any of the men she worked for. So we can take any accusations that attribute her success to being "someone's girlfriend" and throw them into a volcano.

were usually responsible for doing their own makeup. Besides being a lot of extra work for the actor, the problem was that without someone to quality control it, the makeup often looked slightly different from shot to shot, or scene to scene. Having a makeup artist on set made a huge difference to the continuity and quality of the film.

He was great with makeup, but George was a wizard with wigs. He's famous for designing and creating Shirley Temple's curls, which George originally made for a producer and actress named Mary Pickford. She isn't known by modern audiences, but in her day (1910s-1920s), Mary Pickford was one of the most famous actresses and producers in the country. She was one of the founders of the Academy of Motion Picture Arts and Sciences and received the second ever Best Actress Oscar in 1929. Mary's hair was very fine and like nearly everyone in the world, she wanted the opposite of what her hair's natural tendency was. The fat sausage curls George created for her to pin into her real hair became her trademark, and ultimately Shirley Temple's years later when Shirley imitated the look.

Neither Mary nor Shirley ever knew that the curls George originally created came from hair that he purchased from the sex workers who staffed a sexual enterprise called Big Suzy's French Whorehouse. The women supplying the hair to George never knew he was charging Mary $50 a curl, the equivalent of about $650 today. Hollywood doesn't just owe hair innovations to the women of Big Suzy's. George would practice makeup on the sex workers there, too. The women got made up expertly for free and George got lots of beautiful faces to experiment on. The entire world of makeup and hair artistry can thank the women of Big Suzy's.[87]

Constantly honing his formidable beauty skills paid off.

---

87   Apparently, they didn't go underappreciated by George. He spent a large chunk of his earnings there after doing everyone's makeup, so I'm sure George was a favorite customer.

George became a titan of the film industry. He was sought after by the biggest production companies, working on films like *Ben Hur* (1925), *Robin Hood* (1922) and *The Three Musketeers* (1921).

George also became a titan of the parenting industry, fathering nineteen children with his first wife, Ada Savage. Only seven children would survive to adulthood: six sons, one daughter. The daughter, Dorothy, would pass away when she was only twenty-four. The sons, Monte, Percival, Ernest, Walter, Hamilton and Frank—aka Mont, Perc, Ern, Wally, Bud and Frank—would go on to form a makeup empire that would dominate the Golden Age of Hollywood.

Each son would eventually head the makeup department for a major Hollywood studio: Paramount, Universal, Warner Brothers, 20th Century Fox, as well as some now defunct ones such as RKO, Eagle-Lion, Selznick, First National and a dozen more. In midcentury Hollywood, they were the most influential and well-known names in the makeup world, both on-screen and off.

In 1935, the brothers got together and opened The House of Westmore, a beauty salon on Sunset Boulevard that for over twenty years was one of the most famous establishments in Los Angeles. It primarily catered to female celebrities and rich women, but male actors frequented the place, as well. Hedda Hopper, Marlene Dietrich, Joan Bennett, even the Duchess of Windsor were regular customers in the chair at the House of Westmore.

The Westmores were *the* name in makeup and beauty. George claimed that he invented false eyelashes; this accomplishment alone would make him a makeup god. Imagine the Bill Gates of makeup, if young Bill had turned to *Vogue* magazine instead of electronics. If you've ever looked through a judgy article that detailed the type of makeup you should wear depending on which face shape you have—round, square, oval, etc—you can blame the Westmore boys. They were the ones who popularized this famous system of categorization and are directly responsible for years of my own personal angst about eyebrows.

The second generation Westmores were well-known and in-fluential in Hollywood, and not just for their work. Between the six of them, they married eighteen times, won and lost many fortunes, and struggled with alcoholism and gambling. You would think that with all this power and fame at their dis-posal, the brothers would band together to form some sort of fabulous-looking Makeup Voltron. On the contrary, their fam-ily was rife with jealousy and backstabbing, even with their own father. They were ruthless when it came to work and prestige. In 1931, depressed and feeling like his sons' accomplishments were outstripping his own, George Westmore killed himself by mer-cury poisoning, suffering for four days before he passed away.

Being a makeup artist forces you to become intimate with the talent you are working on. Spending hours only inches apart will do that. The Westmore brothers made lots of famous friends during their work and were well-loved by many stars. They were also known for their tempers and hunger for prestige. Those intimate hours sometimes resulted in new enemies rather than close friends. Charles Laughton, after dealing with Perc Westmore for days on end, told him that he was "full of shit."

Hamilton Adolph Westmore—aka Bud—was the second youngest of the group. He was born in 1918, just three years after Milicent Patrick. He went through three marriages, the first couple with actresses he met on the job. Those hours spent only inches apart could inspire more than friendship. Plus, dat-ing well-known actresses didn't hurt to solidify his position in Hollywood.

Martha Ray was his first wife, staying in the marriage for a mere three months. She filed for divorce because she said that Bud "was cruel" and that her strict New England mother didn't like him. Bud's second wife was Rosemary Lane, the woman he was married to while Milicent knew him in the early 1950s. His last wife, Jeanette Shore, he met while judging a Miss California pageant, in which she was a contestant (and later, big surprise, the winner).

While working on her small role (uncredited) in *The World in His Arms* in 1952, Milicent crossed paths with Bud. She was in the makeup chair; he was overseeing his staff of makeup artists' work on the background actresses for the film. At this point, Bud had been the head of the Universal Studios makeup department for about five years. It was a job he had been given only because his brother Ern had been bamboozled out of it.

In 1947, Perc Westmore was living large as the makeup department head over at Warner Brothers Studio. He was so influential with the company that he was sometimes referred to as the fifth Warner Brother (in case you were wondering how many Warner Brothers there were). Bud was the head of the makeup department of a smaller studio, the now-defunct Eagle-Lion Films. Ern Westmore was rebounding from a tough struggle with alcoholism and the executives over at Universal, hearing that Ern was back at work, decided that they wanted a Westmore to head up their makeup department. They set up an interview with him and everyone knew that if Ern could keep on the straight and narrow, he would get the job.

Perc was Ern's twin. Some twins are bound in love and friendship, best friends forever. Perc and Ern were more like ill-fated twins from a fantasy novel: bitter lifelong rivals. Perc heard that Universal was going to hire his twin brother and phoned Ern, asking him out to dinner to celebrate the exciting news. Ern accepted the invitation, both surprised that his twin could overcome his deep-seated resentment and happy at the prospect of finally making up with Perc.

The two men went out for dinner and drinks, chatting about Ern's upcoming job interview. Ern wanted to cut the night short after one drink so that he'd be fresh and ready for Universal in the morning. But Perc keep pressuring him to stay out longer, to have more drinks, to celebrate. Perc ended up dragging Ern to bar after bar, getting his brother absolutely hammered.

Ern showed up for his job interview still intoxicated. As you might guess, it didn't go very well. He didn't get the job. Universal wanted a Westmore, but they couldn't hire someone who wasn't in recovery. The studio head, a man named William Goetz, was still determined to get a Westmore. In the 1940s, getting a Westmore brother for your studio makeup department was like getting a Lamborghini (a very expensive status symbol that definitely performed well, but was still sort of douchey).

Goetz asked his studio managers if there were any other Westmores he could hire. Bud was younger and less experienced but when asked, was happy to give up his job at Eagle-Lion for the cushy and prestigious gig over at Universal. Goetz hired him. Ern, to add insult to injury, was offered Bud's old job at Eagle-Lion as a consolation prize. (He accepted.)

Bud was desperate to prove himself. At this time, he was the fourth Westmore brother to head up a major studio makeup department.[88] But people in the industry knew how he had gotten the job; gossip has always traveled at light speed in Hollywood. He would never shake the story of what happened to Ern. Knowing that he wasn't Goetz's first choice gave Bud a chip on his shoulder that would never go away. He quickly developed a bad reputation among the artists who worked for him. He was cruel, glory-hungry and ruthless. It became clear right away that Bud Westmore had a malicious, insatiable ego.

The first big project he was assigned to was turning actress Ann Blyth into a mermaid for *Mr. Peabody and the Mermaid*,[89]

---

88 Along with Perc and Ern and Bud, Wally Westmore was the makeup head over at Paramount. This situation would last only for a few months. Ern ended up falling back into his struggle with alcoholism and losing his job at Eagle-Lion.

89 He initially panicked because, I kid you not, he wasn't sure if mermaids were real. He consulted with an ichthyologist who assured him that mermaids were just legends based off the stories of freaked-out sailors looking at sea life. I know it was the 1940s, but come on, dude.

a 1948 film starring William Powell about a man undergoing a midlife crisis. While in the Caribbean on vacation with his wife, he meets a sexy, mute mermaid and falls for her. He proceeds to sneak the mermaid into his bathtub so he can cheat on his wife with her. (It sounds like I'm cutting the romance out of it, but that's the plot.)

It wasn't a groundbreaking piece of inspirational film, but the tail created for Ann Blyth to wear looked incredible. Together with his department staff, Bud Westmore crafted a beautiful piece of art that looked fantastic on-screen.[90] Bud, as far as the Universal executives were concerned, had passed muster. When he met Milicent, Bud was riding high in his position.

It was 1952; televisions were everywhere, rock and roll was corrupting teenagers and the civil rights movement was brewing. Everyone was getting nervous about outer space. Milicent was thirty-seven years old. While she sat in the makeup chair, Milicent showed Bud her drawings. He was blown away.

Bud Westmore had some serious issues as a human being, but he could spot talent when he saw it. He had many (male) artists working under him in the makeup department and he wanted to add Milicent's skill to the group. Bud hired her and had her start work right away, making Milicent the first woman ever to work in a special effects makeup department. She was the first to break that barrier and enter the boys' club. Unfortunately, during her time at Universal, she was also the only one.

Her first assignment was to design pirate makeups[91] for *Against All Flags*, a film starring Errol Flynn and Maureen O'Hara. Flynn plays a dashing British naval officer posing as a pirate to infiltrate a ship and he ends up falling in love with the ship's

---

90   Things were rough for Ann, though. Bud told her that the best thing she could do was not drink any liquids in the morning so she wouldn't have to pee during the shoot and have to take off the tail. I think this makes Ann Blythe the world's first dehydrated mermaid.

91   I know "makeups" sounds weird, but it's the plural for makeup designs. So, if Milicent was designing the makeup for multiple characters or monsters in a movie, you could say that she'd be designing the makeups for that movie.

captain, a swashbuckling O'Hara.[92] The designs were mostly sharp eyeliner and sharper mustaches. What more do you need? They looked fantastic. During the shoot, Milicent sketched four different portraits of Flynn. He was delighted with them and bought all four for himself.

Both Bud and the studio heads were happy with Milicent's work on the film. But they weren't just pleased with her artistic output. The publicists at Universal noticed the same thing that all those casting directors did—she looked great in front of a camera. *Against All Flags* was the first film that Milicent took publicity shots for, but as an artist, not as a background actress. There are shots with Milicent, Bud Westmore and Errol Flynn all posed together with Milicent's drawings. The only one of the three who is airbrushed is Milicent. Someone in the publicity department at Universal decided to add a gigantic poof to her cascading dark hair. Photo manipulation and airbrushing to make women look more appealing is not a recent phenomenon.

Her impressive artwork convinced Bud and the executives at Universal to keep Milicent in the makeup department. It was good timing; they were about to need her help. The studio had some ambitious projects coming down the production pipeline. Universal wanted to capitalize on the public's newfound fear of technology and outer space.

My appointment at the Cinematic Arts Library was just days before USC closed the archival reading room for the spring semester. I had to get through all the materials in my allotted time or wait several months for the summer semester to begin. Adding to the pressure was the fact that I found myself considerably ill the weekend before the appointment. Canceling was out of

---

92   This sounds pretty cool until you realize that one of the central plot lines of the film is Maureen O'Hara being jealous of another woman. You tried, Universal. But this is a good movie to watch if you want to see Errol Flynn get attacked by a bunch of bloodthirsty crabs. And not the kind that pirates usually have to deal with.

the question. Luckily, I might not be able to walk in heels or see anything without my glasses, but I'm a wicked fast reader.

The morning of, I dragged myself out of bed and packed up all my research tools. I bought the biggest coffee I could get at a café near the university, along with several bottles of some vile-looking vegetable/fruit juice blend. It looked like the type of mud potion that I mixed up when I was a kid and pretending to be a swamp witch, but I needed to cram as many liquids and vitamins into my sad body as I possibly could. I had only six hours to get through all the materials and I couldn't keel over in the middle of it.

Having grown up in the Boston area, the organized beauty of college campuses is familiar to me. With its brick buildings squatting amidst neat green lawns and stone archways leading to shady courtyards, USC looks like most college campuses in this regard. The palm trees adorning the walkways were a little surreal, though. No matter how long I live in Los Angeles, seeing palm trees always makes me feel like I'm on another planet.

I found the entrance to the Cinematic Arts Library and waited at the counter for Edward Comstock, the archivist assisting me. The room had the same cool, hushed feeling particular to all libraries, but the atmosphere felt different. It took me a moment to realize that I had never been in a library dedicated to something other than books. It was both fun and a little strange, like being in a hip parallel universe. Vintage movie posters adorned the walls and the main corridor was lined with glass cases housing all sorts of old film memorabilia.

"Are you the writer?"

Grey-haired and bespectacled, Edward—Ned—is exactly the kind of guy you imagine working in a film archive. He was friendly and didn't seem to notice that I had crawled out of my sick bed to be there. I was led off to a side room crammed with desks, chairs and piles and piles of file boxes. It looked like the office of a private detective agency in 1980.

Ned laid down the rules. No smoking, no photography, no

food or drinks, no talking, no audio recording. I mentally gri-
maced at the thought of all the illicit bottles of juice in my purse.
He reminded me that I had until 4:00 p.m.—six hours—to go
through all the materials they pulled for me. I couldn't use my
audio recorder to track my findings or my iPhone to take pictures of the papers, but I could copy things down. I asked if
they had a photocopier I could use. Not only could I not use
it myself, but the things I wanted to be photocopied had to be
approved first, by whom, I could only guess. Maybe a shadowy
council of black-robed archivists lived in the basement, feeding
on the souls of people who make too much noise in the library.
I would have to fill out request forms for exactly what I wanted
to be photocopied. If they were approved, they would then send
me an invoice. After the invoice was paid, they would photocopy the materials and mail them to me. I was grateful there
was no blood sacrifice involved.

Still, this was manageable, I thought. I'm a fast note taker and
had brought along enough index cards to shingle a roof. The
sound of squeaking wheels made me and Ned turn. A young
library intern was wheeling a cart toward me, a cart covered
in boxes stuffed full of file folders. Ned cheerfully told me that
when I was ready for the second cart to let one of the interns
know. I gulped. As excited as I was to see so much material, I
briefly pictured a mob of angry interns dragging me outside at
4:00 p.m. while I begged for more time.

Seeing my reaction, Ned smiled and told me that he'd gone
through the files already and marked out mentions of Milicent.
I wanted to hug him, but was pretty sure that wasn't allowed,
either. I explained the project to him: who I was, why I was
writing about her, what she meant to me along with some interesting facts about her life. I even sheepishly rolled up my left
sleeve to show him the tattoo of Milicent and the Creature. I'm
so deeply invested in this project that asking me about it is like
asking a new parent to show you pictures of their baby. Ned was

both fascinated and puzzled that he didn't know more about her. I grinned as I set my bag down near the door.

"That's why I'm writing this book."

I settled in at a desk, feeling that peculiar brand of phantom limb syndrome that comes from being separated from your smartphone. There were a few other researchers in the room, quietly making their way through their own boxes of files. I decided that the best place to start looking for Milicent's monster movie contributions were the *This Island Earth* and *The Mole People* files, both films that were shot and released right after Milicent left Universal Studios. My expectations were fairly low for these particular film archives and I wanted to get them out of the way. They were production files—not preproduction or development files—materials from when the films were shooting.

There are four stages of making a film. Development is the first, which involves writing a screenplay and getting funding for the movie. Preproduction is next, when cast and crew are attached, shooting locations are found and sets and costumes are designed. This is the stage where everything needed to shoot the film is prepared. Production is the actual filming of the movie. Finally, postproduction is when the film is edited, scored and other visual and sound elements are added. Being a special effects and makeup designer, Milicent was involved in the preproduction of these monster movies.

My hunch was right; I didn't find anything about Milicent in *The Mole People* and *This Island Earth* archives. Even still, I had to curb my geeky enthusiasm while looking through the files. I wanted to pore through every memo and budget list. I was touching monster filmmaking history! It was fascinating to see all the minutiae, like how much background actors were paid in the early 1950s (around $19 a day), or all the paperwork producers used to have to swim through. I thought about having to wade through this much physical paperwork on my own films and said a silent prayer of thanks to the austere god of digital spreadsheets. I was grateful for the tight 4:00 p.m. deadline keeping me focused.

By 1:00 p.m., I had conquered the first cart. Besides a thin layer of dust on my glasses and a paper cut, I had little to show for my efforts. I guessed that the only person in the room looking apathetically at a smartphone instead of frantically taking notes must be the intern, whom I asked in a whisper if I could have my second cart. To both my delight and increasingly time-sensitive panic, this cart overflowed even more than the first one, this time with files from *Creature from the Black Lagoon*.

The previous few hours' excitement was nothing compared to what I felt when I opened the first folder. I was probably the happiest person those archivists had ever seen. My fellow researchers kept shooting glances at me, probably wondering if I was high. Considering the amount of cold medication I had taken that morning, I probably was. Glancing around the room at the other researchers, I carefully unfolded a giant promotional poster of the Creature. With a two-foot-high movable cutout of a green monster, whatever I was working on was clearly way more exciting than whatever was at their desks.

Creature from the Black Lagoon has been one of my favorite movies since I first watched it as a teenager. Going through the actual production files from the film was nothing short of magical. I felt like Indiana Jones in a sacred, nerdy temple except I wasn't planning on stealing anything, or wearing a hat. It was the end of the rainbow for me: script pages, production stills, budgets, memos, promotional material. There were so many gems. I found a long list of potential titles for *Creature from the Black Lagoon* that ran from the brilliant to the comical. I wonder how big of a hit the movie would have been if Universal ended up calling it *The Fishman* or *Horror Lagoon*. Yikes.

I read through a stack of comment cards from an early test audience of the film. Even today, before a film is released to the public, it will usually be shown to test audiences to gauge what type of person it appeals to and if anything needs to be changed to maximize audience satisfaction. The test audience is given a comment card at the end of the movie so they can anonymously report their thoughts, good or bad, about the film. My favorite was a viewer who, scandalized by Julie Adams's wardrobe variety, wrote angrily, "Too many costume changes! How many clothes can one woman have on a boat? Terrible movie, ridiculous!"[93]

I was so glad to be able to see all this material firsthand, instead of going through Tom Weaver's photocopies. I doubt he, or any other male researcher, would have thought about this, but to me it was difficult not to notice that every crew member was male. The producers, the writers, the director, the cinematographer, the composers, the set decorator, the editor, the art director, on and on and on. The only women mentioned were the film's heroine, Julie Adams, and Milicent. Even reading about them was frustrating. There was a memo making sure that the famous white swimsuit that Julie wears in the film was specially designed in accordance with censorship regulations and yet would still show the maximum amount of skin. My eyes rolled so hard that I was afraid they would get stuck in my frontal lobe.

If I could, I'd go back in time and buy both Julie and Milicent drinks. Even when everyone is being respectful and polite, if you are the only woman in the room it's impossible not to be acutely, uncomfortably aware of it. This feeling only intensifies if you are a marginalized woman. When I started making movies, I was terrified of being seen as too girly or too emotional. It took me years to stop monitoring my language, my behavior and the way that I dress while at work. I didn't want to remind everyone that I was female and have them kick me out of the boys-only movie treehouse. At best it's awkward, at worst it's isolating and depressing.

---

93   To be fair, they've got a point.

During the production of my first film, I was on my period for the entire shoot—almost a month total. It started the morning of day one and stopped the day after we wrapped. After week three, I was concerned. My own personal horror film was happening and the villain was my uterus. But I didn't say anything to anyone or take any time off. I didn't want to seem weak by going to the doctor and reminding everyone that I was a woman by having "woman's problems." Oh jeez, the only female producer can't work because she's on her *period*, ugh.[94] On set, I felt like a benevolent movie monster, hoping the village didn't notice me and form a pitchfork-wielding mob to chase me off. I've heard countless stories like this from other women in film.

The next folder was full of photographs taken during *Creature from the Black Lagoon* preproduction. There were lots of stills from the infamous "tank test," the day the special effects crew fitted actor Ricou Browning into the aquatic Creature suit and stuck him in a giant aquatic tank to see how well it worked in the water. A camera crew was on hand to shoot test footage to see how the suit looked on camera. Many crew members were pictured working on the cameras, the lighting and the tank. Dudes, dudes, dudes. Suddenly, I hit the jackpot.

It was at the bottom of the pile and I nearly missed it: a single photograph of Ricou in the suit while several crew members worked on it. Barely visible—thank goodness she was wearing an easily recognizable striped dress—is Milicent. You can't see her face because she's behind Ricou. Behind him, applying paint to the Creature suit. She's not smiling for the camera. This wasn't a posed publicity shot; she is working on her art. I wanted to jump on the desk and dance around, which was surely against archive rules. Here was what I was looking for. Hard evidence that she wasn't someone's girlfriend or just hanging around because she was pretty.

Elated, I continued to make my way through the folders. I

---

94   Don't worry, I was fine. My uterus is just evil.

had to pee so badly, but I had only an hour left. I regretted buying all that coffee.

The remaining boxes were full of promotional material, publicity plans for *Creature from the Black Lagoon* and clippings from Milicent's press tour. She was featured in articles about the movie in various magazines and newspapers. There were countless clippings from publications all over the country. I was thrilled and tried to imagine her excitement at seeing her name in print across America. There were pictures of her holding various monster masks she had designed. She looks happy in every photograph. The articles all mention her background, her acting work and her artistic talent. Unfortunately, just like write-ups about women in publications today, they all lavishly describe her looks.

One memo from a publicity manager contained a list of various monster props that were coming with Milicent to be exhibited on the promotional tour. In the inventory was a preliminary sketch of the Creature, done by Milicent. I didn't need anything else to convince me that she designed the Creature. I wanted to take that memo and attach it like a flag to a giant pole and parade it down Hollywood Boulevard.

Those publicity managers at Universal didn't always have great ideas, though. One suggested that they come up with a good technical name for the Creature, perhaps combining it with one of Milicent's previous creations, the Xenomorph from *It Came from Outer Space*.[95]

"How about a combination of man and halibut called the Xenobut?" he wrote. Xenobut, a name to truly strike fear into your heart and drive you to the movie theaters. Thankfully, this idea seems to have died in that memo.

The same manager made another publicity suggestion, this time for an actor from *Creature from the Black Lagoon*, star Richard Carlson. The publicist posited that since Richard "was men-

---

95   That's right, H. R. Giger, eat your heart out. Your Xenomorphs in the *Alien* films are legendary, but Milicent did it before you.

aced by things in *It Came from Outer Space*" and was now being menaced by things underwater that "if he has been menaced in any other recent pictures, it might make an interesting feature." I hope this publicity manager got menaced right out of a job.[96]

Besides printed media, I found a list of TV and radio spots that Milicent appeared in. I imagined her being whisked from city to city to be tossed in front of cameras, microphones and interviewers. I was getting exhausted just reading about all of it, but that could have been the cold medication wearing off.

There were budget breakdowns for the promotional tour: costs for her transportation, for her hotel rooms, for wardrobe repairs. There was one curious memo describing in detail damage sustained to her wardrobe while on the road.

One cocktail dress—completely ruined.
One cocktail dress—beading broken and lost.
One gabardine suit—shrunk and can't be repaired.
One lace coat—burned, torn, and shrunk—ruined beyond repair.
One afternoon dress—torn but repairable.
One pair of earrings—cut in half by pub. man and stones lost.
One velvet blouse—torn, can be repaired.

What happened to her on tour? Who did they send to escort her, a pack of hyenas? Opening another folder of budget lists, a paper fluttered out and landed face up in front of me. I gasped. I was pretty sure the other researchers wanted to stab me with their pencils by now.

The paper was a postcard covered in neat cursive handwriting. It was Milicent's, a note from her to one of the publicity directors, Sam Israel.[97] In my hands was an actual note from

---

96   I'd actually love to read an article like this. "Quick, somebody get me a list of all Richard's menacings!" *Richard Carlson, America's Most Menaceable Man.*

97   Hopefully not the guy with all the terrible ideas.

Milicent. So far, it was the closest I had been to her. I forgot to breathe for a moment. It was sent while she was on her tour; she updated Sam on how well things were going.[98]

My eyes welled with tears. Because directly underneath this joyful postcard was a folder full of the interoffice memos from Universal chronicling the controversy that Bud Westmore started. My heart sank. I had thirty minutes left. I had to pee so badly that my teeth were floating. I read as fast as I could, keeping one eye on the clock and feverishly filling out photocopy request forms.

The memos start out frustrating and become increasingly alarming. They are between various Universal producers, publicity directors and managers. Reading the words Bud Westmore said to these men about Milicent, I was suffused with fury. Decades later, Westmore's resentment still simmered in those pages. It was slightly heartening to read the responses by some of the Universal executives that defended Milicent, her character and her talent. But they didn't make a difference.

Finally at the end of both the archival materials and my appointment time, I packed up in a daze. As I was stuffing index cards and notebooks into my purse, I picked Milicent's postcard back up.

Sam dear, forgive me not writing sooner but as you undoubtedly know I haven't had a minute to myself and when I did I was too exhausted to even lift a pen—(am in the car driving to Kalamazoo now). Enjoying every moment.

She had no idea what was coming.

Women creating monsters—why does it even matter? There are so many glaring women-related issues across the entire

---

98 Presumably not while she was being burned and her earrings were being cut in half.

American film industry. Why does this small facet of the cinematic world mean so much? Monster movies are not the first type of film that comes to mind when people talk about serious art. I get it. It's not a crime that *Killer Klowns from Outer Space* wasn't nominated for an Oscar. But horror movies, and specifically ones that feature monsters, are an important part of the art that is produced by society.

Even if you don't like monster movies, I bet you've used a metaphor involving a monster to express your anger or isolation. Who hasn't seethed in a fit of fury and wanted to be like Godzilla, smashing Tokyo to bits? Or been wrongfully accused and felt like Frankenstein's monster, being chased by an angry, pitchfork-laden mob? Maybe you felt horrible about your teenage appearance, beset by an implacable onslaught of hormones and thought, "I look like a monster."

Monster stories are powerful. They explore prejudice, rejection, anger and every imaginable negative aspect of living in society. However, only half of society is reflected in the ranks of the people who create these monsters. Almost every single iconic monster in film is male and was designed by a man: the Wolfman, Frankenstein,[99] Dracula, King Kong. The emotions and problems that all of them represent are also experienced by women, but women are more likely to see themselves as merely the victims of these monsters. Women rarely get to explore on-screen what it's like to be a giant pissed-off creature. Those emotions are written off. If a woman is angry or upset, she'll be considered hysterical and too emotional. One of the hardest things about misogyny in the film industry isn't facing it directly, it's having to tamp down your anger about it so that when you speak about the problem, you'll be taken seriously.

---

99   Listen, I know it's Frankenstein's monster. You get what I'm saying. I don't
     have to type it all out every time. Plus, wouldn't their last names have been
     the same? Technically you can call both of them Frankenstein.

Women don't get to stomp around like Godzilla. Someone will just ask if you're on your period.

Hysteria is a term that first entered the public consciousness during the medieval witch trials in Western Europe. If you had hysterical symptoms like not having an interest in heterosexuality, having a sexual appetite, or an aversion to marriage—aka being a woman who didn't want to bang your gross suitor—you must have been wearing Satan's class ring. You were clearly a witch and needed to be executed. Hysteria is a ridiculous, bogus medical term that is still in use today. It originated with an ancient Greek belief that all disease started in the uterus, a belief that many Republican lawmakers continue to uphold.

All this shitty, misogynistic history has been reflected in the world of monster movies, a historically male place. Nearly every female monster that's ever crossed the silver screen has been one of those "hysterical" Satan-smooching witches or another brand of oversexed villain—the vampire. There are countless examples of sexy female vampires in the horror world, from the early days of Dracula's brides to Kate Beckinsale's leather-clad vampire in *Underworld*, and nearly all of them were created by men.[100] In horror films, female villains usually fall into one of two categories. Either you're a warty, unfuckable witch who lives in the forest and must be killed for the unforgivable offense of providing low-cost healthcare—oh, I mean eating children and cursing crops. Or, you're a busty female vampire, being punished for your horniness for the rest of eternity by having to cleavage men to death.

Women don't get to be colossal monsters. Women don't get to fuck shit up.

Women don't get to explore their rage on a catastrophic scale

---

100   There are some less well-known examples of female werewolves, but most
      of them are, of course, very sexy and have the same issues that female vam-
      pires do.

on the big screen, at least in a way that passes the Bechdel test.[101] Most female monsters, even outside the horror world, are defined by their relationship to men. Either they've been wronged by a man and now want to take revenge,[102] or they're the bride/ daughter/mother of a male character, or they're jealous of another woman who has the man she wants. Even the most famous female monster of all time, the legendary Elsa Lanchester's portrayal of the Bride of Frankenstein, is created as a nameless bride for the monster.

There are, of course, exceptions to this, but for every one example of an unsexualized female monster, there are quite literally hundreds of sexualized ones. If you Google "female monsters," the results are mostly a slew of lists along the lines of "The Top 5 Sexiest Girl Monsters" and "10 Most Beautiful Female Monsters," sometimes even ranked in order of dateability. They'll steal your heart, ha, get it?

The ones that aren't sexy are, at the very least, differentiated in some overt way as female. This is usually done with a stereotypical feminine marker, like eye makeup or red lips, because when you're living in a cave and eating people, you've definitely got time to apply stylish cat's eyes. I can barely do this in a well-lit bathroom. When I got my female werewolf tattoo, my own mother told me that I should "put some eyelashes on it" so people would know it was a girl.

It's impossible not to correlate these issues with the fact that women are rarely weighing in on these designs and screenplays. But, surprise folks, women get mad about things that don't have to do with men. Women feel anger and isolation just as intensely

---

101   This a feminist test for films. If a film has two women that have a conversation about something other than a man, then it passes the test. You'd be surprised at how few films do.

102   There is an entire subgenre of the horror world for this, usually referred to as "rape revenge" films. That's right. I can cough up a mere handful of examples—using only the most obscure horror films—of unsexualized female monsters, but there's an entire subgenre with hundreds of films about women who have been raped and then go on a killing spree.

as men. Women have desires for power—destructive desires—that aren't satisfied with mean-spirited gossip and a bold lip color. Women need to be able to see themselves reflected in the monsters playing out these emotions on the big screen. Our only options shouldn't be either banishment to a shack in the woods or growing fangs and becoming part of a bloodthirsty sister-wife troupe.

Women rarely get to weigh in on monster designs, but when she got the chance to, Millicent made it count.

At Universal, Milicent had entered the most fulfilling and successful part of her career. Every weekday, she woke up to that beautiful California sunshine and went to work on the studio lot, back in the role of working visual artist. At home, things were wonderful. Earlier in the year, she had met and fallen in love with a man named Syd Beaumont. He wasn't connected to the film industry[103] and more importantly, any other women. It was the healthiest relationship she had ever had. As far as she was concerned, Syd was the love of Milicent's life, a life that was now stable, secure and happy.

A career in the arts is usually an uncertain thing. Artists are typically unsure where their next job is coming from, how long that job will last and what it will pay. But in the film industry, landing a steady job at a studio like Universal was one of the best things you could do. Many professionals in the movie industry move from individual film to individual film, but employment at the studio itself guaranteed work, as long as the studio stayed in business.

She wasn't under contract, but Milicent was pulling in around $250 a week (equal to $2,291 in 2018). That's damn good money. Even though she was married, I imagine it was satisfying to be a woman making enough money to support yourself, especially

---

103 I've been unable to find out what Syd's profession was or many details about him.

considering Milicent's history of romantic turmoil. She was working a dream job in Hollywood and making money with her art. It doesn't get much better than that.

In 1952, Universal—officially known as Universal-International Pictures—had just been bought by the American record company Decca Records. For the years leading up to the sale, Universal's film production had struggled. At the time, Universal was not the media giant it is today. It was famous for creating fun, low-budget movies, the kind you can inhale a bucket of popcorn while watching. Most of the big studios of the time had a roster of talent: Warner Brothers had stars like Doris Day, John Wayne and Gregory Peck under contract. Universal's contracted talent didn't have that kind of star power yet. William Goetz, the studio head in the 1940s, the man who had hired Bud Westmore, had the not-so-brilliant idea to slash the company's production of horror movies, B films[104] and other types of films that weren't considered "serious." His mission was to bring some esteem to the company that was previously known for its (now classic) horror films.

Goetz vastly misunderstood his audiences. Some of these new films were successes, but on the whole, mostly were a disappointment at the box office. People like to be entertained, man. By the end of the decade, he was fired and replaced by studio manager Edward Muhl, who steered the ship back on course. He decided that the best way to get the studio making money again was to make those entertaining films, but to make them look good. Universal started plumping up the budgets for these movies, often creating them in Technicolor, a process utilizing a dye-transfer technique that makes realistic, natural-looking color. These films were not as expensive as the big budget movies

---

104   B films, like B sides on records, were the second movie to appear in the bill for a double feature. Because these films were usually made for a low budget and were typically Westerns, science fiction or horror, the term *B film* was used to describe a cheesy genre movie. The term stuck around even after double features and B movies were no longer part of the moviegoing experience.

of the day[105] or as prestigious, but were successful enough to start luring big-name talent over to the Universal studio lot. It was a good time to be designing things in the makeup department there.

Milicent was a makeup designer, not a makeup artist. Looking at the titles, you'd think they were interchangeable. But there are some big distinctions in the movie industry. Milicent never applied a brush to a person's face. She created designs on paper that sculptors or makeup artists would bring to life.

A makeup artist is someone who actually applies makeup. This can be regular old makeup, also known as a beauty makeup. Or it can be special effects makeup, ranging all the way from fake cuts, bruises and blood to elaborate monster makeups and masks. Special effects artists exclusively do that sort of work. Special effects artists usually work with what is called practical effects—effects that are "in camera," as in, happening in real life. Blood, guts, monsters, squibs (fake gunshot wounds), miniature sets, pyrotechnics, puppets. Anything that you can touch. Visual effects artists use computer-generated imagery—CGI—to create effects outside of the live-action shot. None of the titles for these jobs make a lot of sense, but there it is.

There's been a lot of recent buzz about the value of practical effects versus CGI. They are both tools for a filmmaker to utilize; one isn't better than another. It's true that a practical effect has a certain gravitas on-screen. Your brain can literally tell when something actually exists or not, whether that thing is reacting to light and gravity as a real object would. At least for now, computers are not quite advanced enough to create something that totally tricks our minds. But with CGI, filmmakers can create things with digital imagery that are impossible or unsafe to create in real life. The best is when the two techniques are used in harmony, each method playing to its strengths. A lot

---

105   These lower budget films were made for around $900,000, which is about eight million today. If that sounds like a lot of money to make a genre film, please keep in mind that your average superhero movie in 2018 costs about two hundred million to make.

of horror snobs extol the "good old days" of 80s horror movies with their sometimes cheesy practical special effects. Don't
get me wrong, I love a ridiculous, corn syrup-y zombie blood
explosion as much as the next girl. But CGI can dazzle you. It's
pretty cool to see those giant dragons in *Game of Thrones*, right?
Why not have both?

It gets slightly more confusing when you consider that many
special effects artists are also the designers for the makeup, masks
and suits that they are applying. In the early days, as we saw before George Westmore showed up, actors were expected to fulfill
both jobs at once: figure out their look, apply it and then act in
it. Lon Chaney—nicknamed The Man of a Thousand Faces—
made his name in the world of film by combining his powerful and affecting performances with his deft skill with makeup.
You might know him as both the original Hunchback of Notre
Dame and the original Phantom of the Opera.[106]

Even today, sometimes the artist designing the makeup is the
one to apply it. But not always. The turning point of this practice was actually Bud Westmore. Bud's predecessor at Universal
was Jack Pierce, who was arguably the greatest makeup artist in
film history. At Universal, he designed and applied the makeup
for *The Wolfman*, *The Mummy*, and working alongside actor Boris
Karloff, the iconic makeup for *Frankenstein*. Jack Pierce's designs
were part of what built the reputation for Universal Studios. But
after twenty years of service, he was unceremoniously fired when
William Goetz got the bright idea to make more "serious" films.
Pierce was resistant to pressure to use the newer techniques of
monster makeup, but it's more likely that he was fired because
Goetz wanted to distance himself from the monster movie reputation that Pierce helped establish. Jack Pierce's replacement was Bud

---

106   To create the iconic Phantom makeup, Lon pulled up the tip of his nose
       with wire and pinned it in place, painted his nostrils black and wore a jag-
       ged set of fake teeth. Chaney was hard-core. In 1923, no one had ever seen
       anything so ghastly. Moviegoers fainted in the theaters.

Westmore. Goetz wanted a Westmore, famous for their beauty makeup, to replace the monster king Jack Pierce.

Westmore wasn't applying all the makeups in his department nor was he designing all of them, either. In fact, he spent most of his time doing administrative duties. That's why he needed artistic talent to be in the shop, designing and creating. That's why he needed Milicent.

Milicent would arrive at the Universal studio lot and head for the makeup department, a place far less glamorous than the trailers for background actors. A makeup department looks like an art studio made a big messy baby with a shop classroom. It's an artist's dream filled with foam, monster masks, mannequins, sculptures, art supplies, desks and drafting tables.

Just like when she joined the Disney animation team, Milicent had entered another boys' club. The other designers, the sculptors, her boss—everyone was male. This time around, however, she was a married woman and there's no record of her having to deal with any harassment, at least from her coworkers.[107]

Milicent had a dream job. But when it comes to making the dream a reality behind-the-scenes in Hollywood, you've got to put in a lot of work. As with anything that's designed, monsters and makeups go through many different iterations before becoming the creation you finally see on-screen. How much direction film designers get varies wildly. In a screenplay, the writer might describe a monster in extensive detail, or they might type out "fish-man" and leave it at that. Sometimes the producers or the director will chime in with their own ideas of what they'd like to see, sometimes the makeup department has to come up with something entirely on their own.

This is true for all the departments responsible for the look of the film: the production design, the costume department, the hair stylists, the property masters (*props*). Most filmmakers, studios and production companies hire artists to create something

---

107   This absolutely does not mean that it didn't happen. But I can hope.

called concept art—art that shows the concept of a film. This is especially useful in genre films when what needs to be created, either practically or visually, is fantastical. It's not artwork that is meant to be shown to the public, but rather between members of a film crew to communicate and explore ideas for sets, characters, creatures, props—anything that needs to be created for a film. The art can range from quick, rough pencil drawings to elaborate paintings.

Before Milicent would even put the pencil to paper, she'd do research to come up with some visual inspiration for her impending design. Then she'd start sketching. The guys in the makeup department would check out what she was doing and offer thoughts and opinions. Bud would guide her based on the desires of the studio executives. Some designs go through many, many versions until everyone is happy with the end result. Then, if it's a makeup, it'll be applied to a face to see how it looks. If it's a mask or a suit, it'll be given to a sculptor. The sculptor will create a three-dimensional version of the design—sometimes starting with a scale model out of clay called a *maquette*—and move on to create a life-size version. That life-size version will be molded and cast, usually in something called *foam latex*.

Foam latex is, you guessed it, a foam that's made by mixing liquid rubber latex with chemical agents and whipping it into a foam. This is poured into the mold and baked. Foam latex caught on in the 1930s and is still a staple of Hollywood special effects departments. I guarantee you that most of the fantasy and sci-fi characters you have fond childhood memories of were created in part with foam latex. It's soft, it's lightweight and can be made to look like anything from a suit of steel armor to Yoda's ears.

Once it's out of the oven, the foam latex will be painted before it's finally ready to wear or apply. Sometimes, the director and the producers will see the final product and be unhappy, then it's back to the drawing board to repeat the entire process with a different design. This is why it is important to have a great artist working at the start of the production line. You save time, you save money, you save wanting to murder your picky producers.

Milicent would walk into the makeup department, her ever-present high heels clicking on the tiled floor and she'd take her place at her workstation with a sketch pad, ink, pastels, pencils and paints. Artists, crew members, administrative staff and talent bustled through the gritty air of the shop. Even in this messy, masculine environment, she loved to look glamorous. Milicent didn't let the male-dominated atmosphere tamp down her love of expressing her femininity with fashion.

Milicent wearing one of the masks she designed for *Abbott and Costello Meet Dr. Jekyll and Mr. Hyde*. (*Family collection*)

When my tomboy teenage self saw Milicent resplendent in full-skirted dresses and flashy jewelry, it was the only thing about her that I balked at. With my love of horror movies and heavy metal music, I was struggling to fit into stereotypically male scenes and tried to dress accordingly. I eschewed makeup, nail polish and any sort of hair products. I didn't even like looking in the mirror. What I truly wanted to look like was the lead singer of an 80s heavy metal band, but I probably looked more like the disgruntled survivor of a bleached-denim accident. Seeing Milicent look so inarguably and unapologetically feminine was the only thing that bothered me about her. I associated anything with femininity to being lesser, an idea reinforced by the horror movies I was eagerly gobbling up.

Growing up a horror fan is harder when you're a girl. You have very few role models and they generally all look the same. They're white, they're beautiful, they're thin, they're straight, they're able-bodied, and they only fight the monster because they have to, because everyone else has been killed off. They don't direct the monster, they don't make the monster, they don't go off in search of monster adventures. This makes anything girly and feminine seem weak and I bought into it.

Internalized misogyny is real and it is rampant in the horror community. When you are inundated with images of beautiful women who don't have a lot of clothes or a lot of agency,[108] it implies that women have value only for their beauty. When you see only scream queens[109] and monster victims, those messages sink in and they sink in deep. It puts a lot of women off the genre.

Understanding and empathizing with why women would be put off from the horror genre is something that took me a very long time to get to. As a teenager, I was an enthusiastic carrier of the ridiculous and toxic I'm-not-like-other-girls flag. Look

---

108   Yes, I've seen *Alien*. There are examples of badass women in horror films, but the majority of female protagonists aren't like Ripley.

109   If you're unfamiliar with the term, a *scream queen* is an actress famous for her roles in horror films, usually as a victim. Because of the victim part, there's usually a lot of screaming involved.

at me! I can put up with all the misogyny in horror and still love it! It totally doesn't bother me! I'm cooler than other girls!

What I didn't want to face was the pain caused by loving a genre so deeply and not seeing myself reflected in it. So, I adopted a stance that allowed me to see myself as an exception, as special. If I could play by the rules, if I could swallow all the sexist bullshit, I could be accepted. I could be *one of the guys*. With my *Evil Dead* shirt, no makeup, and obscure horror VHS tapes, I could belong. It was too much work to see that the state of things was garbage. It involved far too much anger and mental anguish. I acted like I deserved praise for refusing to be furious about how glaring and terrible the lack of female and marginalized representation was. I didn't realize that these two states weren't mutually exclusive. I could love cheesy old monster movies while simultaneously wanting them to be better. It seemed easier to mold myself into someone that I thought would be included, to shun women who weren't willing to put up with the misogyny, as if I was better and cooler than they were.

When I became an adult, I realized how harmful this mindset is. I was participating in a toxic culture. I was being a fucking idiot. Identifying as a woman and expressing your femininity is awesome and badass. My feelings about Milicent's wardrobe choices drastically changed. How absolutely incredible that Milicent was creating these masculine monsters while reveling in her lady glory. How marvelous that she refused to try to fit into the boys' club, that she was unapologetically herself and marched into that male-dominated space in her heels. That's some badass shit. It was a revelation to me that you can be a strong woman in a pair of steel-toed boots or a pair of sparkling pumps.

Milicent loved dressing up. She loved looking glamorous. It made her happy. The ways in which women are pressured to look a certain way to attract men are abysmal. It took me years to realize that it was possible to want to look a certain way just for yourself, to want to dress up and wear pretty, fancy things because that's just what you like. Every day that Milicent got dressed in something fabulous, she was high-fiving that little girl in San Simeon who was forced to wear heavy, draping clothes.

That little girl would have been thrilled to see where Milicent was in 1952, in Hollywood, acting alongside all those movie stars and creating makeup looks for them. Now after the dramatic pirate makeups for *Against All Flags*, Bud wanted Milicent to design something very different.

The horror movies we create reflect the fears we feel as a society, and America in the 1950s was no different. That decade was the heyday of science fiction films. In the wake of World War II, America was a shifting country. The Cold War was ramping up. Americans stopped being afraid of a Nazi invasion and started to worry about problems on a bigger and less understandable scale. Anxieties about nuclear war and the explosion of new science and technology crept into the American mind. Government eyes began to turn toward the stars and the gaze of the American public nervously followed. It was the Atomic Age and moviegoers didn't want fantasy films. They wanted to be dazzled and scared by science. With a thin veneer of science covering the plotline of these films, they seemed credible, possible and therefore absolutely terrifying.

The baby boom was, well, booming and suburbanization was in full swing. Everyone was staying home and television was becoming a more popular entertainment medium. Film studios needed gimmicks to draw customers out of their homes and into theater seats. More and more films were shot in color, in widescreen and, excitingly, in 3D. Studios realized there was a giant untapped moviegoing market—teenagers. Teenagers were seen as the perfect audience for horror and science fiction movies that were considered too immature for adults. Plus, teenagers were desperate to get out of the house.

Studios all scrambled to develop sci-fi projects featuring irradiated bugs, alien invasions, nuclear power gone awry, anything to show humans grappling with forces that they had either un-wittingly unleashed or had come to us from other worlds. The entire spectrum of the film industry, from the major companies all the way down to small independents, was trying to get their sci-fi movies onto the big screen.

The executives at Universal saw their chance and they took it. Their reputation for monster and genre films became a boon rather than a detriment. The new films they developed were very simi-lar in plot and feel to monster movies; this time the monsters were just coming from space and wearing weird outfits. The first on the docket was *It Came from Outer Space*, which was shot in 1952.

It Came from Outer Space was an important first for Universal. It was their first venture into science fiction. It was also their first film shot in 3D. In fact, it was the first 3D film made by a big studio. In the 1950s, showing movies in 3D seemed impos-sibly cool and high-tech for audiences. It was an alluring gim-mick. Universal was going into the science fiction genre with all guns blazing.

For such an important film, they made sure to get a heavy hitter in the sci-fi world to write the script: none other than the legendary Ray Bradbury. Bradbury had already claimed his throne as the king of genre fiction in America. His collections *The Illustrated Man* and *The Martian Chronicles* had come out in 1950 and 1951 respectively, becoming immediately popular. He wrote a great treatment[110] for the movie, outlining a story about aliens that come to Earth and can imitate people. America was in the grip of Communist-phobia at this point and McCarthy-ism was in full swing, so this film touched a nerve.[111] Universal gave it the green light.

---

110 A treatment is basically a short, no-frills outline of a film that many writers need to submit to executives or investors before they get the go-ahead to write the full script. That way, big surprises are avoided, like having to shoot the film inside a volcano or needing a herd of angry pink elephants.

111 Spoiler alert—the aliens are actually benign and just trying to fix their busted spaceship, which shows you how Bradbury felt about McCarthyism.

Early drafts of the script describe the aliens' true form as sort of lizard-like, but Bradbury soon scrapped that idea. They were supposed to seem absolutely terrifying to humans and yeah, lizard people are definitely freaky, but they're not boggle-the-weak-human-mind horrifying. Bradbury updated the script to include a description of "something which suggests a spider, a lizard, a web blowing in the wind, a milk-white something dark and terrible, something like a jellyfish, something that glistens softly, like a snake." I can imagine Milicent, Bud and the entire makeup team getting this description and heading en masse to the nearest bar.

Bradbury's suggestion was for the moviegoers to see only the merest, tenebrous hint of the monster. No freaking way, pal. Universal wanted an alien movie that was going to make those popcorn buckets fly. Harry Essex, the writer who did the final draft of the script, didn't help clarify the situation much. He described it as a "horrible creature" and left it at that.

It was left to Milicent to draw it.

Dozens and dozens of designs were drafted up, all variations on giant, amorphous shapes.[112] Most of them look like heads of broccoli with eyes. The design was eventually refined to have only one eye, stubby Tyrannosaurus Rex–esque arms and a whole lot of blobbiness. It looks like an eyeball got trapped inside of a very old Ziploc sandwich bag. This sounds pretty lame, but back in the 1950s, this was some terrifying stuff.

The film was produced by a man named William Alland and directed by Jack Arnold, a team that would go on to become two of the leading sci-fi filmmakers of the day. *It Came from Outer Space* was shot on soundstages on the Universal Studios lot and in the desert outside of Los Angeles. It was released the following year in May 1953 to mild critical and commercial success. It was only the seventy-fifth-highest earner of the year, but it

---

112   Westmore saved all these early designs to use on another, later sci-fi film that also became an icon of the genre. More on this later.

started a cinema trend that would continue for years to come. In 2008, it was nominated for the American Film Institute's top ten science fiction films list. Not bad for a cheesy movie with a weird monster! Milicent had managed to take only the vaguest description of a creature and pull something out of her brain that would help kick off an entire genre of film.

Hedging their bets just in case this new sci-fi thing didn't work out, Universal put another film into development around the same time that was guaranteed to be a success: *Abbott and Costello Meet Dr. Jekyll and Mr. Hyde*. It was the fourth Abbott-and-Costello-meet-a-monster movie for Universal since the 1951 release of *Abbott and Costello Meet the Invisible Man*. The company had done many films with the comedy duo and the horror-comedy formula was a proven hit for them. The films feature Abbott and Costello as characters in a classic horror movie story, but all the frights are replaced with hilarious gags. It works out pretty well. All the emotions and mechanics of scaring someone are very similar to the mechanics of making them laugh. The anticipation, the surprise. It's usually just a matter of perspective.

The formula was also an effective recycling exercise for the studio. The Mummy, Frankenstein's monster, the Invisible Man—these were all characters who were no longer in vogue in Hollywood and sort of passé in the horror world. Bela Lugosi and Boris Karloff were once A-list celebrities because of their iconic monster roles. But nearly two decades later, the most success both actors ever experienced was with those horror parts. Universal could now repurpose these actors in their iconic roles for hilarious results. No longer scary, audiences could delight in seeing them chase around Abbott and Costello. Boris Karloff hated these kinds of films. He felt that they did a disservice to the original characters. But hey, everyone likes money. Boris agreed to do this film and even do a press tour for it, as long as he didn't have to see it.

In *Abbott and Costello Meet Dr. Jekyll and Mr. Hyde*, the come-

dians are in Robert Louis Stevenson's famous tale of split personalities as a pair of American detectives who get involved in
the hunt for the murderous Dr. Jekyll, played by Boris Karloff
sans makeup. By injecting his secret serum, Dr. Jekyll is transformed into the evil Mr. Hyde, who looks like a particularly
violent and horny were-boar. Cue lots of hijinks. Karloff didn't
actually put the mask on and play Mr. Hyde, despite what the
credits of the film say. Eddie Parker, a stuntman, played the
role. Milicent helped design this mask and the several different
makeups that comprise the transformation scene.

That year, after both of these films were finished shooting,
Milicent experienced a personal tragedy. In October, her mother
passed away.

Camille and Elise had been moving around quite a bit since
Milicent had left the house. While living in Glendale, Camille
had been working as an engineer for the State of California. He
helped build a major part of the Angeles Crest Highway, a sixty-
six-mile highway that starts in Burbank (on top of Los Angeles)
and extends west into the San Gabriel Mountains. I don't really
know the best way to compliment a highway, but the Angeles
Crest Highway[113] is a nice one. It's scenic and easy to drive on.
It's used mainly by people in LA who are stressed out and starved
for trees to drive out in the middle of nowhere, get a break from
the city and come back when they miss the juice bars.

Construction on the highway stalled during World War II
and once the war was over, Camille sought work elsewhere. He
was hired by the federal government and his skills were utilized
by the Atomic Energy Commission. The AEC was created after
World War II to control the research and development of atomic
energy and science during peacetime, which considering the fact
that the Cold War was ramping up, is sort of a misnomer. The

---

113   If you're a *Donnie Darko* fan, this is the highway you see much of in the film,
      starting right with the opening scene.

AEC was in charge of things like developing America's nuclear arsenal and eventually nuclear weapons testing. Peaceful stuff.

Camille and Elise traveled all over the country for Camille's new job. They were now unencumbered by children, since Milicent, Ulrich and Ruth had all moved on to their adult lives in Los Angeles. Both Ulrich and Ruth were married and had begun having children. Ruth, following in the tradition of her older sister, was disowned by Camille when she married. She and her husband eloped because Camille would never have given them permission to marry. But Ruth secretly kept up correspondence with Elise.

Over the next few years, Camille and Elise relocated from California to Hawaii to Florida and finally back to California. The couple ended up in their hometown of San Francisco for a while before settling in Oakland, where Camille retired. Both were in their mid-sixties—sixty-six and sixty-seven respectively—when Elise died. Private funeral services were held in Oakland before she was cremated.

The death of Elise wasn't enough to mend the estrangement between Milicent and her family, but Camille did reconcile with Ruth, whose two children had never met either Camille or Elise. Camille apologized to Ruth and her husband, inviting the family up to visit him in Northern California. Camille ended up like many difficult fathers—he became a wonderful grandfather. Ruth's children loved him, despite her insistence to them that he wasn't a good man. Ruth hadn't forgiven him, but kept up the relationship for the sake of her children.

The years hadn't changed Ruth's opinion of her sister. Milicent's siblings and her father both kept up their skewed thoughts about her lifestyle. They were convinced that she was involved in lurid things in Hollywood, that she was a sex worker and that she deserved shame. The tragic way her first two relationships ended, along with the fact that she lived with Frank Graham without being married to him, served as proof that she was an immoral woman.

But Milicent had Syd and she also had her friends. One of the best and closest friends that Milicent had made in Hollywood was a man named George Tobias. George was a movie and television actor, appearing in over sixty shows and films over the course of his life. He is best known as the character of Abner Kravitz from the show *Bewitched*. George was from New York City and was fourteen years older than Milicent. He had been working in Hollywood since 1939.

Milicent and George were a support system for each other and often attended industry events together. Because of this, people always thought that they were romantically involved and carrying on a long-term affair. Neither of them ever publicly confirmed or denied anything, but they were only friends, best friends. George never married and there were many rumors that he was gay. Without some new archival discovery, it's absolutely impossible for me to know. What I do know was that they loved each other and stayed close for the rest of their lives. George would remain a fixture in Milicent's personal and social life.

At this point, Milicent was living up in Beverly Glen, in the canyons and mountains above the city of Los Angeles. Beverly Glen is close to one of the well-known LA neighborhoods, well-known if you liked *The Fresh Prince of Bel Air*, anyway. It's a beautiful area. It's a little tough driving your car through the narrow, winding canyon roads, but it's verdant and lined with gorgeous houses. It was especially tough for Milicent to drive there; she had a love for giant, roomy cars. But Beverly Glen felt like a magical and secret place, and Milicent loved it there.

Despite the family loss, things were otherwise going well in Milicent's life. They were about to get even better. Unbeknownst to her, Milicent had the biggest project of her entire career waiting for her at Universal. Something was in development that was going to change everything.

Abbott and Costello Meet Dr. Jekyll and Mr. Hyde and *It Came from Outer Space* were both modest 1953 box office successes. Everyone was happy with her work. *It Came from Outer Space* would go on to become a classic of the genre, influencing film-makers for generations, particularly Steven Spielberg's *Close Encounters of the Third Kind*.

While she was designing things for Bud Westmore, Milicent kept up with her acting career. She starred in a television series called *Ramar of the Jungle*. On the show, *Ramar* means "white medicine man" in an unspecified native language, so you can imagine the casual racism and white superiority complex that's going to slide in when you turn this one on. It's about two white guys, a doctor and his male associate, who are the sons of missionaries that return to Africa to treat the natives there. Milicent starred as the White Goddess, the revered sexy white lady of an African village who has mysteriously stayed young and beautiful and learned choppy English. She was featured in a three-episode arc (which was later collected into a single story and released as a film in the United Kingdom). Her character is decked out in a leopard print two-piece skirt/bikini set, complete with shell necklaces and a leopard-print cape. She speaks in an accent I can only describe as "grumpy cave woman."

Honestly, it's not great stuff. *Ramar of the Jungle* wasn't a highlight of 1950s television and Milicent wasn't hired for her acting chops. To be fair, she does look fantastic in leopard print.

This was her only role in 1953. Lucky for her, she was busy designing monsters.

Milicent's place as a creature and makeup designer at Universal felt secure. When it came time to design something for Universal's next sci-fi project, Bud Westmore knew exactly who the artist would be.

8

The Beauty and the Beast

I was starting to run out of resources and places to look for traces of Milicent. I had no idea what the rest of her life looked like. So, I decided to go in the other direction completely—I'd look for traces of her death. At least, I assumed it would be her death. At this point, she would be over one hundred years old if she were still alive. I needed to start reverse engineering her life: start from the end of it and work backward. It was something solid I could lean on. There aren't many constants in life, but this was one.

It was time to go and look up her death certificate.

As soon as morning rush hour ebbed slightly, I made the drive to the Los Angeles County Registrar's office. Pulling into the parking lot, I took in another constant in life—gargantuan and slow-moving lines at government buildings. This I had prepared for. There were not one but two books in my purse.

Over the course of the hour and a half I waited in line, I was caught off guard by the realization that I didn't actually know if I *could* look up her death certificate. I didn't know if random people were allowed to do that. Because, make no mistake, in the eyes of the law, I was a random person. I had no familial connection to Milicent. I'm as pale as a nervous ghost and my last name is O'Meara. I'm about as far from an Italian goddess as an actual potato. I was pretty sure that my tattoo of her didn't count as a blood connection, either.

I didn't even know how to ask this stuff. "Uh, hi, can you tell me is this person dead or not?" probably wasn't the way to lead that conversation, especially if I was trying to convince them I wasn't a random creep.

But I had been in line for so long that I was a now legal resident of the Los Angeles County Registrar's office, so I decided to stick it out. When I finally stepped up to the small and grungy window, I blurted out my request to the exhausted woman sitting on the other side.

"Hi, I'm trying to find the death certificate or I guess any kind of certificate but mostly death certificate for this woman I'm writing a book about but I'm not related to her I hope it's okay I don't know if it's allowed but anything you could tell me would be great oh man thank you so much!"

I inhaled and smiled. Instead of kicking me out, the woman ended up being far more kind and patient than she needed to be. She looked up "Milicent Patrick" for me, tapping away on the kind of cumbersome and thunderous keyboard that now resides solely in government facilities and community colleges.

"Hmm, no death certificate exists under that name."

With an apologetic look to the hordes of people waiting behind me in line, I gave her all the combinations of names I could think of. Milicent Trent, Milicent Rossi, Mildred Rossi, Mildred Trent, Mildred Patrick. One l, two l's. This registrar clerk deserved a trophy for letting me take up so much of her time. The people behind me deserved a trophy for not turning into an angry mob and murdering me. After minutes of searching, she finally looked up and said, "Miss, I'm sorry, but no one with that name has ever died in Los Angeles."

I went back outside and sat in my rental car, partially dejected but hopelessly intrigued.

Where did she go? Did she change her name again? Was she still alive?

The idea for *Creature from the Black Lagoon* began many years before 1953. In 1940, a man named William Alland was having dinner at the home of Orson Welles. Welles was in the midst of creating the William Randolph Hearst–inspired *Citizen Kane*[114] and Alland had a small role in the film.

Another guest at the dinner was Mexican cinematographer Gabriel Figueroa, who brought up an outlandish story. According to him—and he insisted the story was true—there was a half man, half fish who lived in the Amazon. He was no myth; this creature was constantly discussed by the inhabitants of the area. More than his appearance, the people were concerned about this creature's annual tradition of entering the village, claiming a maiden[115] and leaving, presumably to eat her, or ravage her, or get her to start darning a mountainous pile of large damp socks. Once this ritual was over, the village would be safe for another year. Safe from creature attacks, I guess. Someone really needed to check the fine print on this deal.

Years later, in 1952, Alland found himself working at Universal, producing and writing. That October, Alland was trying to brainstorm something new and exciting to bring to the executives at the studio. He remembered the crazy fish-man conversation from that dinner at Welles's house and decided to write a script treatment called *The Sea Monster*. The story was basically a wetter version of *King Kong*. Scientists hear a wild tale about a fish-man living in the Amazon,[116] they go out to investigate with a sexy

---

114   The Hearsts have a very weird reach over the life of Milicent Patrick.

115   I'm always curious as to how these monsters can tell, on sight, when someone is a virgin, a trick that nuns have been trying to master for centuries.

116   Considering the title, Alland must have had a tentative grasp on geography.

lady along with for the ride, the fish-man sees the sexy lady and falls in love, they shoot the fish-man and bring him back to civilization, where he escapes and attacks the town but is ultimately brought down due to his weakness for the lady. The end. Alland even acknowledged the similarities between *The Sea Monster* and *King Kong*.[117] The executives at Universal liked the twist on this successful monster movie formula and handed the treatment over to a scriptwriter to see what came of it.

The writer was Maurice Zimm, a man who had been writing radio dramas for a long time but had never written for film before. A detailed treatment emerged that honestly, you don't need to read. It involves a hot heiress funding a scientific expedition to the Amazon. She only cares about seducing men and ends up being used as bait to attract an emotional and human-like fish creature called the Pisces Man. The Pisces Man absconds with her. A lot of escaping and rescuing and capturing happens for both parties until the Pisces Man is weakened and devoured by piranha. Nice try, Maurice.

This story wasn't going to win any awards, but it gave Alland the kind of monster that he really wanted. He wanted a dignified creature full of humanity, something that was barely monstrous. He wanted sad and beautiful, sort of romantic, like something The Cure would sing about if they were mermen. A gross, horrific monster didn't figure into his vision of the film.

Universal thought that the story had promise, but recognized that it needed a lot of work. The treatment was passed off to other writers, Leo Lieberman and Arthur Ross, to be turned into a screenplay. This next version of the story was much closer to the final film than what Maurice Zimm had written, but it wasn't all the way there. It was close enough to be a springboard for the studio to jump off into preproduction, though. In the

---

117 To be fair, the plot of *King Kong* is ripped off from Sir Arthur Conan Doyle's *The Lost World*, so I can't give Alland too much shit.

meantime, Alland and director Jack Arnold shot *It Came from Outer Space* together.

Producers at Universal started to draw up a budget for what was being called *Black Lagoon*, a better and more accurate title than *The Sea Monster*. The first big financial decision that needed to be made was whether or not to shoot in color. This was a unique time in film history. Some films were being shot in color, some in black-and-white. It was similar to when digital technology began to replace analog film in the early 2000s, for both shooting the film and distributing it. There were advantages and disadvantages to both. Color was a draw for audiences, but was more expensive to shoot. Also, when you're making a science fiction film, it's easier to create a convincing monster when you don't have to worry about what color it is.

Universal also needed to decide whether or not to shoot the movie in 3D. Again, 3D was a draw for audiences, but it was more expensive to shoot. The financial breakdown was significant enough to warrant serious consideration. Shooting it in black-and-white would have made the total budget $600,000 (about $5.5 million today); black-and-white 3D, $650,000 ($6 million); color, $675,000 ($6.3 million); and color 3D $750,000 ($7 million).

Much like my buying expensive lipstick and cheap eyeshadow to balance it out, Universal decided to split the difference. The film would be shot in 3D black-and-white. But the version of the screenplay that Ross and Lieberman had written still wasn't right. Alland wanted his *King Kong*–esque story. He wanted a movie with Beauty and the Beast elements. The latest version of the script was all monster movie and hardly any emotion. What that means is there was less of the female character. In this version, the Creature hardly reacts to her. In fact, he hardly reacts to anything at all unless he's attacking it. It's more like an expedition encountering a rabid animal on a safari than a nuanced monster story, with the female role being almost completely insignificant. In the face of the monster, she's terrified and weak. Alland wanted to see more of the female character, more agency and more of an emotional relationship with the monster. Ross disagreed and thank goodness, another writer, Harry Essex (the man who wrote the final script for *It Came from Outer Space*), was hired to do the final script instead.

If you think I'm shooting my Feminist Laser Beams too much, the following quote, from Tom Weaver's excellent book *The Creature Chronicles*, is what Arthur Ross said to Tom about the script and Alland's thoughts. It clearly illustrates how Ross feels about women in film.

> [Alland] wanted to put in *more* of the woman. Here comes this big Creature with his cock four feet long, he's going to fuck her, and she gets away just in time—but she *does* think about him [laughs]!... I had done as much [Beauty and the Beast] as I thought it was correct to do, because essentially that wasn't the story. The fact that the Creature was attracted to the woman was not the reason he fought back... But Bill wanted more of the *King Kong* element in *Creature*, so [Harry Essex came in]. Really, all he did was add more of the girl. Underwater shots, the Creature sees her, the Creature gets an erection [laughs]... I rather felt that the nature of the Creature's relationship to the woman in the picture was quite simplistic.

Ross was proud of his version of the script. He told Tom Weaver that "I wrote intelligent people doing intelligent things." Apparently, Ross doesn't consider women people. Thankfully for future audiences and everyone involved, Harry Essex "adding more of the girl" meant something different than Ross had imagined, instead writing the female character as an actual person, with things like goals and agency and feelings. Essex and Alland worked with Universal postproduction supervisor Ernest

Nims to get the script to its final incarnation. Nims drafted up a list of suggestions to streamline the story and finally get it into the shape that made it on-screen.[118]

The story of *Creature from the Black Lagoon* starts with a geology expedition finding a fossil in the Amazon—a skeletal hand with long webbed fingers. The hand is evidence of a link between aquatic and land animals. The leader of the expedition, a man named Dr. Carl Maia, visits the nearby marine biology institute. There, he meets up with an ichthyologist he knows, Dr. David Reed, and Reed's colleague and girlfriend, Kay Lawrence. Seeing the hand, Reed persuades his boss at the institute, Dr. Mark Williams, to fund an expedition to the Amazon to look for more fossils. Mark, David, Carl and Kay make up the team, along with another scientist, Dr. Edwin Thompson. Kay Lawrence, of course, is the only one who isn't a doctor. But at least she's a smart, capable scientist and not merely sexy fodder for a giant Creature member.

The whole crew hops aboard a steamer boat for a trip down the Amazon. All of these folks are able-bodied white people. The only people of color in this movie are the assistants and the captain of the steamer ship, Lucas, played by Portuguese American actor Nestor Paiva. At first, the team has no luck unearthing fossils. It's when they explore a tributary that empties into a place Lucas informs everyone is called the Black Lagoon that things get interesting. It's an idyllic spot with a small catch...no one has ever returned from it. In typical horror movie fashion, a bunch of people hear about an ominously named place and have to go there. While they're steaming along toward the lagoon, the Creature catches a glimpse of Kay and has immediate interest. The Creature follows the ship into the Black Lagoon and the real adventure begins.

Especially considering what it started out as, and what in the

---

118   Harry Essex would go on to claim almost full credit for the script in interviews, which incensed Arthur Ross. Stealing credit for things is despicable, but honestly anything anyone can do to incense Arthur Ross makes me happy.

THE LADY FROM THE BLACK LAGOON . 185

hands of Arthur Ross it could have been, this is a great story for a 1950s monster movie. It's well paced, it's compelling, it's exciting. As far as early horror heroines go, Kay is one of the stronger ones. She's a scientist, she's brave, she has a moment when she fights off the Creature herself. She's a far cry from the screaming, helpless women being attacked by aliens that other science fiction movies were showcasing at the time.

Alland was happy with this version of the script; he had all his Beauty and the Beast elements. Unfortunately, according to the MPAA (Motion Pictures Association of America), there were maybe too many Beauty and the *Bestiality* elements. You might know the MPAA as the folks who give out ratings to films. Back in the 1950s, there was still something called the Hays Code or the Production Code in effect for films by major film studios. Your film couldn't be released if you didn't pass. The Code was basically a "moral" guideline for what you could and couldn't show in movies. Some things made sense, like a ban on showing children's sex organs. But the list of things you couldn't have in your film was outrageous, from white slavery (but all other kinds of slavery were cool) to dances that were too suggestive, especially since it was all subject to interpretation.[119]

The head of the Production Code Administration, a Roman Catholic named Joseph Breen, had to have a talk with Universal about *Creature from the Black Lagoon*. Breen was infamous for his rigid interpretations and enforcement of the code. He's the man who made Betty Boop hang up her flapper dress forever in exchange for a housewife's skirt. Many filmmakers raged against having to edit their films to comply with Breen's demands and they hated the power he had over their art.

Breen was concerned about the suggestions of bestiality in *Creature from the Black Lagoon*. He wanted to make sure that the director avoided any sexuality in the scenes with the Creature

---

119   It was luckily abandoned in the late 1960s, and in 1968, the rating system we now know went into effect.

and Kay, especially when the Creature carried Kay into his cave. Breen's other concern involved the Creature suit and the anatomy of it. Maybe he read Arthur Ross's version of the script and was terrified of seeing a beastly Creature member. The studio assured Breen it wouldn't be an issue, dooming Creature fans to wonder for the rest of eternity what was under those scales.[120]

Preproduction on the movie went forward when the MPAA was assured that no bestiality would be appearing on the silver screen. The film crew was probably just as relieved as the MPAA. They had their hands full enough creating a family-friendly version of a Creature suit. The design would be unlike anything Hollywood had ever seen.

Alland wanted the Beauty and the Beast elements of the story to be evident in the design of the Creature. But like all crafty producers, he wanted to save money, too. A $650,000 budget for a film was nothing to sneeze at in 1953, but this was a science fiction monster movie that mostly takes place on a boat in the Amazon. They needed every dollar of that budget.

At first, Alland thought that the Creature could be created by the prop department and the folks who handled special effects, with the sculptors from the makeup department making only the head, hands and feet. Those poor guys worked on the design for two months before they came up with something for Ricou Browning,[121] the man who was going to play the Creature in all the underwater scenes, to wear.

The suit, which is an extremely generous word for it, looked ridiculous. It made Ricou look like a mournful guppy that had been forced to wear a spandex onesie. It had a smooth head

---

120   Breen retired from terrorizing movies in 1954, the year *Creature from the Black Lagoon* came out. I like to think that having to debate fish dicks sent him into retirement.

121   Ricou Browning was a twenty-three-year-old accomplished swimmer and diver who the location scouts met while checking out what would be the location for the film shoot, Wakulla Springs, Florida. Jack Arnold loved the way Browning moved when he swam and decided to cast him in the role of the Creature.

and skin—no scales—and big flippers for feet. The hands were webbed claws and while there were some large scales on the belly and sides, most of the skin was just stretchy material. It looked like a terrible Halloween costume that your mom would have made for you in elementary school. To be fair, the prop team was following Alland's requests. But instead of looking romantic and sad and humanlike, it just looked weird and creepy, the missing link that needed to stay missing.

The crew put Ricou in the suit and had him swim in the large underwater tank on the Universal lot. The look was not improved by submerging him in water. They shot some test footage and screened it for the heads of the studio, the makeup department, the prop department, anyone who unfortunately had anything to do with the suit. I'd call it a monstrosity, but that's exactly what it wasn't. Everyone hated it. The heads of the studio declared that it wasn't scary and it looked terrible.

Well, everyone except Alland.

Alland for the rest of his life would prefer his version of the Creature suit. He thought it was both fearsome and elegant, a creature equal parts human and monster. Alland would always wonder what could have been. Which, I can tell you, would probably have been a ridiculous and cheesy monster film that wouldn't have had the impact *Creature from the Black Lagoon* did. Luckily, after the heads of the studio disapproved of his monster, Alland stepped aside and let Bud Westmore and the rest of the makeup department take over. It was time for Milicent to step in.

The stretchy onesie just wasn't going to cut it. No one wants to see a monster who looks like he just got back from his Sweatin' to the Oldies class. The department realized that along with a head, hand and claws, they were going to need to design and sculpt a full suit. The benchmark for a suspension of disbelief was raised with modern audiences. The Creature needed to reverberate with the ring of truth, of possibility.

As an artist for film, Milicent understood this.

"So many people, including youngsters, are so well-informed scientifically that even science fiction has to meet certain standards. Imagination by no means runs entirely riot. Somebody puts a foot down promptly if you ramble too far."

Part of the draw for science fiction audiences was that the films looked like they could be real, that they had some sort of scientific basis. You could take refuge from all the other classic Universal monsters by reminding yourself that they were not real. Werewolves and vampires did not exist. But as far as American audiences were concerned, there *could* be fish-men living in the waters of the Amazon. With all the technological innovations exploding into society on a regular basis, it seemed plausible. The structure of DNA was just discovered that year, in 1953. An amphibian missing link? No less crazy than a human going into space. The Creature had to be an entirely new, convincing type of monster.

For inspiration, Milicent researched prehistoric animals: reptiles, amphibians, fish. She specifically looked for illustrations of animals from the Devonian period, which is when the Creature claw fossil in the film is from. The Devonian period, about four hundred million years ago, was the time period where life began to adapt to dry land from the sea. She spent weeks sketching out designs.

The new version of the Creature that sprang from her pencil was more menacing, more primordial, more powerful. Its body was covered head to toe in armor-like scales. Fanning out from the side of its neck were thick gills, protruding from a bald, textured head with a prominent brow and thick, fleshy lips. There was a version with a tail[122] and a version with an angler fish-esque protrusion from the forehead. These were all rejected. The Creature went through three different iterations before Alland was satisfied. There were several different head

---

122   The tail seems to be Bud Westmore's only contribution to the design. It was rejected and subsequently removed by Milicent.

designs that were in competition with each other and they were all sculpted and molded so that they could be screen-tested. At last, the final design was approved and ready to be created.

Milicent in the Universal monster shop. The staged nature of this photo led many film historians to conclude that Milicent didn't actually design the Creature. This is stupid. It's also a bummer because this is a great picture, even if it is staged. (*Family collection*)

Now, I'm going to pause for a moment here. You're reading this and it's all making sense. Cool, yeah, Milicent works at this place and she got assigned to this task and she did it. Awesome. No problem. But for decades, up until very recently, most people either didn't know she designed it or didn't believe she did for reasons mentioned earlier in this book. So what seems pretty straightforward has been a contentious debate for decades. At this point in the creation process, Milicent's designs were passed down to the sculptor, Chris Mueller. Chris Mueller later insisted that the Creature, the whole monster, was designed by Milicent, who had been working on it as soon as it was assigned to the makeup department. The man who sculpted the Creature from her designs said that she designed it. That is proof enough for me.

Many people—men, it's always men—contend this history on flimsy grounds. There is a memo that exists, granting a one week's bonus to Jack Kevan, who was a makeup lab technician and close colleague of Bud Westmore, for outstanding work on designing and working on the suit. This memo has been waved around as "proof" that Milicent didn't really design the Creature. However, I think it's "proof" of something else.

The Creature suit is unique among Universal Studios' stable of classic monsters. It was the only one that needed to be able to go underwater. Not just splash around in a pond, it needed to be submerged for long periods of time with a person being if not comfortable, at least not miserable or dying inside of it. The Creature is also the only monster that was played by two people.

Ricou Browning was cast to play the Creature in all the aquatic shots, but that's only half of his screen time. The Creature also appears on land—walking around menacingly—during many scenes in the movie. Ricou was hired because of his underwater swimming prowess, but the studio needed an actor to portray the monster on land. Actor Ben Chapman, standing at a menacing six foot five, was cast. Ricou Browning by comparison was just under six feet tall. If you pay close, wildly nerdy attention while watching the film, you can tell that Ben Chapman in his land Creature suit even has an extra chest scale to accommodate his height.

It seems logical that versions of a suit needed to fit two different men of different weights, sizes and heights, and needed to be usable either on land or underwater, should be tweaked by someone with technical know-how. I remind you that Milicent did not actually build this suit. She designed it. She creatively guided it. She didn't sculpt it, she didn't mold it, she didn't apply it to anyone. She wasn't an engineer. It seems almost obvious that after Milicent got the look of the suit right that it would be passed to someone else would could tweak it to make sure that it worked on a technical level. It wasn't her job to do that.

So why, for sixty years, have monster nerds and film historians used this memo as evidence that Milicent didn't design the suit? Why is she the only classic monster designer in contention, the only one that people deem unlikely? Because she is, well, a she.

Ricou Browning has said that he didn't remember Milicent Patrick being around, working on set. This has also been used as evidence that Milicent was there for mere publicity purposes, or that she was just someone's girlfriend (even though she was Mrs. Beaumont at this time), or that she wasn't there at all. No one has taken into account that maybe Ricou Browning had no idea that a woman had designed the suit and since the rest of the makeup department was male, assumed that Milicent wasn't part of the crew. Maybe he thought she was someone's assistant. Browning didn't meet many people involved with the film. He never met Ben Chapman while they were both working on *Creature from the Black Lagoon*, even though they both played the same character.[123]

This is an entirely different type of male gaze, one that I've experienced too many times. I'm sure that voice actor who came into the studio to record his voice parts for my movie, when questioned, wouldn't remember a female producer working on the film.

There were technical issues with the suit after it was built. The eyes were a problem right away for both the land and underwater suits. Goggles under the mask didn't work since they bulged the shape of the face and filled with water after a while. Finally, Ricou had to settle for just looking through the little hole in

123   They were finally introduced decades later at a Creature convention.

the pupils of the mask, making things awkward for him. Different versions of the eyes could be popped in and out of the mask and in most shots, Ben Chapman could wear ones with holes in them. But in close-up shots, he had to wear the mask with no holes at all, making him completely unable to see. He might have looked intimidating in the suit, but he was fairly helpless.

Another problem was that because the suit was made out of foam latex, it floated. The suit wouldn't submerge because it was so buoyant. The crew had to fix thin plates of lead to Ricou's chest, thighs and ankles to get him underwater. The foam latex also eventually began to absorb water, making it heavier. This was good for keeping Ricou underwater, but it made it more difficult for him to maneuver in. Despite all these technical issues, no one's calling out Jack Kevan, saying that he must have been someone's boyfriend.[124]

To sculpt the suit, plaster casts of Ricou Browning and Ben Chapman were made. Most monster suits are made specifically to fit the actor playing them.[125] This wasn't always the case. In the early days of monsters, the suits would just be built to fit some sort of one-size-fits-all frame. This led to some ridiculous cinematic mishaps, though. If you watch the movie *It! The Terror from Beyond Space*, the alien, played by actor Ray "Crash" Corrigan, looks a little weird. Weird in more than an it's-a-cheesy-sci-fi-movie way.

The alien was created by B-movie sci-fi legend Paul Blais-

---

124 Five years after *Creature from the Black Lagoon* was released, Jack Kevan produced an independent film called *The Monster of Piedras Blancas*, where the monster is a blatant rip-off of the Creature, with the exception of the head, which looks like a naked mole rat. If you remember from earlier chapters, Piedras Blancas is where Milicent grew up in San Simeon though, weirdly enough, that's not where they shot the film. I refuse to see this film out of spite.

125 If you are interested in the history of suits and suit acting, I will heartily recommend that you watch the documentary *Men in Suits*, created by my dear friend and mentor, Frank Woodward. The title is a misnomer, though. There's women in there, too.

dell.[126] Corrigan didn't want to travel all the way across Los Angeles to where Blaisdell lived to get fitted and cast for the suit, a reluctance that actors and makeup artists struggle with to this day. The trouble was that Corrigan was a pretty big guy, so when the alien suit was finished, Corrigan didn't fit in it so well. In fact, he barely fit in it at all. His chin stuck straight out of the mouth hole and Blaisdell ended up having it paint it to look like the alien's tongue.

To avoid situations like this, plaster casts were made of Ben's and Ricou's feet in flippers, for Ricou's swimming comfort and ease. Individual foam latex pieces of the suit were glued to leotards so that they would move more naturally, instead of bending awkwardly. This also made the suit more comfortable.

The designs were then sculpted with clay onto the molds of Ben and Ricou. Those clay sculptures were then cast as molds, and those molds were filled with foam latex. The foam latex was baked, dried and then painted. Once painted and assembled all together, they were ready to be worn. Finally, the suit could be submerged in the underwater tank for test footage. Ricou tried out all the different heads and one, the infamous Creature head with all its texture and flaps and gills, was chosen. Creature from the Black Lagoon was born.

Less than a month after the original suit was rejected by Universal executives (and everyone else), the makeup department, led by the design work and creativity of Milicent Patrick, created a totally new suit that was ready for shooting. This new suit would become the last monster to be known as a "classic" Universal monster, and one of the best known and well-loved cinematic monsters of all time. It was the first suit where the

---

126   Blaisdell is known for creating the creatures in such B-movie classics as *The Beast with a Million Eyes*, *Day the World Ended* and *It Conquered the World*. It's not good to be in the world of Paul Blaisdell films. He created the suit for the 1956 film *The She-Creature*, which incidentally has nothing to do with our beloved Creature. Sadly, it's not a great movie. The She-Creature isn't played by a woman and it looks sort of like a giant, angry bug with giant, angry boobs.

creativity and artistry wasn't just on the head or the mask, but covered the entire body, head to claw. It became a part of film history.

Milicent loved her work on the Creature. He ended up being her favorite creation for Universal Studios. She described him in an interview:

> He's a complete monster... The shape he's in now, I think he's cute. But that's because I worked with him so long. He's expected to scare other people. He would probably create a sensation if he walked in here and ordered a drink, but nobody'd even look twice in Hollywood.

The film went into production in September 1953, almost exactly a year after Alland sat down and wrote a treatment for *The Sea Monster*. Initial shooting lasted for three weeks, but finishing touches and extra footage for the opening reel were still being worked on well into November. Up until October, the film was still being called *Black Lagoon*, which, considering all the other possible titles, is pretty good. But by November, the staff at Universal was instructed to call the movie *Creature from the Black Lagoon* and monster history was made. Alland, unsurprisingly, hated the new title. He thought it sounded cheesy and cheap. He also probably wanted the movie poster to be a picture of the Creature sitting on a window ledge, playing an acoustic guitar and looking dreamily out into the night.

In October, *TV Guide* ran a short blurb on Milicent. *Ramar of the Jungle* was still playing and the magazine described her as an artist behind and in front of the camera. There's a beautiful press photo of her in a dress, along with a more intimate, rare shot. The second picture is of her sketching at her home studio. She's wearing a baggy, button-up shirt with the sleeves rolled up, bent over a drafting table covered in drawings.

This period of time was the highlight of Milicent's life as a professional artist, but even when she wasn't working at a studio, she was busy at home. She had a dedicated room in her house that was an art studio and it was always covered in work in various stages of completion. Most of them were portraits and figures. Milicent could draw anything, but people in movement were what she loved to capture and what she excelled at putting on the page. She brought everything to life. Her business cards read simply, "Milicent Patrick: Artist."

While the movie was in production, the publicists at Universal were already cooking up as many schemes as they could think of to market the movie. The studio heads suspected that they had something special with *Creature from the Black Lagoon*. After about six weeks spent working on the Creature, it was time for Milicent to get back to the sketch pad for another film. She was oblivious to the fact that those six weeks were going to change her life dramatically.

Sign of the Pagan was a historical drama about fifth-century Rome being attacked by Attila and the Huns. The film was announced as soon as *Creature from the Black Lagoon* was finishing up production and the makeup department got right to work figuring out what the barbarians were going to look like. Milicent designed the barbarian makeups, which mostly involved making people look fierce and their facial hair pointy. The illustrations and portraits she created for this movie were gorgeous.

For *Sign of the Pagan*, she got into the makeup chair herself and played one of the background barbarian women. This is not as exciting as you'd think it would be, though. Milicent got to stand around and wear a lot of brown and look like she needed to shower. What was exciting, however, was what was brewing over in the screening rooms for *Creature from the Black Lagoon*.

At the start of the new year, January 1954, previews started for the film. It ran seventy-nine minutes, or an hour and nineteen minutes in non-annoying-film-person talk. Right off the bat, it tested very well with audiences. The overall ratings for the picture were high, mostly "outstanding" or "excellent" or "very good." After star Richard Carlson, the Creature was the most popular character. In the test audiences, people complained that the actors playing the Creature were not credited. Overwhelmingly, people were dazzled by the underwater scenes and the fact that it was in 3D. The comment cards were collected into a report that was distributed to executives all over the studio. They started to realize they had something momentous.

After test screenings, *Creature from the Black Lagoon* stayed at seventy-nine minutes. Nothing needed to be changed. It was time to figure out how to market the film across America.

The studio heads had made a promise to Joseph Breen that there wasn't going to be any fish sex, but as soon as it was time to start planning the movie poster, things got pretty suggestive. "Monster from a Lost Age! Raging with Pent-Up Passions!"

I guess you could skate under the MPAA radar by saying that the Creature's pent-up passion was for murdering, but we all know they're just referencing an intense case of prehistoric frustration. You think it's difficult getting a girl to come back to the crappy apartment you share with your roommate? Try getting her to come back to your creepy lagoon.

Besides insinuations of interspecies sexual assault,[127] the publicity team at Universal was hard at work cooking up as many crazy schemes as they possibly could to promote the movie. All sorts of things were floated through the offices of Universal, from lowbrow stunts like getting pictures of the Creature taken with sexy celebrity starlets, to Creature toys, to sellable latex Creature masks, to highbrow ideas like curating an exhibit of prehistoric fossils and footprints to highlight the scientific aspects of the film. Boobs! Toys! Science! Universal was running the gamut trying to figure out how to sell this movie to the country.

---

127 Which, if we can just talk about it quickly, is really screwed up. Many cheesy, beloved genre films use the lure of watching a monster sexually assault a woman for publicity.

This is probably a good time to talk about the Creature's nick-name on the Universal lot—the Gill Man. The Creature is the only Universal monster with so many different names. There's of course just Creature from the Black Lagoon, Creature, Gill Man and my personal favorite—Creech. It makes me feel like the Creature and I are best buddies. In much of the *Creature from the Black Lagoon* promotional material, he's referred to as the Gill Man, which sounds rather cool…until you think about it. That's like calling Superman "Cape Man." There are a lot of other badass aspects of the Creature, but hey, gills.

While the publicity team was brewing up promotional ideas, the makeup department was brewing up designs for another movie. Remember Milicent's discarded sketches from *It Came from Outer Space*? They were pulled out of the drawer for a new film that Universal had in development, *This Island Earth*.

This Island Earth was another William Alland producing, Jack Arnold directing collaboration, although there was a second di-rector, Joseph Newman.[128] It was based on Raymond F. Jones's 1952 science fiction novel of the same name. The story starts with an alien man from a planet called Metaluna appearing to earth's top scientists, inviting them all to come to his cool Earth mansion. He wants them to help him work on a supersecret alien project, which of course, no scientist can turn down. As far as I can tell, the main reason to become a scientist is so you can make yourself available for these types of cinematic situations. The scientists quickly figure out that the alien wants to use their atomic knowledge to build a shield to protect the planet Meta-luna from their enemies over at the planet Zahgon. He piles a couple of the scientists into his spaceship and brings them to the suffering Metaluna, where they must deal with, among other issues, grumpy mutants.

128 Apparently, the heads of the studio weren't happy with the way Newman handled the alien scenes and asked for Jack Arnold, who by now had two major sci-fi movies under his belt.

Compared with most 1950s sci-fi movies, *This Island Earth* is quality stuff. It's generally considered one of the best films of the era, as far as craft and story go. The plot holds up, the visuals hold up. It was shot in Technicolor and besides looking fantastic, it was really dazzling to audiences to see aliens in color. It's one thing to create an alien in black-and-white. With color, you've got both the challenge and opportunity to make something really stand out.

The final design of the mutant ended up as something that looks like a cross between a giant brain and a crab. That sounds silly, but it actually looks pretty cool, especially if you consider that it was inspired by Ray Bradbury's completely nebulous description of an alien. It's a long way from an eyeball in a plastic bag. The exact same team who made the Creature suit made the Metaluna Mutant suit—Jack Kevan and Chris Mueller. It was almost a full suit—the head looks like a gigantic exposed brain with massive eyeballs and a primitive mouth. The torso is a shiny exoskeleton, the arms end in very long pincers and the legs are just sort of waxy-looking pants. Apparently, there were legs (which you can see in some of the press photos and the poster for the film) that matched the exoskeleton on the arms, but the team couldn't manage to get them to fit or move properly, so they abandoned them for the most alien-looking pair of pants they could find. One of my absolute favorite parts about films and filmmaking is that even with big budget films by major studios, everyone is sort of making it up as they go along.

Bud Westmore and the makeup department were immensely excited by the Metaluna Mutant. It's a fantastic collaboration of awesome design work and a great build. Bud was hanging his high hopes on the Metaluna Mutant partly because he had low expectations for the Creature. He deeply disagreed with Alland's vision of a sympathetic monster. In fact, he really hated the idea. And yet, the folks in the test audiences adored the Creature because they developed some feelings for him over the course of the movie, and not in the way that the MPAA was concerned about.[129] They felt empathy for him and saw him as more than a monster. Alland might not have gotten the design that he wanted, but he got the message across that he wanted: the story of a beast that was imbued with humanity.

Bud thought that this was pretty lame. Even before the release of *Creature from the Black Lagoon*, he started disparaging the look of the Creature. In interviews, he complained that the monster didn't look scary enough. He thought that the audience sympathizing with the monster was a bad thing. He hated that Jack Arnold shot the Creature in bright sunlight. Bud thought monsters should be kept lurking in the darkness and that the film wasn't going to do well.

It's strange that Bud was so ready to bad-mouth the Creature and so ready to do it on the record. One of the hardest tests to pass for special effects is to see them in daylight; it's so much easier to hide flaws in the shadows. The fact that the Creature suit was able to be shot in bright daylight and look so damn good is a testament to the competence of the entire makeup department; the design, the build, the painting, the application. Bud should have been proud of the creation of his team.

He should have, if he was a good team leader and artist.

But the thing you need to know about Bud Westmore is that he was a dick.

Remember that Bud was always self-conscious about the way that he got his job at Universal; that he wasn't the Westmore that Universal originally wanted. He grew up in an environment of competition and backstabbing with his father and brothers. Bud spent his career at Universal trying to prove himself, but instead of working hard and creating excellent pieces of art to outshine anyone else, he took credit for the work of others.

Bud was also tough to deal with on a daily basis. He was ego-driven, arrogant and hungry for power. He was abrasive with

---

129   Although, hey, I'm not here to judge. You do you.

his team, once firing a makeup artist because he didn't like the way that the man laughed. Tom Case, a member of the makeup team for *Creature from the Black Lagoon*, quit right when the movie came out because he could no longer stand working for Bud.

This was a man pulsating with insecurity. The youngest Westmore, Frank, wrote in his book *The Westmores of Hollywood*:

> Whenever someone he had hired began to show signs of independent inventiveness, Bud would either fire him or resort to his famous "silent treatment," making the makeup artist's life so miserable in general that he would quit.

If he wasn't harassing his employees, he was taking credit for their work. Bud's time at Universal was mostly spent with administrative tasks associated with running a huge makeup department. When he wasn't prepping for a film by reading scripts and going to production and budget meetings, he was assigning artists to specific jobs, ordering supplies, training new hires.

I'm not disparaging his work here. That's what happens when you're the head of a major department. You don't do as much creative work. It's like that with almost any industry. The showrunner for your favorite TV show isn't writing every episode, the head of the surgery department of a big hospital isn't in the operating room all the time.

What I am disparaging is his habit of rushing into the workshop as soon as there was a camera around so he could jump into a photo of a sculpt or a design and pretend he was the one working on it. He was notorious for this. My favorite picture of Bud Westmore is of him in the makeup workshop with a big cheesy grin, wearing a suit and tie and standing in front of the sculpture of the back piece of the Creature suit. He's holding a paintbrush *backward* up to the piece.

Chris Mueller told Tom Weaver for his *The Creature Chroni-*

cles book, "Westmore signed the checks and got in the pictures. That's about it."

This sort of stuff flew back in the 1950s. Remember, the only one getting on-screen credit was Bud Westmore. There were no detailed public lists on IMDb of who was doing what in which departments. Makeup was Bud's department; it was his domain. He thought he had the right to claim the sole credit for the creations. It was the custom.

Studios never really know how to handle special effects makeup and monster suits. It's a confused place in the film industry. It's makeup, it's special effects, it's sort of like a prop? But it goes on an actor? There wasn't even a category for makeup and hairstyling at the Oscars until 1981. The actors in suits rarely get recognition. Ben Chapman and Ricou Browning didn't receive on-screen credit for playing the Creature, despite sharing one of the main roles in the movie. It's almost a rule that if you can't see an actor's face in a film, they won't be nominated for any sort of recognition, despite the incredible level of skill required to move, act and convey emotion inside of a giant rubber suit.

So, Bud's behavior was tolerated. He was a coveted Westmore after all, and his team created fantastic work. For those working for him, it was hard to let go of a steady position in a major studio makeup department, so they stayed.

If you didn't work for him, or if you were a beautiful woman, Bud Westmore was a completely different person than the jerk lording over the makeup department. Around anyone else, he was a charmer—funny and sweet. This is the man that Milicent was hired by and probably the man she had to work with every day. After all, she was the only woman working in the entire department. I doubt very much that Bud saw her as a threat.

Power hungry? Arrogant? Rough on the people under him? Sound familiar? Even if he was tough on her, Milicent grew up dealing with this kind of man. Putting up with this behavior was second nature to her. Bud Westmore was a Camille Rossi who knew how to work a tube of lipstick instead of a roll of blueprints. So while Bud publicly sneered at her design work and the team's creation, Milicent was unperturbed: she loved her work at the makeup department.

Once he heard about how the publicity team at Universal wanted to promote *Creature from the Black Lagoon*, Bud changed his tune. He changed it fast.

9

Montage

It took Universal a few months before they realized that the best way to promote their new monster film was right under their noses. Maybe slightly above their noses. It depends on how tall they were. At the very least, she was walking around the studio lot every day, wearing heels and charming the hell out of people.

I'm actually surprised it took the publicity team so long. Especially surprised, considering that one of the publicity ideas floated around was to run a feature story somewhere about Julie Adams's "perfect gams," including the measurements of her ankles, calves and thighs. Are there ankle fetishists out there weighing out whether or not to buy a ticket to a film based on the leading lady's leg measurements? The men willing to run an erotic calf-size story were slow to the uptake when it came to realizing that the lady who created the Creature was also a knockout and this was something that could be a great angle for publicity.

Some of the other ideas were to sell free "fright insurance" in the lobbies of movie theaters[130] and to pitch the film to schools, from elementary to college, as semi-educational because of the scientific aspects of the story. Publicizing the gorgeous lady who designed the monster was one of their more solid ideas.

Milicent had been included in publicity photos for the creation of the Creature just because she was part of the makeup team, way before Universal had started hatching plans to use her specifically to promote the film. Some of those pictures that Bud Westmore loved to jump into also feature her working in the makeup shop, surrounded by clay maquettes, rubber masks, parts of monster suits and art supplies, occasionally while Bud is looking on. Instead of featuring Milicent specifically, these photographs highlight the process of the creation of the Creature—designing, sculpting, applying the suit, a process Milicent was an important part of.

But now, Universal wanted to put her in the spotlight.

In January of 1954, someone in the studio had the idea to send Milicent on a press tour to promote *Creature from the Black Lagoon*. She could talk about the creation of the monster, her design and the work that the makeup department did. Milicent was well-spoken, friendly and charming. She'd be perfect for radio shows, television spots and interviews with journalists. She looked polished and professional and would represent the studio well. And of course, she was beautiful. Let's be clear here. Universal wasn't touting Milicent as the most brilliant and talented of monster designers. They weren't even interested in the fact that she was the only woman to ever do her job, even though it made the Universal makeup department an important place at this time in cinematic history. They wanted her because of how she looked.

"The Beauty Who Created the Beast" was going to be the

130　I couldn't find further elaboration on this. What did it help? When you peed your pants? I joke, but apparently musician and horror aficionado Alice Cooper saw *Creature from the Black Lagoon* as a kid and ran out of the theater in terror, so maybe it wasn't such a bad idea.

name of the tour, promoting Milicent as this great stunner (which, to be fair, she was) who was able to conjure designs for all sorts of terrifying monsters, as if being beautiful typically negated any creativity, interest in monsters or artistic talent and Milicent was some sort of standalone wonder. Ironically, because so few women have been able to follow in her footsteps, Universal ended up making that seem true. I certainly thought that was the case.

The publicity team immediately cooked up all sorts of ideas to go along with the tour. Because they wanted to use the word *Beauty*, they thought they could create tie-ins with cosmetic companies and local beauticians. I'm not sure how this would have worked, since the whole angle was that the "Beauty" created the monsters and any Creature-inspired hair or makeup look probably wouldn't be very sexy.[131]

They wanted to send Milicent out with original sketches from all the monsters she had created for her to show off on television, in the lobbies of movie theaters, at exhibits or just to show to fans. This would go along with feature stories in magazines and newspapers about how the monsters were made—from Milicent's original designs through all the approval steps, sculpture and finally, a real-life monster. They even wanted to have a party specifically for photo opportunities that would show all the monsters that Milicent had designed living at Universal and bidding her farewell on her tour, maybe even air it on television. I'm deeply sad that this never actually happened, because this is what my dreams look like.

This tour would have been revolutionary. A woman, not being menaced by a monster, but being showcased as the creator of it, as a talented artist. Yeah, the "Beauty" title is a little lame, but it *was* the 1950s. We're still hung up on that kind of marketing and it's 2018. It would have been an unintention-

---

131   I say this as if I wouldn't absolutely buy Creature-themed lipstick or nail polish.

ally feminist move for Universal. They were using Milicent as
a gimmick. Ha, ha! How novel and crazy! A lady this beautiful creates things that look this scary! Who'd've thunk it? Now
buy a ticket to see the movie!

But for the women and girls getting the chance to witness it,
that tour might have been life changing. Seeing a woman that capable and artistic being praised for her creativity instead of being
chased around by aliens or monsters, whew.[132] That's heady stuff.

Too bad Bud Westmore got wind of this idea.

He put a stop to it immediately. Or, at least he tried to.

When Clark Ramsay from the publicity team called Bud
Westmore to discuss borrowing Milicent for at least a few weeks,
Bud was instantly furious. Just the name of the tour incensed
him. "The Beauty Who Created the Beast" was in direct viola-
tion of Bud's idea that anything that was designed or created in
his shop was his to claim, his to take credit for. The thought of
Milicent traveling around the country, telling the general public that she designed the Creature infuriated him. *Even though
it was true.*

He told Clark that the Creature was completely his own work,
even though the publicity team had taken photographs months
earlier showing Milicent at a drafting table, working on the design herself. Bud's story was that lots of people contributed to
the sketches and designs at the start of the project, but that they
all had left the project because it had become too much work
and too complicated of a design. He claimed that after all these
people had dropped, he had spent about a month working on
the design himself, the design that became the final Creature.

Bud bargained with the publicity team, saying that he'd be
willing to accommodate anything that they wanted to do to
promote the film, except crediting the creation to someone

---

132   I don't mean anything disparaging about scream queens here. Julie Adams is
      a talented actress and I love watching her on-screen. But when that's all you
      see, you start to internalize the idea that that's all women can do.

else. Since it involved his professional reputation, he told Clark that it just wouldn't fly. Stuff like this just wasn't done. No one outed the head of a film department as not doing the work. Especially not a woman. Bud must have realized that if the studio was willing to put that much muscle into the promotion of this movie, it was going to be a bigger deal than he originally realized. I wonder if this phone call was the moment he began regretting bad-mouthing the Creature to journalists.

The publicity team caved. They couldn't do this tour in the first place without cooperation from Bud and honestly, what did they care? It was most important for them to promote the film and make money, not champion women's rights. Bud Westmore had all the power and prestige; Milicent was just some freelance artist.

They went back to the drawing board and had a staff meeting to, as we'd say now, rebrand the tour. This was one of those staff meetings where a bunch of really well-paid men sit around for an hour just to come up with a different word.

The team came up with "The Beauty Who *Lives With* the Beasts" to replace "The Beauty Who Created the Beast." Milicent was being demoted from creator to the monsters' cute roommate who had to deal with their dirty dishes and nag at them to put the toilet seat back down.

This way, Universal could still capitalize on Milicent's beauty and charm by sending her out on tour to discuss the Creature. But now, they could send her out with all kinds of Universal monsters, not just the ones that she created. They crafted a story that she was not only a creative designer, but that she had to take care of these monsters, making sure that they stayed happy and well preserved. How she did this, I can only guess. Brushing out the Wolfman every day? Spritzing mist onto the Creature? Giving the Mummy hand cream? Instead of being an artist, Milicent was relegated to the role of mother figure and caretaker. Because, of course, she was a woman. They posited that she understood the monsters, she liked them. This is true, but not because she was their weird, Munsters-style babysitter. It was because she designed them.

Bud Westmore approved of this idea, because sure he did. A pretty lady going on tour to show how well she takes care of all the monsters that he and his male predecessor created? And he got to keep all the (unearned) credit? He was probably thrilled. He agreed to let Milicent take time out of the studio for the first two weeks of February.

Milicent was excited about the tour. Honestly, I don't think that she even knew that the tour was supposed to be something entirely different. Clark Ramsay called Bud to talk about the initial idea, not her. As far as I know, the "Beauty Who Lives With the Beasts" tour was the only one she knew about. To her credit, she, like Bud, must have realized that this movie was going to be a smash hit. She negotiated to get $300 a week on tour, instead of her regular $250. This was about $2,750 today. That's a lot of money. This is why people want to work in the movies.

Agreeing to go on tour meant that Milicent had to put several projects on hold. As a freelancer, this wasn't an easy choice, but it helped her bargain for a higher traveling salary from Universal. When you're a freelancer, there's never a guarantee that you'll be brought back if you step off a project. But how could she turn down this opportunity? It was full of that elusive and intangible reward for artists—exposure. She hoped that gaining fame as a creature and makeup designer would be great for her career. Gaining fame in any creative occupation is something most artists want. Even if they don't want the dubious reward of being famous, it usually means you're guaranteed that almighty thing: more work. It's invaluable to be known in your field. Most producers and department heads don't look very hard for people to hire. They want artists they already know, or at least know of. Being well-known also means you can ask for more money. It's a win-win, and Milicent knew what choice to make.

She was working on early sketches for makeup and hair for an upcoming Universal film called *Captain Lightfoot*. It was a period piece featuring the budding star Rock Hudson as a nineteenth-century highwayman who robs rich people around the foothills of Dublin, Ireland, until the tables are turned and a lady steals his heart. The film was to be shot on location in Ireland and Milicent had been busy thinking about how sexy highwaymen and their babes would look.

Milicent also had to pause her work on the costumes and monster designs for *This Island Earth*, something Bud assured her she would resume once she got back from the tour.

Outside of Universal, the Westmore brothers had also hired Milicent to do illustrations for their upcoming beauty book creatively titled *The Westmore Beauty Book*. All of the Westmore men contributed to the book, which was a guide containing their makeup and hair secrets. Milicent worked on illustrations of faces, blush techniques, hairstyles, eyebrow shapes. Anything on your face that made you self-conscious, the Westmores had some tips that could help you out. The illustrations were simple and beautiful. Milicent's ability to convey movement and expression with a few bold lines was perfect for this book.

Once Bud approved of the idea and Milicent agreed to the tour, the publicity team wasted no time coming up with what exactly to do with her. They wanted to send her off with a "gallery of monsters"—stills of famous Universal movie monsters. They wanted to manufacture Creature heads in latex for mass production. If you think partnering with McDonald's to make a special sauce or themed milkshake for a big movie is weird, that's nothing. Universal wanted "field men," aka traveling representatives of Universal Studios, to investigate, on a local level, bodies of water that had creepy reputations and rebrand them as "The Black Lagoon." How would anyone even do this? What would this accomplish?

They started scheduling appearances for Milicent on nationwide radio and TV shows, especially ones in the Los Angeles area. Photoshoots were curated. The old photographs they had of Milicent working in the makeup department would no longer do. They staged several shots of her in a "gallery of horrors" working on the Creature design, seated before a drafting table, while all around her were masks, rubber bats and a big rubber Creature head.

The depressing thing about these photoshoots is that their staged nature has, for decades, contributed to the idea that Milicent didn't actually design the Creature. The photographs are, if you are knowledgeable about monsters or creature design or special effects or anything like that, very obviously staged. Why would Milicent be working on the Creature design when the finished rubber version of it was sitting right beside her? Of course, she's dressed up, but it was impossible for people to know that that was how she liked to look every day, even when she was actually designing monsters, not just posing.

I'm always very conflicted about these pictures because I must admit, I absolutely love them. One of them was the inspiration for my tattoo of Milicent. They're really great photographs. During one shoot, Milicent is wearing a stunning, off-the-shoulder, black velvet gown, five strings of pearls and big flashy earrings. In one shot, she cradles the head of the Creature and smiles for the camera. In another, she sits on the floor with various rubber monster masks strewn about on her beautiful dress. One of my favorites has her posing with a drawing of the Creature on a sketch pad on her knee.

In the pictures, Milicent looks proud and she looks happy. She doesn't look like a gimmick, like some kind of crazy maid who lives in a crypt and makes sure Frankenstein's monster keeps his bolts oiled.

My ultimate favorite shot, though, isn't one of the portraits. It's a shot of Milicent with the Mr. Hyde mask from *Abbott and Costello Meet Dr. Jekyll and Mr. Hyde* on her head, but the mask is pulled up to reveal her face. She's looking at herself in the mirror and grinning. That smile is full of everything you could hope for in that moment—joy and confidence. At thirty-seven, she was getting publicized as an artist for the first time. I imagine she was thrilled to do that photoshoot, with all its glamour. The big event she had been dressing up for every day was finally here. Milicent was poised on the crest of a wave of success.

The beauty who created the beast. (*Family collection*)

All the excitement over Milicent was having the opposite effect on Bud. The more fuss was made over her, the more resentful and angry he became. He wasn't proud of a member of his team. He wasn't taking satisfaction in the fact that he was the one who discovered her monster creation talent. He boiled with rage because he wasn't getting all the attention.

Bud stormed into the office of Sam Israel, the assistant studio publicity director (the guy who has to deal with annoying problems so that the actual studio publicity director doesn't have to). Bud told Sam how much the whole plan for Milicent's tour angered him. He refused to admit how much he resented the attention that she was getting, instead complaining to Sam that he was sure that Milicent would claim sole credit for the creation of the Creature.

Sam, to his credit, saw right through Bud. He saw his bluster for what it really was—anger that his limited involvement in the makeup department's creative work would be revealed to the world. Sam, in his letters to Universal's New York office, complained about Bud. As far as Sam had heard, Milicent's work on the Creature was very important and he believed it. But Universal didn't want to risk the tour that they were already pouring funds into because Bud Westmore's cranky baby-man ego was being threatened. Bud had too much clout at the studio. It was a battle of credits that Milicent was destined to lose.

Bud wanted a guarantee that people would think that he designed the Creature. He demanded that Milicent stress the fact that he supervised the process from start to finish and wanted her to say that her job was simply to take his ideas and to translate them into sketches. Bud wanted her to promise to renounce credit for her own work and tell the public that the monster was his and his alone.

She agreed.

A few years shy of turning forty, I think Milicent saw this as her big chance. She'd been working in film, modeling and acting for almost all of her adult life at this point. She was making a decent, hell, she was making a good living at it. She was living in Hollywood, she was living the dream. But she hadn't *made it*. There were no starring roles for Milicent Patrick. Getting sent on a tour all over the country to promote a big-time movie that she had worked on? This was the biggest thing to happen in her life, ever.

Male superiority was the culture. Men's egos came first. Men's everything came first. Welcome to Hollywood, yes, but welcome to the patriarchy. It was probably deeply disappointing to Milicent that she couldn't claim the Creature as her own, but I doubt that it was surprising. The 1950s was a time of sanctioned sexism and racism. The Equal Pay Act (signed in 1963) was years away and most professional jobs were closed off to women, even white women. Having a policy that women were to be paid less than men wasn't an uncommon company practice and overall, women only made about 60 percent of what men did. Again, this was the case for white women. Women of color faced even worse sexism, compounded by all the restrictions and injustices of racism (it wasn't until the next year, 1955, that Rosa Parks would refuse to give up her bus seat to a white man). Politically and socially, women were second-class citizens and less than 40 percent of them were in the workforce. There was an overwhelming amount of social pressure for a woman to focus solely on getting married and raising a family. A lady's role was in the home, not in the monster shop. Milicent was already an outlier for her gender. I imagine she saw giving up credit for the creation of the Creature as a tradeoff for being able to take this opportunity.

There was another problem that the studio was concerned about. Once Sam actually saw Milicent, he got nervous about what would happen when she met the other Universal Studios employees. They were company men all over the country that would be assisting her on her tour. Two years earlier, in 1952, Milicent had been interviewed by the *Los Angeles Examiner* for her design work for the makeup on *Against All Flags* and the article described her.

Mil is a pretty gorgeous creature. She stands a neat five foot four in black mesh stockings, has raven-colored hair and a 41-inch bustline... As she walks through the studios on her way to makeup assignments, she's one of the few gals who

draw wolf whistles from the rather blasé stagehands and elec-
tricians. Perhaps that's no wonder. For she does have a very
enticing gait, these backstage workers will be the first to tell
you. And the overall effect is that 'plate full of jelly' walk.[133]

Sam was worried that the men assisting her on tour wouldn't
be able to resist trying to get some of that "plate full of jelly."
If a journalist couldn't even interview Milicent about her work
without literally measuring her bustline, I'd say Sam was right
to be worried. Milicent being a married woman didn't serve as
creep deterrent because in public, she was *Miss* Patrick. Not Mrs.
Beaumont. All of her film work was done under the name Mil
Patrick or Milicent Patrick. Many married women in show business do not take their husband's last name. When you cultivate an
entertainment career under a particular moniker, you don't want
to change it and lose some of the recognition that went with it.

But it didn't end up being lecherous men that Milicent had
to worry about. As they say in slasher films, the call was coming from inside the house.

If you've never done any press, which most people haven't, it's
sort of like selling lemonade on the side of the road to strangers,
except the lemonade is you. You've got to think of a succinct,
appealing pitch for yourself that can be repeated ad nauseam. It's
got to be something that is easily understandable and doesn't require extra explanation because no matter how clear you think
the information you are imparting is, it's going to get twisted
slightly to make a better story. It's also got to be mostly true, or
true enough. Sure, that's "fresh" lemonade. It was freshly made a
half hour ago with a cup of Country Time powder and tap water.

Milicent had been tweaking her own lemonade for a long
time. She'd been claiming she was Italian royalty for years now

---

133 Reading this ridiculous article was the first time that I had seen someone
     besides Santa Claus described this way.

and had recently reworked the background story so that instead of inheriting her title, she actually grew up in Italy and studied art from Italy's best private tutors. In this version, she had come to America specifically to be a Hollywood makeup designer, dramatically casting aside her role as an Italian baroness. It's a pretty great press angle, especially since no one could fact-check it on the internet. Being estranged from her family also gave her some poetic license with her background. I don't know if the Rossis were keeping up with her through the press, but they certainly didn't publicly refute anything she said.

At the end of January, Milicent kissed Syd goodbye and flew out of Los Angeles. The month before had been a whirlwind of preparation. Armed with publicity shots and a suitcase full of fancy clothes, she was off.

While Milicent was in the skies, filled with excitement, Bud Westmore was in his office, simmering with resentment. He was barely placated by the assurance that Milicent would be crediting him for the Creature. To secure Bud's permission, along with a synopsis of the story and production notes to share in interviews, Milicent was sent off with "proper" credit listings (Bud Westmore's name). The publicity department at Universal didn't want her saying anything that they hadn't already preapproved, knowing that Bud was keeping a close eye on the situation. They didn't want her to "go off the deep end" in interviews. Being a woman alone, everywhere she went she was escorted, or met with some representative from Universal or the broadcasting company she was being featured on. The tour wasn't the exciting free-for-all that you might imagine. It was hard work, it was a lot of traveling, it was nerve-racking—and Milicent absolutely loved it.

She started the tour in New York City on February 1, doing interviews with NBC, ABC and other initialisms of daytime television entertainment. Milicent appeared on radio shows, too, with the publicity team over at Universal constantly scheduling more appearances for her.

Bud was already backpedaling on his earlier feelings, at least publicly, about *Creature from the Black Lagoon*. He realized, in a panic, how much the general public was falling in love with the Creature even before the movie was out. Thinking about people latching on to the monster made him even more furious while Milicent was on tour. He was convinced that she would take advantage of the Creature's popularity and (rightfully) claim her credit. What he hadn't considered was how much the general public would fall in love with Milicent.

Just four days[134] after Milicent started doing press in New York City, feedback started pouring in about how well Milicent was coming off. She was well-spoken, poised and an utter delight to interview. The response from the public was excellent. Universal immediately began to schedule even more press for her—newspaper interviews, photo layouts in the Sunday papers, an interview with the *Associated Press* and a photo press conference for all the New York City papers. One crazy week after her landing in New York, Milicent was off to Detroit, to spend a week in Michigan.

Touring around Michigan doesn't sound particularly glamorous (sorry, Michigan), but Universal was putting her up in style. Milicent stayed at the Sheraton Cadillac hotel in Detroit, a gorgeous historic skyscraper that had been recently renovated. She slept there every night while she was in Michigan and took a car every day to the various cities where she was appearing.

The film was days away from premiering and monster fans were getting excited. Milicent was soaking up that excitement, but also working herself to the bone. Her schedule was intense. An average press day looked like this.

Arrive in Detroit Friday, February 5, 11:00 p.m.
Be in East Lansing (Michigan town) by 9:15 a.m. Saturday,

---

134   In the social media age, this seems like a lifetime, but in the 1950s, it was pretty speedy!

February 6, luncheon interview at noon, followed by three back-to-back interviews.

The week went on like that: lots of driving and traveling and three or four interviews a day. Milicent had to stay fresh, entertaining and enthusiastic while repeating the same thing over and over and living out of a suitcase. She does look a little worn out in some of the photos from the Michigan tour, but she never stopped smiling. Maybe her California body was rebelling against the frigid cold of Michigan in winter.

Milicent carried a collection of rubber mask reproductions of Frankenstein's monster, the Creature and Mr. Hyde. For the television or newspaper interviews, she'd bring them along to show the interviewer and talk about the creation process. Whoever she was speaking to was inevitably shocked and thrilled by the masks. One journalist wrote:

> To look at Millicent Patrick, you'd never believe that she makes people shriek with horror, but she does—as a makeup artist for Hollywood's terror films with monsters. She also does some acting and then the shrieks of horror change to gasps of pleasure.

Press outlets were already getting basic facts wrong to streamline their stories. Milicent was billed as "the Beauty that Loves the Beasts" instead of the approved headline. Her name was frequently misspelled, with two *l*'s. The name of the company making *Creature from the Black Lagoon* and sometimes even the name of the movie itself were left by the wayside. Milicent was what people wanted to focus on. Interviewers just couldn't wrap their heads around the fact that this beautiful, articulate woman created monsters in Hollywood. It was too outlandish. It seemed like a crazy vocation and one that shouldn't or even couldn't be done by a woman. To them, it was like doing interviews with a

Jack Russell terrier that made pies. It didn't matter what bakery the Jack Russell worked for—people were interested in the dog. The interviews weren't even focused on the amount of talent she displayed in her designs—they were focused on her beauty. Almost every article devotes a disproportionate amount of time or space to what Milicent is wearing and how she looked.

In Kalamazoo, Michigan, a press stunt was arranged. Milicent met with a group of teenage art students for a monster luncheon. One of the girls donned a monster mask that Milicent had brought with her. Some of the local (male) theater managers also attended and two of them got in masks, as well. Milicent posed for pictures with the masked female student and the managers, the whole group awkwardly holding their plates of food because they clearly can't see through the masks. It's a weird and silly PR event, but it's sort of adorable to see Milicent in an elegant black dress displaying her artwork and the monster masks to a group of nerdy-looking students. There's a great shot where Milicent holds the Creature head and talks to a group of girls. One of them is in giant goofy glasses and ended up wearing the Frankenstein's monster mask for the photo shoot. It's heartwarming. I hope one of those girls was inspired to explore a career in art.

Back home in Los Angeles, Bud Westmore was keeping tabs on the tour and what he saw in the newspapers enraged him. His was the only name supposed to be connected to the creation of the Creature,[135] but it was absent from most press. Despite his efforts, Bud's worst fears were being rapidly confirmed and the movie hadn't even come out yet. Readers weren't interested in him, they were interested in Milicent. She was the one in the photographs, hers was the face on television, hers was the voice on the radio. And she was dazzling.

Milicent delivered her approved lines, but she had no control over what journalists decided to print. It didn't matter that she credited "Bud Westmore and his staff" with the creation of

---

135   This includes Jack Kevan and Chris Mueller.

the Creature. Articles were listing her as a "movie monster designer" and reporters put two and two together. No matter what Bud wanted, it was ridiculous to think that Universal could send Milicent on tour to promote the film as an artist and have the public not realize she was the one who designed the Creature.

While Milicent was touring in Michigan, reels of the film followed her. Michigan audiences got an advance look at the movie before the rest of the country was slated to see it in March. Many of those limited showings were midnight screenings as a standalone feature, meaning it wasn't double billed with another movie. Moviegoers lined up outside the theater to see *Creature from the Black Lagoon*, even in the cold, dark Michigan nights.

On the night of February 12, the film had its premiere in Detroit. The publicity team pulled out all the stops in terms of ridiculous PR stunts. A life-size cardboard cutout of the Creature was photographed getting off a plane in Detroit that afternoon. Afterward, a man with a Creature mask on and a man wearing a Mr. Hyde mask got a ride around town in a convertible driven by a beautiful woman. The car was hung with banners urging bystanders to go see the movie. For a studio which years before was ready to forsake their monster movie history, Universal was finally back to giving their scary stars the red carpet treatment they deserved.

That night at the premiere, star Julie Adams was in attendance along with Milicent. Having the two female stars of the film—from both in front of and behind the camera—must have been amazing for the audience. The premiere went well; the audience loved *Creature from the Black Lagoon*. Milicent was on top of the world.

A few days later, she wrote the very postcard I found in the Universal archives for Sam Israel back at Universal.

Sam dear—
    Forgive my not writing sooner but as you undoubtedly know I haven't had a minute to myself and when I did I was too exhausted to even lift a pen...

Enjoying every moment + hope the results are okay for you too…

Give my best wishes to everyone + don't forget to include Buddy Westmore + Jack Smith + I'll see you next week—

It's 19° today in Michigan + snowing, leave for N.Y. tonight, then???

My very best—Milicent Patrick.

It was time to leave Michigan and head back to the Big Apple. Milicent's mission had been successful so far and excitement for the film was buzzing. Between that and the growing public adoration of her, Universal amplified Milicent's already-full press schedule for New York City with five more interviews, one of which was with Ern Westmore on ABC TV.[136] By the time she arrived in the city, the New York office of Universal already wanted to add more dates. They wrote to the main office in Los Angeles and let them know that they wanted Milicent to continue her tour past the scheduled end date.

Milicent was reaching a level of fame that was and is unheard of for artists working in film. It's extremely rare for anyone behind the camera, besides directors and sometimes producers, to be well-known. The average person doesn't have a favorite cinematographer or editor or costume designer. Unless you are a filmmaker or a hard-core cinephile, these aren't names you are familiar with. Actors are the most well-known people on a film set for the obvious fact that they're the ones in front of the camera. Their names are the big ones on the movie poster. Audiences see them, they don't see the production designer or the screenwriter or the colorist. Directors become well-known because they're at the top of the production ladder. In many in-

---

136   I couldn't find a transcript for this interview, but I'm willing to bet that as the Westmore that was supposed to be heading up the makeup department at Universal, Ern had some serious schadenfreude watching Milicent get all the attention over the Creature.

stances (if they're good directors), they're guiding all the heads of departments and steering the look and feel of the entire film. They represent all that behind-the-scenes work. Even then, only a small portion of directors are known by the general public.

When it comes time to do press for a film, usually only the actors and the director get sent out to do interviews for the page and the screen. In fact, I can't think of any instance besides Milicent Patrick where the studio sent out the creature designer to promote a film. Because of the confusion surrounding the creation of special makeup effects (Is it makeup? A prop? CGI?), many artists in this field are ignored by mainstream media outlets. This is especially true for monster-suit creation.

The stunning 2017 film *The Shape of Water* is an example of this.[137] Guillermo del Toro's creature masterpiece swept the awards season, ultimately winning well-deserved Oscars for Best Picture and Best Director. The movie was nominated for 234 awards total, winning 82 of them. The film is both a monster movie and a love story, centered on a mute cleaning woman who falls in love with the Gill Man-esque creature being held captive by the facility she works in. The creature, played by renowned actor Doug Jones, is one of the main roles and the makeup/suit that he wears in the film is absolutely magnificent. It's an exquisite visual marriage of digital elements and a practical suit, a technique Guillermo del Toro often employs in his films to great effect. The beauty of that monster is integral to both the film and the film's successes. It's a central part of the look of the film and the character of the creature.

As of the writing of this book, of all those awards, Doug Jones was nominated for only one, by the Austin Film Critics Association, where he was given a Special Honorary Award, instead of, you know, Best Actor. Of all those awards, the makeup team responsible for the creature suit was only nominated for

---

137   *The Shape of Water* is a film that absolutely would not exist without Milicent's work on *Creature from the Black Lagoon*. More on this later.

three Best Makeup honors. *Three*. Mike Hill and Shane Mahan were nominated for Best Special Make-Up Effects in a Feature by the Make-Up Artists and Hair Stylists Guild, by the Critics' Choice Movie Awards and by the Saturn Awards. Hill and Mahan were not nominated for the Oscar for Best Makeup and Hair, even though their creature design and makeup execution played a crucial role in *The Shape of Water* being the filmmaking achievement that it is. This is a heinous crime from which my heart shall never recover. I will go to my grave being furious about this artistic injustice.

So, sixty years ago, in an age before DVD special features and behind-the-scenes featurettes, when people were even more in the dark about the process of filmmaking and creating monsters, it was a historic move for Universal to send out their creature designer on tour to promote *Creature from the Black Lagoon*.

It was poised to change Milicent's life as an artist forever.

Just not in the way she thought.

With Milicent back in New York talking to radio and television hosts and journalists, promotion for *Creature from the Black Lagoon* was reaching a fever pitch. The weekend before she left the city, television audiences actually got to see the Creature for the first time. Our pals Abbott and Costello recorded a short promotional spot where they visit Universal Studios and end up encountering Frankenstein's monster, the Invisible Man and the Creature himself, introduced as Universal's latest horror creation.

Television advertisements for the film started to run in Los Angeles around the same time. The trailers from the film were pretty intense for a 1950s audience: explosions, screams, shots of the monster grabbing at Kay and the insinuation that the Creature wants to carry the heroine off for libidinous purposes. Universal was gunning for the teenage and kid audience, running the commercials between episodes of popular children's shows. This particular placement got the attention of a man named Stockton Helffrich, who worked at NBC and was known as the first censor for network television. He wasn't happy about *Creature from the Black Lagoon*. You can't run bestiality-themed commercials before a show called *Howdy Doody*. NBC cut their own version of the trailer, which Universal hated. Universal cut another trailer and NBC accepted it for scheduling at any time, whether kids were watching or not. This version was quite a bit tamer, but there's not much you can do to filter a horror movie about an ancient, terrifying monster that kidnaps a woman.

Despite their annoyance at having to recut a trailer, the executives and publicity team over at Universal couldn't ask for better promotion than word getting out to the papers that their trailer was too intense for the public. NBC wasn't the only station that took issue with the *Creature from the Black Lagoon* television spots, especially the ones running with kids' shows. These networks pretty much guaranteed a big juvenile audience for the film. When you're a teenager and a trailer for a monster movie gets removed from circulation because it's too scary, you've absolutely got to see that movie.

Longer, slightly more graphic theatrical trailers were playing all over the country and the publicity team was busy getting stories about the film in print. Universal Studios had come full circle from their brief time being ashamed of their monster movie pedigree. Now, they flaunted that legacy. The Phantom of the Opera, Dracula, Frankenstein's monster and the Wolf Man were all featured in articles about the movie, reminding the public that the Creature was just the latest in a long line of tried and true Universal classic monsters.

Milicent's interviews and articles usually included a short synopsis of the film, some information about the process of creating the suit, and some words about Milicent's artistic process. She stuck to the script that Universal gave her, saying things like:

I live with these monsters many weeks before they go to work in front of the cameras. They grow up on a sketch board and sometimes after they come to life in a finished movie, they scare me just as much as anyone else.

Not that they grew up on *her* sketch board, or the sketch board in front of her she was careful to note. The pieces would then include some biographical information about Milicent, crediting her acting résumé and often her work as a designer. Some of them report her as being the first female animator at Disney and the daughter of "C. C. Rossi." One article, featured in *Mirror Magazine*, says: "...daughter of C. C. Rossi, one of America's outstanding structural engineers (which may account somewhat for her startling frame)..."

Milicent likely included this detail about her life to show that, like the Creature, she was part of an artistic legacy, not for some sketchy journalist to make boob jokes about. Unfortunately, lecherous jokes and comments on her looks and her figure usually make up a good portion of all of these articles.

That same magazine article starts out: "Milicent Patrick, a statuesque beauty abundantly endowed by nature to take full advantage of Hollywood's wide-screen techniques..."

America was crazy for the idea that this total babe was making monsters. Readers were eating it up. In almost all of these articles, the Creature and the film itself take a back seat to Milicent. The publicity team was right—she was a hit.

An interview with the *Brooklyn Eagle* titled "Science Fiction Monsters—Who Invents Them? A Girl!" described Milicent as:

> ...languorous Millicent Patrick, her dark eyes dreamy as she sipped a Scotch and soda, ensconced cozily on a corner banquette at Toots Shor's, looked as if she might be trying to decide what to wear for a date. But that is not what she was talking about. 'The Gill Man is my favorite,' she was saying...

Creature from the Black Lagoon was poised to be a hit, too. The Creature was ready to take his place in the pantheon of classic Universal monsters and the movie was ready to make some money for the studio. Moviegoers were excited and the studio executives were pleased. All the members of the crew were proud and happy, except one. Bud Westmore was fed up.

He took matters into his own hands.

Bud scrutinized Milicent's travels. For each city she visited, Bud took note of the newspaper publications that interviewed her. He contacted them one by one and demanded to know the details of the story they were running. Despite what Milicent had said, there was no mention of Westmore, none at all. Bud followed up with more newspapers in cities all over the country, ones that interviewed her and ones that were planning to run stories based on press releases. In each one, there was no mention of him. Bud didn't have time to design monsters, but he seemed to have plenty of time to harass journalists and keep tabs on Milicent. Funny how that works.

He didn't blame the publication, the editor or even the interviewer for printing a story that deviated from the Universal-approved copy. Bud blamed Milicent. Even though she was essentially chaperoned by a company escort in each and every interview she gave, no matter what form of media it was for, Bud assumed it was not only her fault, but that she was doing it on purpose.

To Milicent, her press tour across the country looked like the trail of a rising star. To Bud, it looked like the uncontrollable spread of a wildfire. His greatest career fear was real; his biggest weakness was being exposed to the world. Or, at least so he thought.

The Westmores were a big name in the Hollywood film industry, but they weren't a household name. Fans didn't flock to the box office to see the new movie that a Westmore brother worked on. The public didn't know who Bud was. Nobody was reading those articles about Milicent and laughing as Bud Westmore was exposed as not being as good as his monster genius predecessor. Nobody gave a shit, not even in Los Angeles, not even on the Universal lot. Readers just saw a talented and beautiful lady getting recognition for something that she did. But, as they say, to the privileged, equality feels like oppression. Bud was an asshole who was used to enjoying credit for the work done by others. When one of those artists finally got their rightful moment in the spotlight, to Bud, it felt like theft.

In Bud's mind, Milicent was making a mockery of him and stealing what was rightfully his. She was taking credit for his work, she was enjoying the fame that he should have been enjoying. She lied when she promised to give him credit. She lied and then took off to grab her chance.

She needed to be punished.

On the cusp of the nationwide release of *Creature from the Black Lagoon*, Milicent had been a guest on over forty different television and radio shows all over the country and featured in countless newspapers and magazines. She had been working in the art world for fifteen years, in and out of the film industry. She had been a professional creative for almost her entire adult life, blazing trails for women in film. Finally, she was receiving the public recognition she deserved and her star was on the rise.

Bud Westmore stepped up and shot it right out of the sky.

While she was still traveling in New York, he decided that Milicent would never work in his makeup shop ever again.

Bud told the Universal executives that he would no longer be using Milicent as a designer. He made it known that she was no longer welcome in the makeup department at Universal. Milicent was a freelancer, so it was easy for Bud to get rid of her. Sure, she was supposed to finish her design work on *This Island Earth*, but she wasn't under contract as a member of the production crew for that film. She was just a work-for-hire for the makeup department, despite the fact that she'd been working there for two years. As the head of the department, it was Bud's call whether or not to bring her back. Bud had said that Milicent's job would be waiting for her when she came home, but Milicent had also said that she would credit only him for the Creature. I think that he probably felt justified. In his mind, she broke her promise, so he could break his.

Right away, the guys on Universal's publicity team knew what was really going on. They were the people that Bud complained about Milicent to, so when the news spread, they knew what had happened and why. They knew it wasn't Milicent's fault. They knew the blame lay squarely on Bud Westmore's inflamed ego.

Unbeknownst to Bud, memos began to circulate in the Universal offices.

The publicity team privately acknowledged that if the studio heads forced Bud to bring Milicent back, he would make her life a living hell. If Bud was in the habit of giving the cold shoulder to artists he considered to be too talented, he was certain to make Milicent as miserable as he could. They knew he'd never be happy as long as she was in his employ. But the studio just spent all this money schlepping Milicent around the country because she was such a valuable artist and now it was all for naught.

So, they devised a plan.

Not to get him fired, even though Milicent was just the latest in a line of talented, deserving artists either losing their jobs or quitting over Bud's toxic work environment. Not to get him reprimanded for letting his fragile ego get in the way of the success of his department. Not even to help Milicent find a new job in another makeup department at another studio that wasn't under the influence of the Westmores. (Even though it would have been the right thing to do, being as they were the ones who wanted to send Milicent on the tour in the first place.)

Their plan was to soothe Bud's ego so much that maybe, just maybe, he'd reverse or relent on his decision. Despite the fact that these men privately agreed that Bud Westmore was being childish and that what was being done to Milicent was wrong, especially since it was absolutely not her fault. That's how far big corporations will go to tiptoe around the male ego.

They thought it would be a good idea for Bud Westmore to "spontaneously" receive some letters from higher-ups around the studio praising him, his work *and his decision to choose Milicent for the tour.* These men would rather lose credit for their own hard work and creativity than confront Bud about his toxic behavior. In the letters, they included insistence that Milicent was loyal to the "Westmore organization,"[138] along with some press releases that credited Bud, and Bud only, for his work on the Creature.

Does this sound crazy? It is. Does this seem like something that happens all the time? It does. It happened all the time in the 1950s and it happens all the time now. Corporations, movie studios, any kind of gigantic money-making entity will bend over backward to protect the predators and assholes who make them money and give them prestige.

In the wake of serial sexual abusers like Harvey Weinstein being publicly called out by the brave women who suffered at their hands, people all over the world were stunned. By people, I mean men. How could this be happening? How could men like this be protected, swaddled in power for so long? Why didn't anyone say anything?

All these ignorant people, who, owing likely to their privilege of being white, straight, cisgender, able-bodied or some combination of the four, could not believe the horror stories they were hearing. Women, people of color, disabled people, LGBTQ+ people and anyone who was from a marginalized group were less surprised. They weren't surprised at all. They know how much corporations value money over human rights.

Bud Westmore was a trophy piece for Universal Studios. They

---

138   It was a big deal to piss off the Westmore family. They might have all been constantly trying to stab each other in the back, but they also stuck together. For a very long time, they were a powerful and influential presence in Hollywood, for good or bad.

wanted a Westmore like someone might want a Rolex or a Chanel purse. As long as Bud was decent at his job (and not drunk like Ern), he was fine. They didn't want him for his personal portfolio. They wanted him for his name. Universal Studios, as a growing film company, wanted to show that they were the real deal. Bud Westmore wasn't even that great at monster makeup. The Westmore dynasty was founded on beauty makeup and it was a well-deserved reputation. That's what the brothers were good at. That's what Bud was good at. But once Universal switched studio heads and decided to get back in touch with their horror movie roots, they weren't going to give up their flashy makeup department head for someone who might have been better at the job, but not as well-known. His reputation was an asset.

It's the same reason why all those dirtbag actors and producers and directors who sexually abuse women were able to stay under the radar for so long. Many, many of them are still under the radar. The bravery of the victims coming forward is the only reason the tide is slowly, *slowly* turning. Ultimately, the important thing to companies isn't ethics. It's money and power. For decades, they've been happily complicit in this bullshit system as long as money was being made. Men like Harvey Weinstein aren't losing their careers because movie studios are growing spines and hearts. They're losing careers because of the Everest-esque mountain of damning evidence stacked against them and that the public outcry might make those studios lose money. Even then, men like Casey Affleck win Oscars, and women like Brie Larson have to award those Oscars to these scum buckets.

If it seems insane that the publicity team would bend over backward to keep Bud Westmore happy, this was just par for the course. Sixty-four years after Bud Westmore fired Milicent Patrick, it still is. We are just beginning to chip away at this problem.

This was all happening while Milicent was finishing up the tour, in the last part of February. *Creature from the Black Lagoon* was set for nationwide release on March 5. Letters were sent back and forth across the Universal studio lot as the publicity men fought for Milicent. Maybe they felt responsible, maybe they felt guilty, maybe some of them genuinely were repulsed by Bud's reprehensible behavior. It didn't do any good.

Milicent landed back in Los Angeles. After nearly a month away, she was finally home to recuperate from the press whirlwind. The excitement for the future that filled her and pride she glowed with over her accomplishment were all destroyed when Milicent got word from the studio that she no longer worked for Universal.

While she was processing Bud's treachery, the fight continued. The "spontaneous" complimentary letters to Bud were not enough to change his mind. So, one of the publicity men—Charles Simonelli—put together a memorandum from the man who handled all of the television and radio interviews that Milicent did in New York City. It detailed Milicent's "cooperative attitude," confirming that she followed the instructions that Universal sent and never "went off the deep end" at all. It also testified that Milicent had plugged Westmore in each and every interview, giving him sole credit and that she never, not once, sought to give any publication any idea otherwise.

Other field representatives involved in Milicent's tour gave full reports, saying what a wonderful job she did, how hard she worked and how successful she was in achieving her goal of creating tremendous buzz for *Creature from the Black Lagoon*.

The publicity team sent Bud the biography that they used for Milicent. It was given to every publication she spoke to and was the basis for all the stories run on her. They also sent him the press copy which named Bud as the sole designer of the Creature and as the man Milicent worked for. They insisted that she conducted herself "beyond any criticism." The only other thing they could have done was hired an airplane to write "BUD WESTMORE DESIGNED THE CREATURE" across the bright Southern California sky. These men, for whatever reason, virtuous or practical, felt strongly about this situation and wanted to do anything they could to help Milicent.

It was also revealed that besides being interviewed by Ern Westmore in New York City, Frank Westmore was in Detroit during the premiere of *Creature from the Black Lagoon*. The publicity team speculated that both brothers reported back to Bud to tell him about all the attention Milicent was receiving from the press and stoked the fires of his rage.

On March 5, while the publicity team was pleading with Bud on Milicent's behalf, *Creature from the Black Lagoon* finally hit American theaters.

Theater lobbies all over the country were decorated with posters and promotional material featuring the frightened faces of the actors and the scaly glory of the Creature himself. All that promotional muscle paid off; the film was an instant success. *Creature from the Black Lagoon* pulled in about $1,300,000 domestically (about $12 million today). Although it wasn't as big of a success as many involved in the film would claim. Jack Arnold liked to say that the movie saved Universal from bankruptcy, but that's just not true. Quite a few other Universal films made a lot more money that year. Don't get me wrong though, it did do well. Bud Westmore, according to Tom Weaver's *The Creature Chronicles*, started calling the Creature his "bread-and-butter monster."

Reviews of the film were mostly positive, quite the accomplishment for a monster movie. The *Hollywood Reporter* called it "solid horror-thrill entertainment" and the *Los Angeles Examiner* said "the underwater scenes are fantastic." Not all publications were impressed with the story or the monster (or the acting), but generally *Creature from the Black Lagoon* was well received by the country.[139] Plus, let's face it. Horror fans don't usually

---

139   Today, in 2018, the movie sports a rating of 84 percent on the popular film review site Rotten Tomatoes. The movie has withstood the test of both time and the internet.

go see films based on what newspaper reviews are saying. You want to see monsters, you go see monsters. We're used to the press not considering our favorite films highbrow entertainment. Monster enthusiasts were thrilled with the movie and enamored with the Creature. The underwater scenes blew audiences away, especially when shown at late night drive-ins, where some theatergoers reported that it looked like the Creature was floating through the night in front of them.

Publications praised the underwater sequences, the terror and above all—the Creature. Star Julie Adams credited the movie's popularity to the humanity of the Creature, likening him to King Kong. She was convinced—and I think she's right—that true classic monsters inspire a feeling of compassion from their audiences. Even though the suit was much more terrifying and monstrous than he originally wanted, William Alland got his wish for a sympathetic Creature.

Compassion for the Creature is what separated *Creature from the Black Lagoon* from many of the other sci-fi monster movies of its time, and indeed, many other monster movies across cinema history. Sure, watching giant monsters pulverize buildings is cathartic and fun. But there's something deeply compelling about more nuanced empathy elicited from *Creature from the Black Lagoon* that has kept audiences coming back again and again for decades. It made the film an instant cult classic. The Creature earned his place among the pantheon of classic monsters right away.

There's a scene in the film where the Creature is swimming underneath Julie Adams as she paddles around on the surface of the lagoon. It's probably the most famous moment in the entire movie. It's iconic. At first, it's a scary scene, *Jaws*-like, before *Jaws*: big claws and scaly skin hiding in the murky darkness. But soon, something shifts. The Creature watches Kay from the watery depths, looking up at her with such longing and sadness that it's hard to remember that it's just a rubber mask and not a fully articulated facial makeup. Instead of feeling like a frightened victim, ready to bolt out of the lagoon, you start to remember moments in your life when you were in the role of the Creature.

The first time I watched *Creature from the Black Lagoon* and I got to this scene, all I could think about was my teenage self. Covered in acne, awkward, feeling fat and ugly, I didn't know how to approach people I found attractive. I looked at them in my high school hallways the same way that the Creature looked at Kay. Thanks to my generalized anxiety disorder, my palms were also the same level of clamminess.

I felt an overwhelming empathy and understanding for the Creature. It gave the film an emotional depth that's rare in any genre. The best monster films don't just parade some sort of terrifying beast in front of your eyes. They pull at a hidden element of your mind, a part that feels ugly, or afraid, or lonely. They give it flesh and blood, and sometimes sharp teeth.

The power of a monster movie is in seeing that dark part of you running around on-screen. You get to watch it wreak the havoc and devastation you should never effect in real life. It's cathartic to see what happens if you let that part of yourself loose instead of shunning it and banishing it to its own Black Lagoon.

Thanks to Milicent's design work, Jack Kevan and Chris Mueller bringing it to life, and Ben Chapman and Ricou Browning embodying it, the Creature became one of these special monsters that are so much more than a scare. The Creature's place in both horror and cinema was secure.

Milicent had come back from her tour to promote *Creature from the Black Lagoon* happy and excited for what was to come. She was looking forward to a wonderful career with Universal Studios, designing monsters and makeup by day and returning home to her loving husband every night.

What Universal had created in Milicent Patrick was, there's no other word for it, a star. Their next science fiction film on the docket, *This Island Earth*, now had a famous name attached to it. They had invested a lot of time and money hyping up

Milicent's name, and the public had responded. She was now a commodity for the studio, a special name they could attach to projects, a personality and a talent they could use to promote their monster movies.

Milicent also had become an ambassador for a little-understood realm of the filmmaking world, the makeup and special effects industry where Universal was pushing boundaries and making history. Her successful tour was a major opportunity to tout the studio's monster-making pedigree. Not even the legendary Jack Pierce was sent out to promote his films. For a company that was fully embracing its horror heritage and using it as a way to attract audiences, what better person to have in their employ than an electric and talented monster designer and spokeswoman who had already proved herself a draw for crowds and press?

But Bud Westmore didn't care about the makeup and special effects industry as a whole. He didn't care about Universal. He didn't even really care about the welfare of his own department. He cared about his ego and his reputation, two things that in his mind, Milicent had wounded grievously and irreparably.

A week after the film's release, Bud stayed firm in his decision. Despite the urging of the men of the publicity team and the grand success of *Creature of the Black Lagoon*, Milicent was out of the makeup department, permanently. The heads of Universal did not deign to involve themselves in the matter. No one with more power than Bud stepped in. Instead of spending that March celebrating the release of *Creature of the Black Lagoon*, Milicent spent it adjusting to unemployment.

She didn't fight back. Milicent took her removal from the makeup department with the grace that was expected of the women of her time. There was no storming into Bud's office, there were no angry letters or phone calls to executives over at Universal, no reaching out to the press. There wasn't too much that she thought she could do.

Milicent was removed from the development team for *This*

Island Earth. She wasn't credited for her illustrations in *The West-more Beauty Book*. *Captain Lightfoot* and *This Island Earth* went forward in production, still utilizing the makeup, hair, costume and monster designs she helped create.

She would never work behind the camera in Hollywood ever again. With Milicent gone from the Universal makeup department, Bud was free to spread the word that he created the Creature, a myth that would persist for decades to come. Since he was a well-connected Westmore, it meant that Milicent would no longer be welcomed in most makeup departments. At this time in Hollywood, being out with the most famous dynasty in makeup was a career-crushing blow. For years, Bud would continue his reign at Universal.

Meanwhile, Milicent's life was about to take another drastic turn.

10

Iris

It took me a long time to forgive Milicent.

I wanted her to demand Bud Westmore's head on a spike. I wanted her to be an Amazonian monster goddess, hand in hand with the Creature, as together they pushed Bud over the edge of a waterfall. Or maybe into a volcano.

At first, it made me so angry that she, as I saw it, took this gross offense to both her and her career lying down. She should have made a giant stink, she should have fought back, she should have, she should have, she should have.

So often, the onus of these situations is placed on the victims. You shouldn't have been wearing that miniskirt if you didn't want to get groped. You shouldn't have been rude to that cop if you didn't want to get harassed. You should have said something when your boss was making sexual advances. You should have fought harder, been smarter, been more careful. The truth is that these situations shouldn't happen at all. Milicent Patrick should have triumphantly returned from the Creature tour and gone on to a long and successful career designing monsters for Universal Studios.

Yes, it would have been absolutely badass if she marched into Bud Westmore's office and dumped a bucket of manure on his head. Yes, it would have been amazing if she went back to all those newspapers who interviewed her and gave them a new story about what a turd Bud Westmore was. But why was I being so hard on her? Wasn't she allowed to say "fuck this"?

At what point are women forgiven for not being supernaturally resilient Amazons who spend all their waking hours fighting injustice? Milicent was thirty-seven and had been working in and out of male-dominated artistic industries for fifteen years. She had a more successful and varied creative career than many people could dream of. My frustration with her was just a way of protecting my broken heart.

I needed to forgive her and direct my anger at a place where, instead of corroding my insides like battery acid, it could actually accomplish something.

After my dead-end visit to the Los Angeles County Registrar's office, all my resources were dried up. I didn't know it was possible, but I had finally run out of monster nerd friends to pester. The internet held nothing for me and I had exhausted the Los Angeles Public Library's search engines.

I was getting a good hold on Milicent's career, but I felt like there was a part of her personal life, a part of her as a person, that I was missing. I had written letters and emails to people who might have known her and received no reply.[140] I had discovered the scope of her incredible career, but I was just skirting the edges of her personality. Who she was as a person remained a mystery to me.

Venting my research woes to Belinda, the kind and wonderful friend who let me live with her and her business partner, Chuck, when I first moved to Los Angeles, I got a surprising break in my case.

---

140   I think most of them have actually passed on.

"Well, you know what you need to do. You need to go to the Mormons."

"The Mormons? I don't want to drive to Salt Lake City."

"No, really, you need to talk to the Mormons. They're here in LA, too."

I laughed. I thought she was joking. But Belinda insisted that I go visit the Mormon center in Los Angeles. I grew up in a non-religious household, so I didn't know much about Mormonism besides the fact that they really like Utah. Little did I know that Belinda was right. The Mormons were going to be my savior.

If you've ever utilized the website Ancestry.com, you've also gone to the Mormons for help. Family ancestry and genealogy are definitely their jam. When there's polygamy in your church history, big families happen. What I didn't realize is that something called necrogamy is also their jam. Yes, you read that correctly. Necrogamy. The process of marrying the dead. Not in a necrophiliac/*Beetlejuice* sort of way, but in a spiritual way. There are several reasons for this practice and they're all weird.

Mormons believe marriages, or "sealings," last all the way into eternity and beyond. They don't want anybody being left behind and lonely. They believe that you can get married when you're dead, either to a living person or another dead person.[141] Those two souls will meet up in the afterlife and Netflix and chill for all eternity, I guess. So, it behooves the Mormons to know about as many people as possible, as a sort of necro-dating pool.

Belinda told me that if I went to the Los Angeles Mormon temple and offered them my personal information, I would be granted access to their extensive genealogical archives. In exchange for being a potential ghost bride to some lonely Mormon man, I would get to search through one of the best family databases in the world. For a short moment, I weighed the annoy-

---

141 The good thing is apparently if you, as a dead person floating around in the Mormon idea of space afterlife, get offered the marriage, you can turn down your potential spouse.

ance of an eternity of turning down advances by random dead dudes against finding Milicent. Hey, I was desperate. Don't ever say I wasn't dedicated to writing this book. I decided to do it.

Whenever I go somewhere "serious," I always find myself struggling with what to wear. This wasn't just me trying to get taken seriously in a work environment. As someone unfamiliar with religion who was throwing themselves at the mercy of these nice, proper Mormon people so they would hopefully let me use their archives, I didn't want to be turned away because they thought I was a tattooed degenerate. I put on black boots, long black pants, an oversized black sweater and a black beanie. This served to cover up all of my tattoos and a large portion of my blue-and-purple hair. In the car service on the way to the temple, I realized that it also made me look exactly like a cat burglar.

Besides some restrained eyebrow raising on the part of the very polite clerk at the front desk of the archive building, I didn't have any problems. This might be because they were afraid I was going to rob the place. Within minutes of my arrival, I was set up on a computer. I had envisioned the Mormon genealogical archives as a dusty, holy place, filled with towering stacks of tomes and labyrinthine aisles. The room that I ended up sitting in looked more like my middle school computer lab, with probably the exact same type of computers.

I sat down in front of the ancient, clackety keyboard and entered my brand-new log-in information for their digital archives.

It was absolutely worth it to sell my peaceful afterlife.

I slid down the uncomfortable Mormon rainbow and landed in a pot of research gold. I found Camille's birth certificate and draft papers, Milicent's birth certificate, articles about her as Mildred Rossi, census papers with her parents' names, and addresses where she lived all over Los Angeles. I almost stood up and high-fived the tiny old lady doing family research at the computer next to me, but as the person who looked like a cat burglar, I felt like I should stay in my own personal space.

Hours passed as my flash drive filled up with all kinds of invaluable digital documents. The archives are made up of a group of different genealogical search databases. Some are regional, some are general. Almost every single one held at least one piece of information about Milicent for me. Thanks to her propensity for name changes, it took a while to input all her known names into each database. After nearly the entire morning spent hunched over that keyboard, I had a treasure trove. I was regretting my earlier hesitation about becoming a ghost bride. Take my afterlife.

I clicked through a database that organized names into little family trees. It was pretty cute. Nothing had popped up for Milicent's names, so I started searching under just Rossi. I didn't know much about her siblings at this point. She never spoke about either one of them in any interviews. The only family member she ever really talked about publicly was her father.

A tree graphic appeared for Camille Rossi. I clicked with low expectations. Camille and Elise's records were from long ago and fairly spotty. I had hit many dead ends over the course of the morning. So, when two little branches extended down from Ruth's name, I was intrigued. Her name wasn't listed as Ruth Rossi, but as Ruth Green,[142] the first time I had seen Ruth's married name.

I stared at those two branches for a moment before the calculations started whirring in my head. If Ruth was a few years younger than Milicent and she had two children, they couldn't be older than...

Two slots, but only one name. Lawrence Green. The other slot was blank.

The numbers in my head were ringing a bell, an alarm, a siren echoing off the inside of my skull.

This guy could still be alive.

I searched for his name in some of the databases, but noth-

---

142   This name, and the names of her children, have all been changed.

ing was coming up. I took a breath and tried the digital Swiss Army knife—Google. I typed his name into the search bar and one of the first hits was a YellowPages.com website listing. He lived on the West Coast.

There was a phone number.

I must have ejected my flash drive from the magical Mormon computer and packed my things up and waved to the nice desk clerk. I must have found that bench near to the entrance and sat down in the sun. But all I remember is staring at my shaking left hand as my right held my iPhone up to my ear. The number worked.

Milicent was finished working behind the camera and the movies she had started designing for continued on without her. But she would never publicly disparage Bud Westmore. Even to her friends and family, once it was all over, she never complained. She didn't harbor any anger. While I would have at least made a dartboard with his face on it, Milicent accepted her fate and moved on with her life as best as she could.

With the Westmores against her, Milicent's makeup design career in Hollywood was dead. However, Bud didn't have any influence on the casting directors at Universal, or anywhere else. For the next year, she continued her work as a background actress, both at Universal and a host of other studios, such as Columbia and MGM.

During the rest of 1954, only one movie came out that she had a role in as a background actress, the film *Living It Up*, starring Dean Martin and Jerry Lewis. It was a singing, dancing, crazy film billed as "the wackiest movie ever made," made by York Productions, meaning that Milicent got a break from the Universal lot. She wouldn't have to return until the end of the year, to shoot the film *Man Without a Star*.

It was a Western starring Kirk Douglas. Milicent is in the film as the uncredited Boxcar Alice. She's a "saloon entertainer" alongside her friend, fellow actress Mara Corday. Milicent shows up in a lot of the behind-the-scenes set photos wearing some adorable "Western lady" outfits, meaning gingham. Lots of gingham. She's always laughing and smiling in the candid shots. Milicent still loved being on set, even after what happened with *Creature from the Black Lagoon*.

Milicent in her Western gingham explosion sketching Kirk Douglas on the set of *Man Without a Star*. (*Family collection*)

The incident with Bud Westmore didn't diminish her love of drawing, either. While she didn't do any design work for *Man Without a Star*, she continued her practice of drawing portraits of a film's stars on set. I found a single press photo of Milicent holding a—very well done, might I say—drawing of Kirk Douglas wearing a cowboy hat. She would do this on sets for films done by other production companies, but it never landed her a job again.

Otherwise, it was a tough year for Milicent and not just because she was cheated out of her dream job. 1954 would mark the start of a long, slow decline. Her husband, Syd, was diagnosed with cancer. Everything in Milicent's life was coming to an untimely end.

Syd ultimately succumbed to the disease. He had no children from previous marriages, so Milicent was taking care of him on her own. For the rest of her life, she would miss him and consider him to be her one great love.

Milicent was always susceptible to mental health issues, something she might have inherited from her mother. But after Syd's death, she began to slide into depression. The only thing that helped was getting out of the house, seeing her friends and returning to work.

By the next year, in 1955, background work perked up a little bit. She had an uncredited role in MGM Picture's *The Prodigal*, a biblical epic starring Lana Turner, written by our pal Maurice Zimm from *Creature from the Black Lagoon*. Monster movies, bible movies, they're sort of similar, right? Lots of drama, powerful forces, the eating of flesh.

Milicent had another uncredited background role in *The Kentuckian*, an adventure film directed by and starring Burt Lancaster. She also had a couple of small roles (salesgirl and waitress) in a television sitcom called *It's a Great Life*.

Along with the depression and the loss of her husband, there was something else affecting both Milicent's mental health and her acting work. In 1955, Milicent turned forty. This is the age that is, as comedian Amy Schumer calls it, the turning point into "unfuckability" for women. At forty in Hollywood, you're old. You're a hag. You might as well go live in the swamp and make tea out of moss. Get ready to start scaring the neighborhood children with your warts. As an actress, this was a huge professional problem for Milicent.

Wait! you cry. There are all sorts of sexy older women! Look at Helen Mirren!

There are a few exceptions, but it's true. After forty, roles for women in film drop off dramatically, especially roles predicated on sexiness, which most of Milicent's were. Roles for women over forty were even scarcer in the 1950s. Most female characters in film are related to men in some way, anyway, so they are limited from the start: girlfriends, mothers, wives. According to a recent study by the Center for the Study of Women in Television and Film at San Diego State University, women make up only 12 percent of movie protagonists. Even in secondary roles, women make up only 29 percent. Women make up only a third of the speaking characters in films. The majority of these women are in their twenties and thirties, whereas men over forty make up over half of on-screen characters. I can name approximately five million films where a younger woman is with a much older man, or a younger actress is playing a role meant for an older woman.[143]

Young women get more roles than men do. But this sharply reverses around the age of forty. Men are considered mature and sexy with their unkempt dad bods and women are sent out to pasture. *Time* magazine did an analysis of over six thousand actors and actresses, and found that men's careers peaked at about forty-six, while women's peaked at thirty.

In the roles that women do get, male characters get twice the screen time, on average, and twice the amount of dialogue. Even if you finally make it and get a part, when you're a woman you're still more likely to be seen and not heard when you are seen at all.

For someone whose self-worth was so tightly tied to her appearance, like many women, turning forty was a trying time for Milicent. As a young woman, her parents taught that her looks were something to be hidden, that they were something to be ashamed of. When she broke away from them as an adult and started work in the film industry, her beauty became the focal point for most people's interactions with her. Throughout the years, she became more and more convinced that her appearance was the only thing people cared about. She believed it was the most important thing about her and now she was losing it.

The thing about depression is that it lies to you. Depression

---

143   Let's be real. We all love Jennifer Lawrence, but who decided she needed to start playing mothers and older business women at twenty-two years old?

will find the one thing you are worried most about and convince you that it is real. The added problem with Milicent's fears is that they weren't entirely misplaced. Looking over all the articles written about her, you would come to the same conclusion. That's what everyone focused on. Her art is almost always an afterthought to some weird journalist too busy leering at her boobs. She was often hired as a background actress based on her looks. That wasn't the only reason, but it was certainly a main factor. Working in front of the camera isn't an easy job when you have fears like these.[144]

If you read almost any article about any woman in Hollywood at any point in time, it's the same way. In fact, it's not just Hollywood. It's most industries. It takes a very strong person not to succumb, to stand up to the ridiculous sexist bullshit. It's constant hard work resisting the pressure to think that your only value as a woman is in your youthful looks, even for someone who isn't dealing with mental health issues. This wasn't a time when getting mental health support was societally accepted or even widely available. Without her work at Universal to bolster her self-esteem, these fears began to overwhelm her.

Milicent wasn't quite alone during this awful time, even without Syd. She kept up with her friends, especially George Tobias. They helped her through this tough period. She kept making art. Milicent pushed through 1955, not giving in to the depression that told her that she was worthless. She continued on until she met the last man who would change her life.

The phone rang for a few seconds. While it was ringing, the realization that I had absolutely no idea what I was going to say flattened me like an anvil in a Road Runner cartoon. My mind struck a perfect blank.

"Hello?"

---

144   And almost everyone has fears like these.

Oh, god.

Lawrence Green sounded like a nice, older man. He was probably mowing a lawn and drinking homemade lemonade. Definitely not doing anything out of the ordinary, like searching through secret Mormon archives dressed like a night prowler. How was I going to make this not weird?

"Hi! My name is Mallory, Mallory O'Meara, and I'm a writer. I'm writing a book about Milicent Patrick and I was doing research about her life and found you listed as one of her relatives, along with a public phone number,[145] so I, uh, figured I'd call." All of this was said in one shaky breath.

There was a pause.

"You mean Aunt Mid?"

Lawrence was a little off-put and confused. This was understandable. After a few minutes of talking and convincing him that I wasn't crazy, his tone warmed. He explained that he hadn't been close to his aunt, but his sister was. He said he'd call her and give her my phone number so she could call me later. I thanked him profusely and he hung up.

Aunt Mid. Aunt Mid!

In a car service on the way back from the archives, one important fact finally floated to the surface of my excitement. Lawrence was confused *because no one else had ever contacted them about Milicent*. No one else knew they existed. I was venturing into unknown territory. This wasn't just the scoop on Milicent Patrick. This was the whole... I don't know. Pint? Gallon? What is it actually a scoop of?

When I got home, I had to lie on the floor for a very long time. I was too excited to do anything else. I kept trying to remember that this might not work out. This family might think I'm a weirdo and never want to speak to me again. They might not know anything. They might be crazy cannibals. But some-

---

145 I almost said that I found the phone number online, but that made me seem even more like a creepy stalker.

thing told me that anyone who referred to Milicent as "Aunt Mid" must have more to say.

Lawrence's sister did call me that night. When I picked up the phone, an older woman introduced herself as Gwen and apologized for calling a little late (it was around 7:00 p.m.). She explained that she worked as a therapist at a college. Gwen was kind and patient and not freaked out in the least by me. She told me that she did some research beforehand and that I seemed like a nice girl.[146] I went weak in the knees with affection for this woman.

I took a big breath and explained the project to her. I went into more detail than I did with Lawrence, telling Gwen about how Milicent was my hero and that I worked in the same industry that she did. Then, I had to ask the most important question.

"Is she still alive?"

"Oh, no, sweetie. She passed in 1998."

I was nearly two decades too late.

The chance that I'd find Milicent alive had always been a slim one. But I'd held out hope, even though she would have been over a hundred years old. After all this time, I wanted so badly to talk to her. It took a few seconds to swallow my grief.

But there I was, talking to her niece! This was the closest I had ever been to Milicent and now, knowing she had passed away, probably the closest I ever would get.

We continued to talk and Gwen answered some of my big questions. After a few minutes, we both realized that this wasn't something that could happen over the phone. Gwen very graciously asked if I wanted to visit. She had all of Milicent's effects stored in big plastic bins at her home in Northern California and offered to take everything out so that I could go through them. Gwen just needed to talk it over with her husband, Frank, and she would get back to me about a good weekend.

---

146 Artists and writers, this is an excellent example of why it's important to have a professional website that absolutely does not make you seem like a stalker.

We hung up and I leaped around the room while simultaneously calling and texting all the people closest to me. This was it.

In 1955, a widowed Milicent Patrick met Lee Trent. She probably saw him before she actually spoke to him; he stood out in any room he was in. Lee was forty-two years old, standing six-foot-five with a full head of the kind of thick white hair that probably made other men want to punch him directly in the face. He was charming and gracious and the electricity between the two was immediate. Milicent and Lee started dating right away.

Lee Trent was born in San Antonio, to Texas sharecroppers. He grew up in poverty, the only child of his parents who survived childhood. At nineteen, he decided that the farming life was not for him and he traveled to Chicago to try his luck in the entertainment industry. For a year, he struggled to make a name for himself in Chicago, so in 1933, he went to Detroit to try out for a brand-new radio drama. Hundreds of men tried out for the part, but Lee was chosen for the main role. The program was called *The Lone Ranger.* That's right. The Lone goddamn Ranger.

If you're unfamiliar with it, *The Lone Ranger* is a story about a masked man, a former Texas Ranger, who fights rogues and bandits in that old, wild American West. He's helped by his Native American friend, Tonto, and his trusty horse pal, Silver. The phrase "Hi-ho, Silver, away!" comes from this show. It spread to be a vast media empire of radio shows, television series, films, novels, cartoons, video games and toys. But the whole thing started with a radio show out of Detroit and Lee Trent.

Lee was the voice of the Lone Ranger for the first three and a half years of the program. The show quickly gained popularity and Lee's ambitions grew along with his salary. He decided to do what anyone who has any success in media does and try his luck in Hollywood. Another actor put the black mask on (although I guess it doesn't matter since it was the radio) and Lee headed out to California.

After a few months, the man who replaced Lee died in a car accident and the radio studio asked Lee to come back. He agreed, and played the role for another four years. I'm assuming that things were either not going well in Los Angeles or they offered him a lot of money. Maybe both.

In 1941, another actor, a man with the manliest name in the world—Brace Beemer—took over for Lee as the Lone Ranger and Lee set out once again for the West Coast. This time, his luck was better. He ended up acting in many films, mostly Westerns (trading in on that *Lone Ranger* fame). There were no big starring roles, though.

He also traveled to New York City to do a few stage productions. The write-ups about his performances were always heavy on the physical descriptions, describing his robust head of black hair and how the women in the audience swooned over it. Lee was, by his own admission, not a great actor, but he was definitely a looker. Lee was a smart man. He guessed that his show business luck wasn't going to strike big again, not like it had with the role of the Lone Ranger. He wasn't silver screen material. He had looked at the well-dressed businessmen in the audience while he was performing, envious of what he thought they had—respect.

Lee started looking for other work in New York City. He was offered a job in the garment industry, which sounds a lot fancier than it was. He became a traveling salesman of women's clothing throughout the South. I'm sure that his looks and charm helped boost his success. Lee worked his way up in the company, eventually becoming vice president. But he still wanted to be in California, so he quit and headed west.

Back in Southern California, a friend got him a job as a sales manager for another clothing company. By 1953, Lee was doing well and had his sights set even higher. He partnered with a

male friend who worked in the same company and they created a small door-to-door cosmetic business called Con-Stan.
Con-Stan sold makeup and beauty products and all sorts of the
shady, pseudo-scientific cosmetic cures that you could get away
with in the 1950s. They had names like Nutri-Moist, which
sounds like an awful brand of wet cat food. Terrible branding
aside, Con-Stan started to grow and make a lot of money. They
bought some smaller companies and soon sold women's clothing, vitamins, food supplements and household cleaners. By the
mid-1950s, there were thousands of Con-Stan salesmen roving
around the country, hawking cans of Nutri-Moist.

Lee was a rich man, but stayed a little bit bitter about never
making it in Hollywood. He wasn't a fan of the *Lone Ranger*
television show or any of the newer movies. He became one
of those crotchety old dudes who constantly lament the passing of the "good old days."[147] Lee didn't lose his love of Hollywood glamour, though. He still kept up with his friends in the
entertainment business and attended a lot of industry events in
Los Angeles. Movie openings, charity events, opening galas,
you know the deal. This is what led to his crossing paths with
Milicent Patrick, someone who might finally draw eyes away
from him.

In Lee, Milicent had finally found an equal, in both personality and accomplishments. He liked to do things big. Milicent's
grandiose sense of style, her magnetic charm and love of social
activities appealed to him. But what Milicent loved most about
Lee was that he was attracted to her personality. He made her
feel loved for more than her looks. Lee was the first man that
Milicent felt truly saw beyond her figure.

The next year, 1956, was forty-one-year-old Milicent's last
productive acting year. She was in a musical comedy called *He
Laughed Last* by Columbia Pictures, in an uncredited role as a
secretary. She also had a small part in MGM's *Lust for Life*, a

---

147   I'm doing that jack-off hand motion here.

film about Vincent Van Gogh, starring Kirk Douglas. Milicent drew another fantastic portrait of Kirk and MGM took a press photo of her presenting it to him.

After that, what took up most of her time over the next few years was a relocation. She and Lee moved into an opulent home together in a neighborhood near Beverly Glen called Sherman Oaks, where Milicent had free rein to decorate as she pleased. They weren't married yet, but as two people in their forties with Milicent a divorcée and widow to boot, I'm guessing that neither of them were concerned about a scandal. Lee had never been married and had no children.

Milicent brought her love of glamour into her new home in a big way. You could call it flamboyant and over-the-top, but Milicent grew up on the Hearst Castle estate. She knew how to make the excessive look good. The walls were covered with beautifully framed paintings, artwork and pictures of friends. Each room was huge and filled with appropriately sized furniture, all in white and gold. Her sofa was longer than some studio apartments. She and Lee shared a massive bedroom with a walk-in closet and a separate vanity for Milicent. Nearby was a bathroom with a tub big enough for more than four people.

With gorgeous armchairs, a marble fireplace, carved wooden sideboards, giant mirrors and a piano,[148] the space was extravagantly decorated. Thanks to Milicent's artistic eye, the home felt airy and classy instead of stuffy and garish. In the spacious backyard was an in-ground pool and a garden. Friends referred to it as Lee and Milicent's "Sherman Oaks Shangri-la." As sort of a whim, Milicent created an interior design business, which she called "Milicent's House of Imperial Design."[149]

She spent her youth living in the shadow of Hearst Castle, admiring its opulence. Now, Milicent finally had her own lavish

---

148 Milicent was still playing the piano recreationally.

149 I can't find any evidence of clients. Gwen thinks that Milicent wasn't actually serious about this, even though Milicent had business cards made.

home. She could wander down the hallways, covered floor to ceiling in framed photographs of friends and celebrities, and feel like the woman she named herself after. She became her own version of Millicent Hearst, basking in the splendor of her own miniature castle, wearing gorgeous dresses, playing hostess to extravagant parties. She even had her own version of William Randolph—a large, tall, party-loving man with a business empire.

There is always a part of us that longs for the things we couldn't have as a child. We'll always desperately want them. A lost parent, financial security, beautiful things, a sibling. Milicent grew up in the most extreme version of this. Sometimes, it's as big and indefinable as love. Sometimes, it's as opulent as your own Wonderland. Her Sherman Oaks home didn't have its own zoo or three guest cottages or land as far as the eye could see, but it was her own slice of paradise. It was a space to be admired, to awe those who visited. Most importantly, it was hers.

It wasn't just Lee and Milicent enjoying this space. Milicent was working the least she ever had and for the first time, focused on leisure. She was still making art and had a designated studio space in her new home, but she was able to concentrate on the other things that made her happy. She loved parties and having friends around, so the couple threw lavish parties, sometimes with over thirty people in their home. There was always wine and cocktails, and Milicent was a wonderful gourmet cook. She was an extremely generous woman, a trait that was enhanced by her newfound prosperity with Lee. Milicent loved being a hostess and excelled in the role. She and Lee made fantastic entertainers. They also hosted game parties. Card games, bridge, poker—the couple loved having people over to play with them. Milicent liked the games, but she liked the company more.

She had been making her own clothes for most of her life and now she got to truly indulge in her love of bombastic fashion. At these parties, she'd sport over-the-top, almost theatrical outfits. She wore furs, mink stoles, giant hats; her closet was her own dress-up box. Milicent loved throwing costume parties, even when it wasn't Halloween. I have an adorable picture of her and George Tobias, with her dressed as a life-size cocktail and George dressed as Julius Caesar.

One interesting affectation that Milicent had was her way of speaking. I don't want to call it an accent; it was more of a character voice. Her voice was naturally deep, but she pitched it lower to sound even more regal and sonorous. She sounded like she was addressing royalty, even calling people "darling," as if she were playing the part of a fancy Hollywood actress in real life. As Gwen described it, "Even when she wasn't acting, she was acting." This habit became more pronounced during this time.

Milicent found an objective happiness in her new life, but she still battled with depression. Remember, depression is a mental health issue. When you have depression, you don't need a specific trigger or thing to get depressed about. Depression takes care of that for you, finding worries in your life or inventing reasons to be depressed. You can be depressed during the times in your life when you should be happiest, whether because of work success or finding a great romantic partner or going on a wonderful trip. Milicent was also struggling with the migraines that had tormented her since Disney. These two malefactors would sometimes keep her laid up in bed for days at a time.

Loneliness plagued her in the spaces between parties and visiting friends. Lee was frequently out of town for work, leaving Milicent with her art to keep her company. Even when Lee was home, their relationship could be fraught. They were two big personalities and clashed frequently. They repeatedly—and publicly—called their relationship off and Lee would move out of the house. Soon, they'd inevitably run into each other at a party or an event and get back together.

Besides parties, Milicent did get to use her time to indulge in other passions. There was always music playing in the house, mostly classical and big band records. She retained her adoration of films, fostered as a kid up at Hearst Castle when William Randolph Hearst would screen his movies. She didn't have a favorite actor or actress or director. She just loved film so much, loved the experience of watching a movie.

Milicent's entertainment tastes weren't limited to the screen. She was a reader, too. In the den of her home and above the gigantic bed were shelves upon shelves of books. Milicent loved literary fiction, romance novels and history books. Her tastes ran the bookish gamut.

Lee and Milicent remained childless. Both being with an older man and being in her early forties must have taken some of the social pressure off, but it didn't make her want children less.[150] With her newfound spare time, she gave a lot of herself to charities.

Milicent had always been active in SAG (what was then just the Screen Actors Guild, but is now SAG-AFTRA). Now through them she often attended charity events, most of them specifically for children and children's hospitals. Lee traveled frequently for work,[151] so when he couldn't accompany her, she would bring George Tobias or just go by herself. She loved being out and she loved doing good for children. Milicent always offered her services as a babysitter to her friends with kids. With a really nice pool and a massive house filled with shiny things, I'm guessing that she was a popular choice.

In addition to SAG events, Milicent also got involved with the West Coast chapter of ANTA (the American National Theater and Academy), the Italian American International Club[152], the American Institute of Fine Arts, and in a very fancy move, the Opera

---

150   As far as I know, Milicent never considered adoption in any of her relationships or marriages. I also don't know how her infertility affected any of her relationships.

151   Con-Stan opened a Canadian office that Lee helped run and he spent a lot of time there.

152   I assume that she didn't try to pass herself off as an Italian baroness with these folks who, I would think, knew better. She did make friends through this group, including a couple that lived in Italy and would visit her whenever they traveled to Los Angeles.

Guild of Southern California. Milicent was busy. ANTANS was the fund-raising arm of ANTA and Milicent dedicated a lot of her time to it. She loved theater[153] and wanted to help support the arts in any way.

She still acted, enough to at least keep her SAG membership, though she was in only one role a year for the rest of the decade—1956, 1957, 1958 and 1959. Milicent played the bit part of Island Woman in the film *The Women of Pitcairn Island* made by Regal Films, a drama about an island made up only of widows and children, now beset by sailors. In 1960, she was a background actress in *Raintree Country*, an MGM drama starring Elizabeth Taylor. The two years after that, she had small roles in single episodes of two television shows, *Westinghouse-Desilu Playhouse* and a Western called *The Restless Gun* starring an actor called John Payne, with no relation whatsoever to John Wayne. In *Westinghouse-Desilu Playhouse*, she appeared in the episode *The Killer Instinct* with *Creature from the Black Lagoon* actor Nestor Paiva.

In 1958, Camille Rossi passed away at seventy-three years old. He was buried in San Francisco. Camille was survived by his second wife, Lima, a woman who Milicent had never met. He definitely made his mark on the world. He made his mark on Milicent, too. She didn't just lose her estranged father, she lost the possibility of reunion, of his realizing the error of his ways, perhaps even apologizing and reconciling with her. Camille died with so much left unsaid between him and all his children, especially Milicent.

Gwen and I spent weeks trying to pick a weekend that worked for both of us. Finally, a date was set. I booked a rental car and stared impatiently at my calendar.

---

153   When Milicent passed away, Gwen donated all of her clothing to a college theater company, partially because that's what she wanted, but partially because that was really the only suitable venue. Not a lot of people are looking to pick up a forty-pound full-length leopard-print coat and pillbox hat set at Goodwill Industries.

In the meantime, there were still blanks to fill in. I had been searching for Milicent for nearly a year and had a lot of material collected: newspaper clippings, Universal Studios memos, magazine articles, pictures and interviews. None of them were dated past the mid-1950s.

There was a scanned copy of one newspaper article that a friend sent me where Milicent was referred to as "Milicent Trent." It was a tiny write-up of some charity events and Milicent was listed among the attendees. This was the most tantalizing lead I had. She only took the name Trent after her time at Universal, meaning the article had to be from the late 1950s, maybe even 1960s. Sadly for me, the top of the scan was chopped off. No date, no publication name. This chunk of newspaper floated in reference purgatory.

The only clue was that the article had to be from sometime around Thanksgiving, because it was surrounded by ads for turkey. I couldn't even go to the library and ask to see old newspaper archives without having to go through every single Southern California newspaper issue from the mid-1950s onward. It would take me approximately a decade to do and I would die long before that from paper cuts or ink poisoning.

One afternoon, I went through the treasures I had carried home on my flash drive from the Mormon archives. I was so overwhelmed by finding Lawrence and Gwen that I'd completely forgotten about all the documents I found. One of the things I saved was a scan of a newspaper page, a full page. Reading it over, I noticed a very familiar cartoon of a smiling turkey, morbidly showing off an advertisement for its own flesh at only ten cents a pound. It was the same article I had been frustrated over for months, except this one didn't have anything cut off the page.

The *Van Nuys Valley News*.

Off I went down a research rabbit hole.[154] I hadn't thought

---

154   Later on in my research journey, I discovered the glory of a paid subscription to Newspapers.com, which is a tool of wonder. I could have just typed the contents of that stupid turkey advertisement into the search bar and Newspapers.com would have scanned millions of copies of newspapers and found me the right one.

to look under merely Mrs. Trent or Mrs. Lee Trent, somehow forgetting how much journalists and news publications love to forget that women have first names or agency. Lots of articles popped up, all in the society pages of the *Van Nuys Valley News*.

I figured out what Milicent was up to in her unwilling retirement from life as a professional artist. She had taken after her mother.

11

Cross-Cut

No longer in front of film cameras, Milicent now grinned for the flashing bulbs of journalists as they chronicled the social goings-on of Southern California. She stepped elegantly into the 1960s as a society lady.

This decade was a strange time of upheaval for America. The economy was booming again, but the Cold War was center stage in American politics. Change was rippling across the country. Milicent's privilege as a well-to-do white woman afforded her the luxury of ignoring the turmoil happening in the rest of the country. She loved helping charities, but never sought to learn too much about the issues causing the need for them. Milicent was never a political person and the focus of her world was small. As she got older, her world shrank even more.

Milicent liked to stay close to home. She didn't travel much, even outside of Los Angeles, even outside of her neighborhood. Most of the events she attended and friends she saw all lived in the area of Hollywood and Beverly Hills, less than five miles from her home in Sherman Oaks.

She also stopped seeking out professional artistic jobs and

spent her time on portraits and small, personal projects. Milicent stepped off the crazy carousel of the creative hustle. When George Tobias wanted a custom book plate for his home library, Milicent designed one illustrated with an erudite depiction of him.[155] She'd sketch friends in her home studio, where the walls were covered with portraits she'd completed.

Milicent working in her home studio in Sherman Oaks. (*Family collection*)

Milicent did try her hand at writing. She wrote little nonfiction articles on Hollywood life and celebrities that she had known and sent them in to various publications. They were always rejected. The rejections depressed her (don't they depress

---

155   He is smoking a pipe in the drawing, which is probably 100 percent of the reason I think he looks scholarly.

everyone?) and added to the narrative running in her head that she was only good for her looks.

Even though she wasn't getting much acting work, Milicent was experiencing a new type of visibility. She frequently attended the kind of events written about in society pages, with guest lists and elaborate descriptions of what people were wearing. Milicent was usually wearing the most extravagant outfit in the room and many mentions of her at these parties and dinners describe her fashion choices. One Fourth of July saw her decked out in a show-stopping red, white and blue dress.

At the start of 1960, Milicent and Lee's relationship was in one of their regular dips. During their off periods, she had no trouble finding another man's arm. She was forty-five years old, extremely social and still looked incredible. In fact, sometimes it is difficult to date photographs of her; Milicent might have been some sort of vampire. She tended to her looks with military precision, especially her skin. She didn't drink through straws because they caused lines, and had an odd way of smiling that wrinkled her eyes as little as possible. Her smile would be dazzling, but sometimes photographs of her look like she's being held hostage and pleading for rescue using only her eyes.

She was seeing and being seen with a businessman in the steel industry named Jimmy Percival. But soon she and Lee were back together, as one reporter would say, "for the umpteenth time." They were never apart for very long. With Milicent's tumultuous relationship history, this break probably didn't seem like a big deal. The two had been together on and off for five years at this point.

Her only on-screen work this year was a small role in a single episode of a television series called *Lawman*. Milicent plays the Native American[156] wife of a white man, who gets angry at her

---

156 Hollywood will jump through the tallest and most intensely flaming hoops in order to not cast people of color in film and television. Milicent also played Hispanic women and Pacific Islanders.

and pushes her so that she falls against a rock and dies. Yikes to all of that. The next year, she had another small role as a saloon girl in another Western series called *Laramie*. This time, she didn't fall on a rock and die, so that's a plus.

Despite not getting the acting work that she desired, Milicent wasn't bitter like Lee was about not "making it" in Hollywood. Now in middle age, she considered her life well spent.

It's easy to speculate about Milicent's life and happiness. What if she could have had children? Was her life empty because she couldn't procreate? Would things have been better if she had worked in a different industry, one where her life was more normal and average? How would her life be different without the relationship trauma? But I'm not here to make those calls. As far as I can tell, Milicent did the things that she wanted to do as best as she could do them and made up for the things that she couldn't.

No, she didn't get to "have it all" in the patriarchal way that women are pressured to strive for. Get a husband, a stable job, buy a house, have children. Some of those things or all of those things might be what some women genuinely want. I do not believe that there are better or worse kinds of happiness and fulfillment. For one woman, raising children as a stay-at-home mother can bring just as much satisfaction and joy as being a traveling artist might be for another. My partner and I are working creatives and are childless by choice. This is our life and we do not feel that we are missing out on anything. It's simply what we want. I don't look upon mothers with families and feel pity or superiority or longing. I just hope that they find happiness on their own terms, like I do for everyone in the world. They are experiencing a kind of joy that I won't experience, just like I might experience kinds of joy that they might not. Some of these experiences are not mutually exclusive, either. It's ridiculous to speculate on whether or not Milicent would have been happier with children, or more acting success, or more artistic work or a different relationship history. One of the things I admire most about Milicent Patrick is her unwillingness to define her life based on anything but her own satisfaction. She dressed the way that she wanted to, did the work that she wanted to and dated the people that she wanted to. This fierce hold on her own desires is what is important.

Everyone's happiness looks different and everyone's access to this happiness differs depending on a myriad of factors like their privilege, health, luck and personality. Milicent didn't get a choice in some of the factors that shaped her life, like her infertility or the early death of Syd Beaumont. But she made the best of what she had, which was being a beautiful, talented, ambitious, healthy white woman. In America, even back then, that was a whole lot of currency. She made it count as well as she was able.

While Milicent was turned inward in Sherman Oaks, the work that she created was creating ripples outward.

There are two ways to drive up California: the scenic, coastal drive where you can catch glimpses of sparkling waves and sandy beaches, and the way I took to visit Gwen. When people think about the Golden State, they think about it the same way people think about New York, that it's mostly just New York City. They think of all the big cities: Los Angeles and all the Sans. San Francisco, San Diego, San Jose. But there's a lot of stuff in between. California's a big state.

Being from New England, where you can drive through all the small states in one day, it took me a long time to get used to the fact that you can start at the bottom of California and drive for eight hours and still not reach the other end. All that stuff you're driving through is mostly farmland and because California is in a terrible drought,[157] it looks more like you're driving through a postapocalyptic wasteland.

I don't like to drive long distances alone because I listen to too many podcasts about serial killers, so I press-ganged my

---

157 Which means I wasn't "forgetting to shower" while finishing this book, I
      was conserving water.

friend Zane into accompanying me. Zane woke up that morning feeling ill and needed to study for a nursing test, but I gave him my best "but I might get murdered!" look and he agreed to come along. It probably helped that it was before dawn and he was so exhausted that he'd probably agree to anything as long as I provided him with some coffee.

As the day went on and we got closer and closer to the northern part of the state, I got more nervous. What if they didn't like me and decided not to talk to me? What if the number was wrong and they were actually very convincing murderers? I *did* get that number off the internet. What if it was a dead end?

I learned my lesson from the Mormons. Dressed as conservatively as possible, I had all my tattoos covered with a long grey cardigan and leggings, not burglar attire. I almost looked respectable. Over the course of the drive, I drove Zane crazy trying to decide whether or not to show Gwen and Frank my tattoo of Milicent. On one hand, they were still getting used to the idea that some random stranger was dedicated enough to their aunt to write a whole book about her. It might be a little much to roll my sleeve up and show them Aunt Mid's face inked into my arm. On the other hand, it is a great tattoo. I decided to play it by ear and Zane went back to sleep in the passenger seat.

When we pulled up at the address Gwen had given me, my hands shook. I took a big breath and looked out at the lovely home sitting in front of a well-kept lawn. I was so nervous; I really needed to impress these kind people. It was like a first date, except instead of the possibility of getting laid, the fate of the project I had dedicated the last year of my life to was on the line.

An older woman stepped out onto the front porch. I managed to hold in the "Holy shit!" before it flew out of my mouth. Gwen looked like Milicent. Her cheekbones, her smile. Obviously, the two women were closely related and I should have realized before this moment that they might look alike. But looking at this beautiful, grinning lady really brought it all home. *Wow*, I said in my head, *this is really her family.*

★ ★ ★

The short amount of time Milicent had in the spotlight as an artist made a big impact around the country. People who watched her talking about her work on television were entranced and inspired. After the release of *Creature from the Black Lagoon*, she started getting fan mail from people wanting to know more about her and her art, and from people who wanted to see more of her.

The letters and postcards took a long time to get to Milicent because the only way that fans had to contact her was to write to the makeup department at Universal, which means that Bud Westmore had to take in praise for Milicent even after she left. This probably helped fuel his quest to erase Milicent from Creature history. People didn't forget Milicent, as much as Bud hoped that they would.

There were quite a number of fan letters from men complimenting her beauty and asking for signed photographs. Some of them demanded to know why she didn't do more acting and why she was spending time designing monsters instead of being on-screen because, of course, women are only good for one thing. One guy wanted to know why she was wasting her time "behind masks" instead of being pretty for the camera. This is the fan letter equivalent of asking a woman to smile more. It implies that Milicent's real value is in her attractiveness, and as a pretty woman, her imperative is to be available for people to look at and enjoy. I can guarantee you, these fans considered themselves "nice guys" who were just trying to compliment her. I also guarantee you that's total garbage.

But not all her fan mail was from thirsty dudes. A lot of it, in fact the majority of it, was from people writing in as fans of Milicent as an artist, people who loved her personality and her artwork and wanted to see more of that.

From letters addressed to Bud Westmore at Universal Studios:

This card is really for a Miss Patrick that my husband and I saw on your brother's show… She spoke with such ease, is so charming and so lovely we would just love to see her on programs when we go home.

Dear Miss Patrick,

I have *never* written a fan letter in my life but I just happened to see you on the "Ern Westmore" show & truly enjoyed your talk...

—Mrs. Kaufman.

Dear Miss Patrick,

After seeing some of your handiwork in Universal International's shocking 3-Dimension film *It Came from Outer Space*, I thought that it was the ultimate in makeup; but now I find that it was only the beginning—I mean the terrifying *Creature from the Black Lagoon*...after reading an article about the filming of *Creature from the Black Lagoon* I made up my mind that I would write to you commending you on your creative [sic] and originality...

These letters came in from men and women, boys and girls. One ten-year-old boy wrote in because he heard his mother say, after seeing Milicent speak about the Creature on television, that Milicent was going to be a famous artist. He wanted a picture of Milicent to hang on his wall.

They kept coming, as the months and years went by. Not all the letters sent to Bud Westmore reached Milicent (I wonder why!) but fans would write in multiple times, sometimes from overseas.

The best letters by far are from the little girls who looked up to Milicent as an artist and a purveyor of the weird. It must have been so unbelievably powerful for young girls who were into strange things that only boys are "supposed" to like, seeing a woman like Milicent Patrick on national television talking about monsters.

Dear Milicent,

I have seen many movies in which monsters you created appeared. I like weird movies very much. My favorite
though, is *Creature from the Black Lagoon*. I also saw *Revenge
of the Creature*,[158] which I liked just as well.

I have a scrapbook in which I keep many odd-looking
things and I would appreciate very kindly if you would
send me a few pictures of the Gill Man for my scrapbook.
I would gladly pay the cost, if any...

I am 13 years old, in the 8th grade and I love to draw...

Very yours truly, Maria[159]

Milicent answered all her fan mail, even from the dudes who
just wanted pictures of her, sending headshots and pictures of
the Creature.

Time went on and the fan mail didn't stop. It wasn't constant,
but it would continue to trickle in, year after year. Bud Westmore was claiming credit for the Creature wherever he could: in
interviews for the two *Creature from the Black Lagoon* sequels, in
books (his brother Frank Westmore's book about the family has
no mention of Milicent and credits the design to Bud), in magazine articles about the monster. But those who fell in love with
the Creature and went looking for more could find those original articles about Milicent. Bud couldn't fully squash her impact.

---

158   The Creature in *Revenge of the Creature* (the sequel to *Creature from the Black
       Lagoon*) is nearly identical to the Creature in the first film. Milicent didn't
       work directly on this movie, but the design was obviously taken from her
       Creature from the Black Lagoon work. The only cast members to return for
       the second film were Ricou Browning, reprising his role as the underwater
       Creature and Nestor Pavias in his role as the riverboat captain, Lucas. Jack
       Arnold and William Alland teamed up again for it. It wasn't as successful
       as the first film, but successful enough to warrant a third film, *The Creature
       Walks Among Us*. As much as I love the Creature, the sequels are lukewarm.
       You don't have to watch them. They're not good enough to be great mov-
       ies and they aren't bad enough to be amazing cheese fests. *Revenge of the
       Creature* is notable for being Clint Eastwood's film debut as an uncredited
       lab technician.

159   I tried desperately to find the writer of this letter, but was unsuccessful. I
       hope that she made a life out of weird art and odd things, and wherever she
       is, I send her a high five.

Many other Universal monster movies came out after Milicent's work at the studio. *Tarantula*, *The Mole People*,[160] *The Monolith Monsters*, *The Thing That Couldn't Die*, and more. But the Creature remained the last great Universal monster. He was the final creation to become an icon, up in the monster pantheon along with Frankenstein's monster, the Bride of Frankenstein, Dracula, the Wolfman, the Phantom of the Opera, the Mummy and the Invisible Man.[161] *Creature from the Black Lagoon* had that magic combination: a quality film and a fantastic, unique monster.

When the 1950s came to an end, so did Universal Studios' reign in monster films. The merger of Universal with Decca Records/MCA (Music Corporation of America) was finally complete with Decca/MCA fully taking over Universal in 1962. Decca/MCA wasn't interested in making B movies, or anything less than big budget, big-name commercial films. The new Universal Studios also wanted to get in on what had drained its ticket sales for years—television. Between these two goals, there was no room for monster movies.[162]

The Creature's popularity only increased with time. Even though Milicent wasn't credited and only a few dedicated fans knew she was the designer, her creation went on to a permanent place in the cinema hall of fame. And whenever female fans discovered the existence and work of Milicent Patrick, she changed lives.

The 1960s passed as a quiet time for Milicent. When she wasn't nesting in her home or making art, she was attending local events or seeing friends. The most excitement was her

---

160 A few film historians think that some of Milicent's designs were used for the monsters in *The Mole People*, but I've never been able to find any proof of it.

161 Lots of monster nerds have variations on this group, but this is my book and that is my pantheon.

162 In the 1960s, Universal distributed a Godzilla film and two King Kong films, but they were produced by the Japanese production company Toho, most famous for creating *Godzilla*. Universal wouldn't have another big monster hit until 1975 with *Jaws*. Yes, *Jaws* is a monster movie. Fight me.

roller-coaster relationship with Lee. But by all accounts, they absolutely adored each other.

At the end of 1963, on December 29, the two decided to make it official after eight years of on and off romance. Lee had proposed several times by now—and Milicent always said yes—but the engagement was always called off at the last minute due to some kind of explosive argument. This time, as Milicent told the press, they decided that "they were truly meant for each other."

The couple drove to Las Vegas[163] to have a small, cheesy chapel wedding with Lee's business partner and his wife in attendance as witnesses. With her and Lee both in middle age, and Milicent on her third marriage, why not make it easy and fun? Sadly, there was no Elvis impersonator in attendance. Milicent was forty-eight years old. She wore a snow-white, form-fitting dress with a high collar in the back. She looked stunning.

Lee and Milicent during their Las Vegas wedding, somehow making a cheesy wedding chapel look classy. (*Author collection*)

---

163   It's only a four-hour drive from Los Angeles if you leave at a decent time.

Lee and Milicent spent the first part of their honeymoon in Las Vegas, then they were off to travel around Mexico. Milicent had a wonderful time there, but it must have been bittersweet. She always had wanted to see the place where her father had spent his youth, but now he had passed away and Milicent was still ostracized by her siblings. The couple spent most of the trip in Acapulco, sightseeing and dining. Milicent made a point of taking in the Spanish architecture that reminded her of her childhood on the Hearst estate.

It was short-lived wedded bliss for Milicent and Lee, though. Within a year, they had separated. Milicent, beset by loneliness, could never quite get used to all the traveling Lee had to do for work. She hated his being away so much. They had adopted a very fluffy cat, but it wasn't quite a stand-in for a husband.[164]

Soon, she was seen being "wooed" by Henry Morgan, an American comedian popular on both radio and television. Milicent had appeared on his New York City-based television show, called, take a guess, *The Henry Morgan Show*, ten years earlier and evidently made an impression on the man. Henry Morgan was famous for his cranky and biting wit, but it didn't go far with Milicent. She went back to Lee pretty quickly.

Milicent's final acting role was in 1968, at fifty-three years old. She had a bit part in the comedy/adventure film *The Pink Jungle*, a Cherokee Productions film that was distributed by Universal. It was about a fashion photographer—played by James Garner—on a shoot in South America who goes diamond hunting with his model. Fifty-three isn't old, not by a long shot. But when your primary work consisted of roles like Sexy Saloon Girl and Hot Island Woman, it's not long before you age out of Hollywood.

She tried to stay active in film, but this was the last background role she was hired for. Work had been either slow or nonexistent for the past eight years. The migraines that had har-

---

164   Trust me, I've tried!

ried her for decades were getting worse. Now that she was no longer focused on acting work, she turned to something that had been out of her life for many years: her family.

While I was coming back to reality on her front stoop, Gwen gave me a big hug. I couldn't believe how much she looked like Milicent. I told her so. She grinned, taking it as "one of the biggest compliments I could give."

She led Zane and me through the house and into the kitchen, where she was getting set up. When she had told me over the phone that she had some containers of Milicent's things, I was picturing a folder of papers, maybe some small cardboard boxes. Waiting for me in the kitchen were huge Tupperware tubs, the kind that you pack all your winter clothing in and stuff under the bed. I was absolutely floored. Zane seemed mildly impressed, but he was also on at least three kinds of cold medications and was desperate to be left alone with his anatomy textbook.

Before I sat down at the kitchen table, Gwen brought me into their spare bedroom. Hanging on the wall next to the bed was a framed photograph of Milicent when she was about my age, one I had never seen before. She's looking off camera, glamorous in a black satin dress and feather boa, her dark hair swept back into a low bun. She looked like a goth Jessica Rabbit, smoldering in the frame. Well done, she seemed to say, you finally found me.[165]

Gwen and I talked for a bit, but I was practically squirming with excitement to get at those boxes. They were sparkling like an unlooted treasure chest in a video game.

When I went back to the kitchen and sat down at the table, I made sure to tug the sleeve of my Respectable Person cardigan down over my Milicent tattoo. I completely chickened out about showing it to Gwen. Everything was going so well and I didn't want to make it weird.

---

165   A copy of this photograph now sits in a frame on my desk and has accompanied nearly the entire writing of this book.

You could roast marshmallows over this picture. (*Author collection*)

Gwen dragged the first Tupperware tote over and started taking items out and stacking them on the table. The tote was stuffed with papers, folders, photographs, envelopes. When Milicent died, she left everything to Gwen: her house and all her possessions. What remained in these totes was what was left from Milicent's life, decades of collected ephemera and memories in an age before digitized documentation. The answers to almost all of my questions about Milicent were in these boxes.

I cannot overstate the kindness that Gwen showed me. She sat with me the entire time, almost four hours, with a break for a lunch that she graciously prepared in between. Gwen explained—when she could—whatever item I was holding, answered my questions, told me stories.

After nearly a year of fumbling around in the darkness of the past, trying to uncover a life and legacy that was purposely hidden in some parts and merely obscure in others, I was stunned. If I had a question, I just asked Gwen. I could just *ask*. What a wonderful thing. How had I managed up to this point? It was the same feeling as getting a smartphone or an indoor toilet or eyeglasses. It made things so laughably easy that I could hardly remember what it was like before. I'm so lucky not just that I found Gwen and Frank, but that they welcomed a blue-haired weirdo obsessed with their aunt into their home and offered to help in any way they could.

Adding to my joy was how thrilled Gwen was to talk about Milicent. I had clearly found the right family member to talk to. It's no wonder to me why Milicent left everything to Gwen, why she adored her so much. Gwen simply radiated love and admiration for her magnificent aunt, even when talking about the darker parts of her life.

I took photos of everything on my iPhone, nearly eight hundred different items in total. Halfway through the cataloging/talking/gasping, Gwen's husband, Frank, came home from golfing. Frank is a sweet, tall man with grey hair and a gentle manner. He was just as warm and kind as Gwen, with stories about Milicent of his own.

"Millie was truly an individual, and truly a free soul. A free spirit. She was a sweetheart."

Gwen added, "Frank, I told Mallory how much Millie loved you. She'd be talking to me and Frank would walk in the room and she'd just say to me, 'I want to talk to that handsome man!'"

Gwen and Frank have been married twice. After they divorced, they got back together, realizing they were meant for each other. When Milicent heard about the remarriage, she laughed. "What, you think you're going to have more husbands than me?"

For the first time in my entire search for Milicent, I felt like I was getting to know her as a person, not just as an artist or an actress or a hero. I don't want to say that I felt her presence in that room. That's not quite what the feeling was. It was more like I'd been hearing her voice from far away, just barely making out the words. But now I could hear her clearly.

"Gwen, do you think this book is a project that she'd get excited about?"

"Oh, my gosh. Yeah. Yes. I'm sure she's up in heaven smiling and clapping her hands and saying, 'Yay Mallory! Gwen, give her anything she needs. Help her.'"[166]

After Milicent's parents had passed on, her siblings continued to disapprove of her lifestyle, even though she was no longer active in the entertainment industry. But toward the end of Camille's life, Ruth had let her children, Gwen and Lawrence, visit him despite the fact that she still thought he was, as she put it to Gwen, "a bad man." So when Milicent contacted her, Ruth decided to let her children see their aunt Milicent, too.

For Lawrence, "Aunt Mid" was just that, an aunt he wasn't close with. But for Gwen, she was a wonder. To a young girl who had been hearing stories of this apparently evil and wild woman all her life, Milicent was fascinating. Combined with Milicent's larger-than-life personality and her over-the-top glamour, Gwen was entranced by Milicent, and Milicent absolutely loved Gwen. Gwen grew up wanting to be a ballerina, something Milicent supported wholeheartedly. Milicent knew what it felt like to want to be an artist and have your family disapprove. When Gwen started ballet lessons, Milicent was so proud.

Ruth wasn't happy about Gwen's adoration of Milicent, but she didn't want to take away something that made her daughter so happy. She was deeply concerned that Gwen was going to follow in Milicent's footsteps and get carried away with the pursuit of beauty and fame. Ruth was convinced that looks were the only thing that Milicent valued, that Milicent had a need to be gorgeous and sexy. She didn't want those to be Gwen's val-

---

166   I'm not crying, there's just a pen in my eye. Maybe a book. Or one of my cats.

ues. Ruth valued schooling and smarts more than anything else. Even as a little girl, when Gwen played dress-up with Ruth's clothes and asked her mother if she was pretty, Ruth would reply, "Pretty doesn't matter. It's what's in your heart. Beauty is as beauty does."

What she was teaching Gwen wasn't wrong. But Ruth's disdain for Milicent pushed her philosophy on beauty to an extreme. Being perceived as pretty shouldn't have to be a priority, but feeling pretty for yourself can be if it makes you feel good and it's not destructive to other parts of your life. Feeling pretty, just for yourself, can be amazing.

That's where Ruth was wrong about Milicent. Milicent liked feeling pretty for herself. She didn't follow fashion trends or spend exorbitant amounts of money on brands to impress other people. She made her own clothes according to her own tastes because it made her happy. Milicent liked looking glamorous. It was her style. But she dedicated her life to art and friends. That's where her values lay, which were reflected in the developing relationship between Gwen and Milicent. Milicent was Gwen's cheerleader, encouraging her dance and ballet career.

As soon as Gwen was old enough to write, she'd send Milicent cards, letters and photographs from her dance recitals. Milicent would always respond with warm enthusiasm. She was so proud of her niece. Even when Gwen got older and started asking for beauty tips (something she couldn't get from her mother), Milicent insisted that she didn't need to change anything about herself. "You're perfect. Just be you," Milicent would tell her, not the answer of someone who cared only about looks.

Hearing this meant so much to Gwen. She looked up to Milicent. She thought that Milicent was "the most amazing woman I know." It doesn't get much better than having the most amazing woman you know say "don't worry, you're good as you are."

Milicent was overjoyed to have her niece and nephew in her

life,[167] but she still wished she could reconcile with her sister. Ruth wasn't having it, though. Her opinions on Milicent hadn't changed. Ruth didn't want anything to do with Milicent or her career. At least, she acted that way to Milicent's face.

I mentioned before that her family would always watch Milicent's appearances in film and on television, even the really cheesy stuff. On the surface, this seems like evidence that they really loved and cared about Milicent. But to me it seems insulting and awful. To make Milicent feel so terrible about herself, to make these assumptions about her life and then turn around and enjoy the fact that someone they were related to was on the big (or small) screen is, not to put too fine a point on it, shitty. It's not sweet at all. Ruth spent more time watching Milicent do something she was ostracized for than actually talking to and supporting her.

I'm estranged from my own parents for similar reasons. My mother has spent a large amount of time obsessively following my career in the creative world on various social media platforms and she has spent absolutely no time supporting said career. Some people try to convince me that this means that she really cares. It doesn't. It's just weird. Knowing that she's seeing everything I do but not acknowledging anything about it to me feels terrible. Whether it's resentment or disapproval or jealousy or something else I can't understand, I don't know, but the Rossi family subjected Milicent to the same thing. It's especially sad in Milicent's case because she's a much better person than I am, forgiving her family, reaching out again and again over the years. I just found a great therapist and adopted some cats.

Milicent could have used that support after everything she had been through in the past few decades. She would need it more than ever in the years to come.

---

167   Ulrich and his family didn't have a relationship with Milicent.

12

Cutaway

By the end of the 1960s, Lee and Milicent were both getting tired. They wanted off the roller coaster they were riding. After six years of marriage, in January 1969, they filed for divorce. The society papers and Hollywood gossip columnists were mostly uninterested in the pair at this point, but a few papers reported the split. "Lee is out of the country most of the time, anyway," Milicent told one reporter. She kept the house in Sherman Oaks.

Milicent was used to the fluctuations of love, and not just with Lee. The only truly solid relationship she had was with Syd Beaumont. It was the healthiest relationship she would ever have.[168] Lee was her longest relationship, but also the most tumultuous. Granted, Paul Fitzpatrick and Frank Graham gave Lee a run for his money, but Lee and Milicent were on and off again for longer than I've currently been alive.

Finding true romantic love was never the focus of her life, though. Milicent wanted her life to be glamorous, filled with

---

168 Which, unfortunately is why I don't know much about Syd. There were no big public blowouts and Milicent didn't keep photographs or reminders of the part of her life with him. It was too painful.

friends and fun and art. That's what truly mattered to her. Now, in middle age, living in her gorgeous, miniature Hearst Castle, surrounded by friends (and her fluffy cat), doing art on her own time, she was living the life she wanted to live. Not bad for a woman who had her career purposefully crushed.

For Bud Westmore, however, things were not looking so good. I'd like to pause Milicent's tale briefly to update you on how Bud's life fared after she left Universal.

Milicent always referred to what Bud did in vague terms, saying simply that there were "problems" with him, never addressing the incident directly. Milicent didn't think badly of Bud Westmore for annihilating her career.

But I do.

On the surface, Bud's next fifteen years at Universal were successful.[169] He continued taking sole makeup design credit on lots of major films and television series, some of which stand today as cultural icons: *Spartacus*, *To Kill a Mockingbird*, *Dragnet* and *The Munsters*. Behind-the-scenes at Universal though, a noose was tightening slowly around Bud's neck.

Men who recently witnessed the #MeToo movement[170] were surprised not only by how widespread the problem of abuse and harassment is, but also by how long it has been allowed to continue. Some of the men being called out had been active garbage piles for decades. They hadn't just been garbage piles to women and marginalized voices, either. Many men have also

---

169 In yet another blow to women's history, in 1957 Bud Westmore was hired to design the original makeup look for Barbie, helping to throw generations of young girls into self-esteem crises.

170 If you don't have social media, the #MeToo movement is a social media movement that went so viral in 2017 that it started making real change. Women who experienced sexual harassment and assault in the workplace posted #MeToo to show how prevalent it is, me and quite literally every single woman I know included. Men were stunned, women were unsurprised. It led to some brave women calling out famous men in the entertainment industry for their abuse, most notorious of which was producer Harvey Weinstein.

come forward with reports of abuse at the hands of these human dumpster fires.

This toxic nightmare has been allowed to continue for the simple fact that these steaming human diapers make movie and television studios lots of money. It's more expensive and more of a hassle to fire them and handle the problem correctly than it is to cover it up and get rid of the victim involved. Until very recently, as in 2018, victims who were gutsy enough to come forward and try to report their harassers or abusers were usually met with silence, or the loss of their jobs. Other people, mainly women, witness this backlash time and again, and put up with whatever abuse they face because they are certain that the only consequence of reporting it will be the loss of their hard-won jobs. So the harassment continues. This treatment is commonplace and perpetuated in the media, so many women assume it is just part of life, something to deal with like rain or pimples or cancer.

There was a film that I worked on with Dark Dunes Productions which was a disaster from the start. One of the major players on the project, who had pitched it to Sultan, my boss, was an utter shit show. He talked a great game and got Sultan to agree to fund his film, but what quickly became apparent was that the budget he originally estimated was far too low. It was so low that even if we doubled it, we still couldn't make the film. The project was a money pit. Things got worse quickly. The script (that he wrote) was a mess, the development in shambles, all while this guy tried to pump Sultan for more money.

When he wasn't harassing Sultan, he was harassing me. He'd call me every day, sometimes multiple times, to talk about the project and often, just life. Occasionally, he'd be drunk when he called. He increasingly wanted to know more and more about my social life. When my boss was hesitant about sending him more money, he'd dial me up to complain, calling Sultan a "rag head" or a "camel jockey." He started asking for pictures of me, no matter how many times I refused. Things got more and more inappropriate, to the point that he suggested that during the shooting of the film (which was getting less likely to happen every day) I should sleep in his room, you know, to save money.

I knew what was happening to me was bad, but I didn't know what to do about it. At twenty-three years old (he was over twice my age), I was brand-new to the entertainment industry. I thought this was just something that I had to put up with, like catcallers or creeps on the internet. It was my lot in life as a woman and I should just feel lucky that I had the job at all. For months, I told no one and tried to brush it off.

Finally, it became clear that the project was dead in the water. Sultan had enough and didn't want to make the movie anymore. He didn't want to deal with this guy anymore. One of the other producers on the project, a man named Frank Woodward, agreed that it was a disaster and needed to be terminated.

During a meeting in Los Angeles between Frank, Sultan and myself, we talked about how to get Dark Dunes out of this awful situation. I was adamant in my support of Frank and Sultan. I told them how much I, too, wanted to never have to think about this film ever again. They both noticed that I was more vehement than they were. They wanted to know why.

I took a deep breath and told them what had been going on. I got lucky. They believed me. My story sealed the deal and we terminated the project. Sultan kept me on at Dark Dunes Productions, promoted me and assigned me to another film. I even got to mail the guy the notice for the termination of the project myself. To this day, Sultan and Frank[171] are two of my closest friends. As far as I know, that project still hasn't been made.

---

171   Frank Woodward is an immensely talented director, writer and editor; the kind of filmmaking genius that has forgotten more industry information than I'll ever know. He took me under his wing and taught me how to be a producer and a screenwriter. There are a lot of scumbags in the world. Some of them are written about in this book. But don't lose hope. There are Frank Woodwards in the world, too.

A lot of people don't get so lucky.

Most of the time, projects don't get terminated. Once a studio or a company had sunk a lot of time and money into someone, they consider them an asset. They want to keep that asset. For Universal Studios, Bud Westmore was an asset.

But times were changing in the film industry. Along with that Decca/MCA takeover of Universal, things were changing in the makeup world, as well. Studios were getting thriftier. Executives were starting to realize that maybe they didn't need a gigantic, expensive makeup department led by an even more expensive department head. During the 1960s, Bud saw the shifting tides. His response was to double down on his cruelty, ruthlessly firing any employee that spoke against him.

In 1970, after over two decades with Bud Westmore, it was finally their wallets and not their morals that made Universal get rid of him. The industry had changed and now there was an abundance of freelance makeup artists for hire, film to film. Many stars had a preferred makeup artist that they brought along on each project. These freelancers came much cheaper than Bud Westmore.

When Bud's neck came up on the budget chopping block, he might have been saved. He was just shy of twenty-four years with the company. Twenty-four years is a long time to work anywhere. Most people would make close friends in that time, close friends that would rally to support them. Not Bud. Bud had years of angry artists and assistants that he had ripped off and abused, years of Universal staff members hearing about his terrible behavior. He was let go.

Bud immediately slipped into a mental and physical decline. He became a recluse, dreading going out in public and facing people after he had fallen so low. He managed to get a few free-lance makeup jobs based on the strength of his name, but he was embarrassed to do them after reigning for so long as the king of makeup at Universal. He told his brother Frank Westmore,

"I can't. I haven't got the guts. I don't know how to do daily makeup anymore." Bud knew people thought he was getting what he deserved.

He let his health go and within a couple years, started struggling with heart problems. In 1973, at age fifty-five, Bud died of a heart attack.

After his death, Milicent updated her résumé. For the first time, she included her work on *Creature from the Black Lagoon* in her artistic credits, actually saying that she designed the Creature and did the final paint job on the monster. *Famous Monsters of Filmland*, the preeminent monster fan magazine (it still is) even ran an article on her in July 1978. "Queen of the Monster Makers" it was called, written by visual effects artist Robert Skotak. It reported not only her work on the Creature, but her work for *It Came from Outer Space* and *This Island Earth*. The best part of the article is that it barely mentions Milicent's looks. It's more progressive and respectful of Milicent than most articles written about female artists today are. It focuses mostly on the creation of the Creature, and the only downside is that it features only one picture of Milicent, smaller than the picture of Bud Westmore.

This article brought in a whole new crop of fan mail for Milicent, which she was only too delighted to answer. Because *Famous Monsters of Filmland* is not what you'd call a mainstream magazine—fine, yes, it's for nerds—the story wasn't picked up by any other publications. It was the last piece of publicity on her artwork that Milicent would see.

For the next few years, Milicent continued life as usual, though without Lee. At fifty-five years old, she was still being called "a knockout" by the journalists reporting on the events she attended. Milicent was an active member of the women's auxiliary of ANTANS and she had a lot of friends in the group. Milicent wasn't just getting dressed up and buying tickets for expensive, fancy dinners, either. She was more deeply involved now, helping make invitations, designing signs and planning events. I bet the women appreciated both Milicent's artistic eye and talent. An event invitation designed by Milicent Patrick was sure to be a beautiful thing.

More than theater, she focused on charity events for orphans, which is just about the most charitable thing you can focus on, unless those orphans are also starving and stuck in trees, holding kittens. She got involved in WAIF (World Adoption International Fund) events, which was the children's division of the International Social Service, an international children's adoption program.

Milicent would go to these events by herself or with George Tobias. Instead of Mrs. Trent, she started going by Milicent Patrick Trent. Her name was legally changed to Trent after the marriage, but she decided to add the Patrick back in. For a couple of years she stayed single, focusing on her own life and friends. It was the calmest romantic time in her life since college. She went to one party of a close friend of hers, Monique Fischer, with a business mogul named LaFayette Utter, but that was the only time she was seen publicly with him.

Along with Monique Fischer, Milicent had a lot of other close friends. Speaking from experience, this can be a symptom of being estranged from your family. You end up leaning a little harder on the friends in your life for love and support. Especially if you are as social as Milicent was, you find yourself not with one best friend but several, and behind them, a whole group of people who you consider close to you. You have the extra emotional bandwidth and time that you don't spend dealing with parents or siblings and in both my and Milicent's case, children. Although, I will admit that Milicent spent way more time with orphans than I do.

The calm didn't last long, though. By 1971, Milicent and Lee were seeing each other again. Their on and off again romance had been going for nearly two decades at this point. It was practically a habit. Whenever Lee found himself back in town for a long period of time and ran into Milicent, sparks were almost guaranteed to fly. Now, Lee was living at least partially in Canada, having surrendered the "Sherman Oaks Shangri-la" to Milicent in the divorce. There was no way he was taking that house away from her.

Milicent was still making attempts to connect with her family, mainly Ruth. When Gwen got married at age eighteen, Milicent was one of the guests and showed up dressed to the nines to celebrate her beloved niece. She was stunning in all black—high heels, giant sun hat, dress, even a fur. Gwen was married in Simi Valley, a small town to the north of Los Angeles, and the residents weren't used to seeing people like Milicent. Everyone kept asking Gwen who Milicent was, in awe. "That's my aunt," Gwen replied proudly. Ruth was exasperated by the spectacle, but Gwen was overjoyed to have her fabulous aunt at her wedding, dazzling the guests.

Milicent was determined to still be Milicent Patrick. Turning sixty didn't end her propensity for dramatic presentations, high heels and over-the-top outfits. Everywhere she went, Milicent still wore something fantastic, her hair in an elegant updo. It was 1975 and she was almost ten years past her last acting job. This wasn't Milicent Patrick's look for the big screen. This was her look for life.

Throughout the rest of the decade, Milicent stayed ensconced in her private wonderland in Sherman Oaks. The 1970s swirled around her and Milicent mostly paid events in the outside world no mind. Nixon, the Vietnam War, the oil crisis. At least she missed disco.

If you hide from the world long enough, it eventually comes to your door. It came knocking for Milicent in 1980.

It seemed like only a half an hour had gone by, but before I knew it, I had hit the bottom of the last Tupperware bin at Gwen's house. She had been telling me stories about Milicent for four hours. My iPhone was filled with photos and my purse was filled with keepsakes that Gwen insisted I take with me. Photographs, drawings, prints of portraits that Milicent had done for films, even two books of piano music that Milicent loved.

Feeling much more comfortable with Gwen than I had when I first arrived, I thought it was time to ask about some of the harder things. I told her about my struggle to find a death certificate for Milicent.

"Oh, she didn't pass away in Los Angeles. She wasn't buried there, either."

"I couldn't find her gravestone in any online databases."

"That's because there isn't one. She was cremated."

Mystery solved. What I had been searching for didn't exist.

"But you can go visit her, in a way."

Gwen told me where I could find Milicent's final resting place and gave me a copy of the eulogy that she wrote for Milicent, along with the funeral program that she designed. She even gave me a copy of the death certificate. When I said I couldn't overstate the kindness that Gwen and Frank showed me, I wasn't kidding. They opened their home and their hearts to me and I will forever be immensely grateful.

After everything was packed up, I asked for a picture with Gwen. I was filled with gratitude, sadness, excitement and triumph, but I held it together.[172] Gwen gave me a final hug before I got into the rental car. Once again, I marveled at how much she looked like Milicent. Now, I also marveled at how much she was like Milicent. Kind, gracious, funny, charming, loving. She was carrying Milicent's best traits on. Milicent might no longer be living, but I still found her.

The year 1980 began with a devastating blow to Milicent. At the start of the year, George Tobias went to the hospital. He

---

172 I totally pulled into a grocery store parking lot on the way back to the hotel and cried all over the rental car steering wheel.

had been suffering from a blockage in his intestinal tract and could no longer stand the pain. Doctors agreed to go in and do exploratory surgery to find out more about what was going on. In his stomach, they found a tumor. George had cancer. Milicent stayed by his side in the hospital.

A month later, on February 27, George died at Cedars Sinai Hospital in Los Angeles. Milicent was with him when he passed. Afterward, she was on hand to talk to journalists, informing them about how he died and that he was a working actor right up until his diagnosis. She put together a memorial service in Los Angeles for him, after which he was sent to be buried in New York City, where he was born. Milicent never got to visit his grave.

Milicent had lost her best friend of over thirty years. This tragedy happened during a downswing in her relationship with Lee and he was out of the country. The two men she normally counted on to get her through tough times were no longer there. Milicent's other good friends were there to bolster her, but tragedy wasn't done with her. It was coming straight to her door. Or, rather, smashing through it.

Just after the memorial, heavy rains in Los Angeles caused a mudslide to sweep through Milicent's home.[173] The deluge of thick dark mud took out walls, windows and furniture and covered the floor of her home. Outside, it annihilated her garden. Nearly the entire back of the house was destroyed. Milicent's Sherman Oaks sanctuary became a hell of mud, mold, broken glass and wrecked furniture. Devastated, Milicent went to stay with friends.

She was dispirited further when she discovered that her home insurance wouldn't cover the damage. Milicent even went on

---

173 We always need rain in Southern California, but we're rarely equipped to handle it. The soil, especially after wildfires caused and amplified by the dryness, has a hard time actually absorbing the water. Mudslides are common after heavy rains and are frequently fatal, causing damage to lives and property.

television to be interviewed by Consumer Reports about what happened and how she was stuck paying the cost for the disaster, but it didn't make a difference. She was on her own.

Up to this point, Milicent had survived like many self-employed artists: she saved and spent wisely. Repairing the damage to her home completely drained her savings. Neither Lee nor her family helped her. It was an intensely stressful time and her longtime adversary—migraines—got worse.

Fixing and refurbishing her home became Milicent's focus for the next few years. The loss of George, the mudslide and the financial stress overwhelmed her. She saw friends at parties and social gatherings, but no longer attended the lavish formal industry events she had once enjoyed.

In 1983, a sixty-eight-year-old Milicent was at a meeting for one of her women's theater charity groups called the Round Table. A woman named Adela Rogers St. Johns was being featured as a special speaker. Eighty-nine-year-old Adela had been an important and influential writer and journalist in California since 1912. Her career began at the *San Francisco Examiner*, one of the papers owned by William Randolph Hearst. During her speech, Adela talked about Hearst and San Simeon, raving about the place and extolling its beauty.

After the talk, Milicent approached Adela. They had met a few times before at different film industry events and the two women were friendly. Adela was also a prolific and talented screenwriter, penning an episode of *Alfred Hitchcock Presents* and films like *What Price Hollywood?* and *The Single Standard*. Milicent said to Adela, "You know, my father built San Simeon. I lived there for ten years. I haven't been back since."

Adela looked at Milicent and whispered, "Don't go. You'll be so disappointed."

Milicent was surprised to hear Adela's warning, especially after she gave such an emphatically positive speech about the place.

Apparently, when Hearst Castle was first given over to the state, the Parks and Recreation department didn't quite know what to do with it. It's not your average state park. It's like a cross between a nature preserve and Disney castle. When Adela visited after it became a historic site, she was saddened to see how rundown and weedy it had become.

It's hard to imagine a splendid place like Hearst Castle being described as rundown. But Adela was used to seeing the place in its heyday when William Randolph Hearst was there and the place was lively with parties. Now there were safety railings everywhere and Public Works garbage cans dotting all the pathways. It makes sense that Adela thought Milicent, as a person who grew up there, would have an even stronger reaction to the changes.

By the time Milicent turned back around though, all the women of the group had taken Adela's speech to heart. They wanted to schedule a trip to Hearst Castle, and they wanted Adela to come. This was a bunch of older, rich women. Older, rich women love going on group trips.

Adela really didn't want to go, but after her insistence just minutes earlier that all these women had to see Hearst Castle, she couldn't refuse. You can't mess with a bunch of strong-willed old women. A trip was scheduled, and Milicent went along, as well. Milicent packed some fabulous outfits, got into her giant Cadillac with her friend Elvie, and hit the road.

The Round Table women traveled in style. They weren't going to stay in a hotel. The group rented the home of George and Phoebe Hearst, the site of the original Hearst Ranch. This was a home that Milicent had seen but never stayed in, and it was still in beautiful condition. The trip took place in March, when things are starting to bloom in Southern California. Fortunately, the weather was mild, since Milicent arrived back to her childhood home dressed like a queen.

Milicent hadn't been back to Hearst Castle in over fifty years.

During that time, she had an eventful, successful life. She made it to Hollywood and made a living there, working alongside movie stars and socializing with the rich and famous. Milicent returned to the estate with her head held high, dressed in a floor-length black gown, topped with a wool cape, a massive golden necklace and a fur hat the size and floofiness of a fat, sleeping raccoon. She didn't just look like she belonged there. She looked like she owned the place. She looked like Millicent Hearst.

Milicent in front of the Neptune Pool. Look at that floofy hat! (*Author collection*)

Adela, Milicent and the rest of the group got a full tour of the Castle. Milicent took pictures in nearly all of the rooms, smiling and posing proudly. She even got to visit her old one-room schoolhouse down at the base of the hill. The best pictures of her from that day are the candid ones. In those, she smiles a different, smaller smile, the effect of childhood memories plain on her face.

Milicent was overjoyed to be back at Hearst Castle. When she asked the tour guides about her father though, she had the same experience that I did. No one had heard of him. Camille Rossi wasn't mentioned anywhere in the pamphlets or literature about the estate. He wasn't featured in any of the talks. His architectural feats were, but not his name.

She was upset. Milicent had been telling people about her

father's work at Hearst Castle for over five decades and finally back to see it again, she saw Camille's legacy everywhere. But his name was absent. It was as if her personal connection to all that grandeur didn't exist. She had always been proud of her childhood at Hearst Castle, coveting and trying to emulate the splendor there. It was disheartening to discover that her own claim to its history had been erased. For nearly her entire adult life, Milicent had been uncredited for the part she played in artistic history. Now, thanks to Camille's reprehensible behavior, her association with the history of Hearst Castle was unknown, as well. She spoke to some of the historians at Hearst Castle and offered her time to them, in which she could tell her father's story and consequently, her own.

Uncovering Camille's legacy became Milicent's project over the next year. She tracked down workers and artisans who knew her father—the ones who were still alive and didn't hate Camille's guts. Then, she interviewed them over the phone and through written correspondence about what they remembered of Camille and his work. Milicent wrote a long article about her childhood at San Simeon for the Hearst Castle historians. One of them traveled down to her now-rebuilt Sherman Oaks home to interview her about it, the same interview I got to hear thirty years later in the Hearst Castle historical library with a pair of old headphones.

Milicent had been going by the name Milicent Patrick Trent, but now she put the Rossi back in her name. She referred to herself as Milicent Patrick Rossi Trent, reclaiming her own heritage and history, even though her family had ostracized her. It was her name and her history, too. Even though I'm estranged from my own family, I've never changed my last name. It's my name, too. Like Milicent, I can make it my own. This final name change reflected Milicent's remarkable life in all its changes and experiences, marvels and tragedies.

A journalist at the *Los Angeles Times* found out about her quest and ran an article about it at the start of the new year, January 1986. This was the article that became the key to my finding Milicent's post-Universal identity. Milicent told reporter Evelyn Wolfe all about Camille's adventurous life.

"'He was flamboyant, all right,' Trent smiled. 'But he was much more than that.'"

She went on to talk about Camille's engineering accomplishments, including the famous tree-moving story.

Milicent worked so hard to unearth her father's legacy at Hearst Castle and it saddens me to say that it really didn't work. Camille still isn't mentioned on the tours of the estate and is barely mentioned in any of the books or literature on the subject. It's sad for Milicent, but honestly, I don't feel that bad for him.

What Milicent did unearth was her own happiness, something that had been buried since George's death. Publicly talking about her childhood at Hearst Castle made Milicent feel pride in her life again. In the recorded interview, she talked enthusiastically with the historian about her work as an actress and an artist, although she did admit that she hadn't been in any movies recently. Milicent still had her SAG card at seventy-one years old.

Milicent was reinvigorated and finally got back to the social life she had retreated from. Before long, she crossed paths with Lee. The two started dating, picking up their thirty-year-long relationship, even though Lee was still in Canada most of the time.

A quiet year and a half later, the couple planned to get married again. Legally, it would make things easier for them, especially with Lee gone so much. Romantically, they figured that since they were both in their seventies and couldn't seem to get rid of each other, they should tie the knot a second time. But before they could, tragedy struck.

In January 1988, while Lee was in Canada on Con-Stan business, he passed away suddenly.[174] He was seventy-eight. Milicent was devastated. She would never have another serious relationship or marry again.

The heartbreak marked the beginning of the end of her life.

---

174   I was unable to find his cause of death.

13

Fade Out

In 1988, while still grieving for Lee, Milicent's health went into decline.

Along with the migraines, Milicent had developed Parkinson's disease. Parkinson's is a neurodegenerative disorder and its progression is often slow. There is no cure and the cause is unknown. There are some treatment options, but there are a lot of complications from Parkinson's and they are often fatal. She began to move more slowly and have issues with muscle stiffness, tremors and keeping her balance. It made walking difficult and her limbs sore. Not only was it impossible to drive and difficult for her to travel, but she no longer wanted to be seen in public. She needed a cane to walk and she traded in her beloved fitted gowns and glamorous outfits for loose, flowing black slacks and dresses that helped hide it. Milicent didn't feel like herself anymore and rarely left the house.

Time was running out for Milicent to reconcile with her sister.[175] Ruth would sometimes visit with Gwen, but they were

---

175 Ulrich had passed away in 1966, without reconciliation.

still not close. Ruth kept her low opinion of Milicent, even though Milicent was seventy-seven years old, walking with a cane, and clearly not living whatever crazy Hollywood life Ruth imagined. She was concerned, even though Gwen was now a responsible, successful therapist and mother, that Milicent's ways might corrupt her daughter somehow.

In 1992, when Parkinson's started making her life really tough, Milicent called Ruth and asked her to come stay with her in Sherman Oaks. Gwen had moved to Northern California and Milicent wasn't very close with Lawrence. Ruth refused and within a year, at seventy-two years old, passed away.

Everyday life became difficult for Milicent. Between the Parkinson's and the migraines, she took a substantial amount of pain medication to stay comfortable. She mostly read, watched movies and slept. Tremors in her hands prevented her from drawing. Her pens and charcoals lay dormant in her unused art studio.

Friends would come stay with Milicent and take care of her for brief periods of time, but there's only so much that non-medical professionals can do. Eventually, Milicent was forced to hire in-home care and sign up for Meals on Wheels, a daily meal delivery service for the elderly.

The next time Gwen visited, she was horrified. Milicent was eighty years old and living in filth. The home care people she hired were there only to take care of Milicent. They barely did anything to keep up the house. Milicent, frail and barely mobile, could not clean her home on her own. She wasn't eating well. She'd have a Pop-Tart for breakfast, half a banana for lunch, and whatever the Meals on Wheels service brought her for dinner.

That night, Milicent wanted Gwen to sleep in the bedroom with her. Gwen made up a bed on the floor next to Milicent. A little while later, she woke up to the horrifying sensation of something crawling over her. Gwen turned on the light and discovered a horde of rats running over her, over the bedroom, over the entire house. That was that last straw. She couldn't let her aunt live like this.

But Milicent was adamant about staying in her home. She desperately did not want to move into a care facility. Milicent's house was the last remaining part of her identity. It was her castle she had been curating for over twenty-five years. Gwen talked to the home care people and organized a schedule. She would fly down from Northern California every weekend and take care of Milicent. They would take care of her during the week. Milicent was overjoyed to see her niece so often, but she was reluctant to let Gwen take over her care. She hated being so helpless. She felt humiliated.

The first weekend, Gwen cleaned the entire house, top to bottom. She called an exterminator to take care of the rats. She cooked hot meals and to Milicent's displeasure, she gave her baths. But after a few weekends of this, Milicent's happiness overcame her humiliation. Her house looked like a home again.

Gwen couldn't tell if Milicent was happy in the beginning. At the first doctor appointment she took Milicent to, she spoke to the doctor privately. She told him that Milicent never smiled, never looked happy. She wanted to know if Milicent had said anything to the doctor about being upset with Gwen taking care of her.

The doctor set her straight: "She can't smile anymore, Gwen. The muscles in her face make it impossible."

He told Gwen that Milicent absolutely loved having her there and that she wished Gwen would move in. But Gwen had a great job up in Northern California and couldn't give it up.

Once Gwen realized that Milicent only looked unhappy, she took it upon herself to make sure Milicent was enjoying life as much as she could. Gwen and Frank set up big Christmas trees and decorated Milicent's home for the holidays. They'd stay with her for New Year's and fix mimosas for her. She was able to keep her sense of humor.

"Darling, I'll have another." Milicent would say to Frank, and he'd pour the champagne. When he reached for the orange juice, she'd say, "Oh, no juice. No juice."

"Well, Milly," he'd say. "That's not a mimosa."

"That's correct," she'd agree.

Now that her situation at home had improved so much, friends came to stay again. Couples from the Italian American club, women from her women's groups, and close friends like Mara Corday would visit occasionally. Milicent loved regaling people with tales of her life and all the adventures she had in Hollywood. She'd reminisce with these visiting friends or entertain Gwen with stories about famous people that she knew. While talking to Milicent's friends, Gwen finally got the family rumors disproved.

Milicent's friends were horrified when Gwen told them that her family had assumed that Milicent was a prostitute. They couldn't believe what the Rossis thought of Milicent, that she had a shady, immoral life in the film industry.

"Shady? Mil? No. Everyone loves her."

At age eighty-two, Milicent was living comfortably and she still had her spirit. One day, Gwen wanted to make sure that Milicent had her affairs in order, so she called an attorney to come and talk to Milicent privately.

When he arrived, he was a tall, handsome older gentleman and Milicent was immediately aflutter. As Gwen was leaving the room, he asked Milicent how old she was. She looked him right in the eye and said, "I'm sixty, darling." Gwen's jaw dropped as Milicent shot her the best hold-your-tongue look she could manage with her Parkinson's. Gwen said, "Mum's the word, sweetheart. If you're sixty, I'm about thirty-five," which made Milicent laugh.

Later that year however, things took a turn for the worse. Milicent began to lose her ability to communicate. Gwen took a week off from work and took her to the doctor. He called

Gwen back a few days later, after he had run some tests. Milicent had breast cancer and it had already spread. He told Gwen that Milicent was going to be in a severe amount of pain, if she wasn't already. She needed to be moved to a hospital immediately; home care was no longer an option.

The doctor knew Milicent would not agree to move out of her home. He insisted that it would be unconscionable for her not to go, though. Milicent was not going to live much longer. She needed a hospital to manage her pain. Gwen agreed.

It wasn't just the pain that forced Milicent to move out of her Sherman Oaks home. It was also her love for Gwen. It wasn't possible for Gwen to uproot her life to spend every day in Los Angeles. So Milicent finally agreed to leave Hollywood forever and move to a hospice care facility in Roseville, California, a location close to Gwen's home.

Every morning and every night, Gwen would visit her at the facility. But being away from her home drained what little spirit Milicent had left. Not even two weeks later, Milicent started to slip away.

The day that Milicent died, Gwen got into the hospital bed and held her. Gwen told her how much she loved her and how much God loved her. Milicent shook her head. Gwen insisted that God loved her always. Milicent started to cry.

"God doesn't love me."

It was the last thing she said. She took her family's message to heart, right to the end. But she wasn't alone.

On February 24, 1998, at eighty-two years old, Milicent Patrick passed away.

The sun was out with all its California splendor when I drove to San Francisco Bay. It was the day after my visit with Gwen and with me was a pile of papers: a copy of Milicent's death certificate, the eulogy and the funeral program. I didn't want to read them until I was at her final resting place.

After Milicent passed, she was cremated. Gwen and Frank organized a memorial service for her a few weeks later at a church in Hollywood so that all her friends and colleagues could attend. Instead of traditional white lilies, Gwen ordered long-stemmed red roses. Milicent's life couldn't be represented by something demure. She was a long-stemmed red rose.

The program listed every name she ever called herself, from Mildred Elizabeth Fulvia Rossi to Milicent Patrick Rossi Trent. No matter the name, she was always Milicent Patrick.

I sat down on the edge of the sparkling water and read the words Gwen spoke at the memorial service. "She lent her presence to art, society, humanity and to those she held dear."

Gwen didn't bury Milicent in Hollywood. She and Frank brought her back up to Northern California. They hired a small airplane to take her ashes up and over the San Francisco Bay. Milicent was always larger-than-life. In death, she needed to be as well. It's the perfect spot for her, part of the picturesque and expansive waters of the Pacific Ocean. But she is so many other places, too. I spent so long looking for her final resting place, not realizing that I was in it.

Milicent Patrick's final resting place is in every single *Creature from the Black Lagoon* T-shirt, every Metaluna Mutant toy, every VHS tape of *Fantasia*, every DVD of *The Shape of Water*. It's on the desk of every female animator and in the pen of every woman doodling a monster in the margins of her notebook. It's always been there. It's just been hidden, purposely obfuscated.

Now, it's in every copy of this book, in your hands or in your ears.

Guillermo del Toro wanted to create *The Shape of Water* because when he saw *Creature from the Black Lagoon* as a child, all he wanted was for Kay and the Creature to end up together, to have a happy ending. *The Shape of Water* is a reimagining of that story, where the woman loves the monster. Instead of sinking to the bottom of that black lagoon, the Creature becomes a hero. He gets his happy ending.

With this book, Milicent gets her happy ending, too. I didn't have to reimagine anything, though. I just had to bring what was always there to light.

At Milicent's memorial service, Gwen shared something that her aunt would always tell her.

"Everyone is beautiful. Some choose to share it, while others hide it. It's much better to share!"

The beauty of Milicent's life and work was, like that of many other women, purposefully hidden to rob her of her power and her influence. Milicent Patrick is the lady from the black lagoon and she's not alone. She's raised out of it now, but there are so many other women—in every industry, living and dead—who are still in there. So many other stories are sunken in the depths of history and so many women are still shouldering the burden of harassment and abuse while trying to create. Thanks to technology and the bravery of countless women, the tides are finally changing.

When I was a teenager, Milicent showed me the way forward into the creative life that I wanted to live. She demonstrated that it was possible for me to make the art that I wanted to make. Now, as an adult, she has shown me the way forward to help create the world I want to live in. Uncovering her life over the past two years has helped me see the things I need to do to protect more women from her fate. It's helped me be brave, be strong and be loud.

Every day, having Milicent's portrait on my arm doesn't just remind me that I belong in the monster world. It reminds me not to put up with all the bullshit that comes my way. It reminds me to be fearless and demand the things I deserve.

Milicent Patrick deserves to be known as the artistic pioneer that she was. But she's also a symbol for why we need to work harder, to speak up and to help other women. Milicent never saw the renown she should have during her lifetime and she was a beautiful, able-bodied, straight, well-off white woman. She had all the privilege that a woman of her time could have and it still wasn't enough to protect her from men like Bud Westmore. I can only imagine the number of female artists not as privileged as Milicent who didn't even get in the door.

Thousands and thousands of women are out there, feeling alone in their creative passions. Thousands more haven't even entertained the idea of making art because they can't imagine a place for themselves in that world.

Milicent Patrick's legacy isn't just a body of influential work. It's also an invitation.

EPILOGUE

Years after Milicent's death, her legacy got an interesting ally. Bud Westmore's obfuscation was no match for the internet.

With the rise of the Web, hard-core cinephiles started to post and share more detailed credits for films. Obscure memorabilia that had lived for decades in the moldy basements of fans was now widely available for anyone with access to the Web. Coincidentally, the year Milicent died was the year Jeff Bezos, Amazon.com founder, bought IMDb and superpowered the online film database.

Monster nerds on the hunt for information uncovered the truth: the Creature wasn't designed by Bud Westmore, who has sole credit for the makeup in the film's screen credits, but by Milicent. Female fans were now able to discover her.

When I was a teenage monster fan, there were a few women horror filmmakers that I knew of and they all seemed like outliers. Years later, when I moved to Los Angeles I was thrilled to discover that I was wrong. I met countless other women in the industry, in the genre film industry, no less. Along with actors, there were directors, fellow producers, cinematographers, editors, writers, special effects artists, prop makers, any film job you could think of. All huge fans of horror. It was a legion of women who grew up thinking that they were the only ones because the film industry didn't showcase or hire them. I realized that they had always been there, making art, making films and smashing down the doors of that boys-only clubhouse. That's when I truly felt at home in Los Angeles.

These filmmakers were the smartest, most ambitious and supportive women that I had ever met. They worked so hard and constantly reached out to their community of other creative women to offer advice and support, a community they welcomed me into. For the first time in my life, I truly understood the value of female friendship, of a support system of women. Not just being able to gripe about tampon brands and the best kind of black eyeliner, but to talk about being a woman in business, about what it felt like to get catcalled, about learning how to word emails so men wouldn't talk down to you. It was revolutionary. I felt like a gigantic weight had been lifted, a weight that I wasn't aware I had been carrying.

For so long, I thought of Milicent as being on her own in a sea of male colleagues. But her story seems less sad to me now when I think of her surrounded by other female creatives to share her frustrations and joys with—at Disney, in modeling and as an actress.

Many of the women I met are now my friends, colleagues and always my inspiration. I can't imagine my life without this network of brilliant, creative women who are always ready to offer work advice, listen to me complain and make me laugh. Like me, some of these women were inspired and encouraged by Milicent's work. Also like me, some of these women went on to use that inspiration and encouragement as they entered the film and television industry.

Horror director Chelsea Stardust (*All That We Destroy*, *Satanic Panic*) had a very similar experience when she discovered Milicent:

I have been a huge fan of the Universal monster movies since I was a little girl. *Dracula*, *The Wolfman* and *Creature from the Black Lagoon* were always my favorites. When I learned Milicent Patrick was the actual creator of the Gill Man design it opened my eyes to the possibilities that were available for women in the entertainment industry. She helped pave the way for women like me and I am forever grateful for her perseverance and dedication.

Eryn Krueger Mekash, Emmy-award-winning makeup artist best known for her work on the television series *American Horror Story* was inspired by Milicent on her road to success in the special effects world:

Milicent Patrick set her mark on Hollywood as a true Renaissance woman; she was creative in all aspects and paved the way for other artists to continue through her successes even if she was never formally acknowledged for it. Today would be a different scenario; she would be hailed Queen.

Award-winning illustrator, concept artist and painter Karla Ortiz was encouraged by the existence of Milicent Patrick while she was already working in the male-dominated world of film. Her concept art has been used for many films, including Marvel blockbusters like *Doctor Strange* and *Black Panther*:

When I was younger, all my artistic inspirations were men. It's not something that you do on purpose, one just simply tends to admire that which one has access to. The desire to paint, to be an artist, for me was strong enough that I pushed through, even if everyone who I admired as a successful artist didn't look like me. I found out about the many incredible women and minorities in my industry entirely too late in my career, but even so, it was deeply heartwarming... Stories of people who made great things are inspiring and motivating, because they give us the ability to see ourselves doing those great acts. Their stories give us the strength we need when life demands it the most. Which is why digging through the remains of history and shedding light on the incredible Milicent Patrick is an immensely important act for so many of us... She pursued her passion and was brilliant at it, creating one of the most iconic monsters in history... Her story can and will inspire so many of us to shed our fears and pursue our craft without hesitation, possibly as Milicent herself would have wished for us to do.

It wasn't just the Creature that brought people to Milicent, either. Filmmaker and journalist BJ Colangelo (*Powerbomb*) found her through her work on *This Island Earth*.

I fell in love with the work of Milicent Patrick before I was old enough to comprehend the revolutionary woman she was. My father was a closet sci-fi geek and showed me *This Island Earth* when I was about four years old. The Metaluna Mutant was the most terrifying and fascinating creature I'd ever seen. It was a very real nightmare that would haunt me for years. As I grew older and began to learn the mechanics of creature design and the artists behind them, I was always a little disappointed to see male after male credited in creating the monsters and killers I dearly loved. I felt alien for being a female-identifying person in love with horror, which appeared to be molded and maintained exclusively by men. It wasn't until college when I fell headfirst back into the Universal monsters, namely *Creature from the Black Lagoon* (my all-time favorite), that I became aware of Patrick and her impact on horror iconography. Making the realization that my favorite monster was created by a woman was like a sign from the universe making me feel welcome in a genre that held my heart. Subconsciously, it always makes me smile a little more knowing that two of the monsters that have resonated with me the deepest were made by a woman.

The Metaluna Mutant is loved by many creators, including bestselling comics/animation writer and artist Kate Leth:

Like many others, I first saw the Metaluna Mutant in *Mystery Science Theater 3000: The Movie.* It was a staple in my house as a young teen, to the point that quotes from it became part of my family lexicon. Of course, the crew of the Satellite of Love were riffing on *This Island Earth*, but I developed such an incredible love for the weird, nonsensical movie and its aliens; particularly the Metaluna Mutant. He's such a goofy, wonderful, endearing creation—part bug, part man, all slacks. The experience of watching that movie with my parents, long before our family dissolved and things got ugly, is such an indelible memory of a time I felt safe and happy. The Mutant became a symbol of that, for me, I think. I started collecting figures of him in my early twenties and continue to do so to this day. I have a tattoo of him that is either mistaken for the aliens from *Mars Attacks* or makes me an instant friend when people recognize it. Finding out that he was created by a woman who had her credit taken by a man has only increased my affinity for him—I can certainly identify with that. I guess I love him the way some people love the Wolfman or Frankenstein's monster, but to me he's the underdog of Universal monsters. He doesn't get as many figures. Nobody's dressed as him at Universal Studios. All the same, he's my favorite monster, and I'm forever grateful to Milicent Patrick for bringing him into my life.

And it's not just women, either. Milicent's legacy has rippled through the film industry, even for male creators.

Mike Hill—the award-winning sculptor and special effects artist who was the lead creature designer for *The Shape of Water*—has drawn great artistic inspiration from Milicent's work:

Creature from the Black Lagoon is a perfect monster movie… It's a story that is reminiscent of some of the great monster movies, but what set it apart was the Creature itself. It's a perfect design. Not too subtle, not overthought. A man-fish, complete with armor, gills and deadly talons. The blending together of a human being and a fish is actually not as simple as it sounds and can easily come off as cartoonish or grotesque. But Milicent Patrick's design was the perfect amalgamation. Beautiful, lithe, deadly and believable. The face itself is compelling to look at and although seemingly devoid of expression, somehow it speaks to us. We read into it. An extremely convincing composition. There have been various fish-people since and in the future there will be surely more to come, but there will only ever be one Creature from the Black Lagoon.

Milicent's legacy continues in the work of all of these fantastic artists. It continues in all of the women who saw her contribution to film history and realized that they could do it, too. No, Milicent didn't bring the Creature into the world single-handedly. Yes, she was part of a team. That's the point. She was part of that team. She was *there*. Many women have been there, behind-the-scenes in the film industry, from the very beginning. Because their contributions have been obscured and their presence discouraged with harassment, generations of potential female filmmakers have been impeded from being there, too.

Things are slowly improving in the film industry. According to Women and Hollywood statistics, in 2017, 11 percent of directors of the two hundred fifty top-grossing films were women, up from 2016, when it was only 7 percent. In 2018, Greta Gerwig became the fifth woman in history to be nominated for the Oscar for Best Director.

It's improvement, but it's paltry improvement. Eleven percent is pathetic, especially when more than half the population identifies as female. Women still make up a small percentage of almost every single behind-the-scenes role in Hollywood. On top of struggling to get hired, they deal with abuse, harassment, fear, intimidation and credit theft every single day. We have such a long way to go. The good news is that we've got the same ally that Milicent Patrick's legacy had.

Thanks to the internet, women can communicate, organize and create more than ever before. The #MeToo movement could not have happened without the power of the internet. There's a sea change going on. The reign of men like Bud Westmore is coming to an end. Good riddance, motherfuckers.

White men have always held sway over the world of monsters. In film, they're the majority of the ones writing about them, designing them, sculpting them, playing them, directing them, fighting them. That needs to change. Milicent designed one of the most iconic monsters of all time, but the Creature is still male, played by white dudes. Everyone deserves the catharsis of seeing themselves crushing a building. Everyone deserves to see themselves with terrible power and agency. Everyone also deserves to see themselves battling the creatures with terrible power and agency. We need female characters, asexual characters, fat characters, nonbinary characters, queer characters, characters of color, disabled characters, trans characters as both monsters and the heroes fighting them.

Why? Because monster stories are cool. They're fun and exciting and sometimes cheesy. But they can be important, too. As Guillermo del Toro said during his 2018 Golden Globes acceptance speech for Best Director:

> Since childhood, I've been faithful to monsters. I have been saved and absolved by them, because monsters, I believe, are patron saints of our blissful imperfection, and they allow and embody the possibility of failing.

Milicent's life was shaped in part by real-life monsters and the obstacles put in her way by a patriarchal culture. But the lives of future artists and creators don't have to be. It's up to female filmmakers to keep making great art. It's up to those who find success to hold the door open for aspiring female filmmakers. It's up to male allies to call out their scumbag male colleagues and make spaces safer for women and marginalized voices. It's up to actors to demand inclusion riders that require diversity on a film's cast and crew with their contracts. It's up to fans to demand films that are more inclusive, both in front of and behind the camera.

Milicent Patrick was a woman before her time. That time is now.

★ ★ ★ ★ ★

AFTERWORD

Chasing down Milicent Patrick was a researcher's nightmare. Or maybe a researcher's dream, depending on how much of a masochist you are. She often got no credit for her work, and just as often, she fabricated parts of her life. Between the two, I had to be careful about what I could put down as fact. I wrote only about the work and events that I could verify the existence of.

That said, Milicent, in her usual way, had many different versions of her own artistic résumé.

She claimed involvement in many more projects for the screen—both animated and live-action—that, try as I might, I could not find evidence of, like being a "Bugs Bunny Expert" for Warner Brothers and designing Kim Novak's makeup for Alfred Hitchcock's *Vertigo*. Some of them have some grains of truth. On a couple of the résumés, Milicent claimed she was the youngest ever costume designer for Paramount Studios at age fifteen, working as a "ghost designer." I can only assume this means that she worked for no credit, as opposed to designing sheets with holes cut in them for people to wear. Milicent was still living in San Simeon when she was fifteen, so that can't be true. But with the boxes of Milicent's effects that Gwen let me look through were many fashion illustrations. It was possible that she was designing costumes in an uncredited position at some point in her career in Hollywood.

I'm never going to stop keeping my eyes and ears open for information about Milicent and I hope that someday, I'll have more answers.

While that's not particularly satisfying, to find something that is, all you have to do is look at the cover of this book. Matt Buck, the artist whose vision for an awesome Milicent Patrick tattoo set in motion a series of events that would change my life forever, illustrated the cover. I'm telling you, finding a talented tattoo artist is worth it.

It meant a lot to me to have Matt as the cover artist for this book. It's strange that the first thing readers see is the end of a nearly three-year journey and it's strange to have it all come back around. It's just like in the movies.

But as this story shows, sometimes life just works out like that.

ACKNOWLEDGMENTS

Holy shit.

Telling Milicent's story required a lot of help behind-the-scenes and I have so many magnificent human beings to thank. First off, my terrific agent, Brady McReynolds. You're a champion and this book wouldn't exist without you. I'll never be able to give the JABberwocky Literary team enough high fives. My editor, Peter Joseph. From the first time we talked about this book, you really fucking got it. Thank you for being so marvelous and making this book so much better. Thank you for making my fish dick jokes funnier. Natalie Hallak, Linette Kim, the entire Hanover Square Press team. You're all gems. Laura Gianino, you helped bring this book to the world and I will be forever grateful.

David Schow, you were the one who handed the torch to me. A thousand thanks and a thousand slices of pie. Tom Weaver, for all the initial help that sent me on my way. The Hearst Castle librarians, historians and tour guides, for all your time and assistance. Ned Comstock at the USC Cinematic Arts Library. You went above and beyond. The countless Los Angeles Public librarians. You're all heroes. Mindy Johnson, you fucking goddess, for the wealth of information and kindness. Michele Wells and Ken Shue, you saved my ass. Carol McKenzie for her stellar transcription services.

To the countless friends who went on trips with me and made connections for me, thank you, thank you, thank you. Kate Gaffney and Mick Ignis, especially. Belinda Cases and Chuck Martinez, you helped both me and this book land on solid ground in Los Angeles. Ross Blocher, for the early reading, typo hunting and finally getting me into Disney. BJ Colangelo, Chelsea Stardust, Eryn Krueger Mekash, Kate Leth, Karla Ortiz, Jovanka Vuckovic and Mike Hill. You're all bad motherfuckers. Thank you for sharing your love for Milicent's work and for bringing your art into the world.

My therapist, Chris. I wouldn't have been able to write this book if you weren't always keeping my brain from spontaneously combusting.

All of the magnificent listeners of *Reading Glasses*, thank you for coming on this journey with me and for all the support you've given this book. Brea Grant, for being a stellar cohost and an even better friend.

Adam and Candace Cultraro, for being my California family. Sultan Saeed al Darmaki, my brother from another mother. I'm lucky to have you as my boss and I'm even luckier to have you as my friend. Frank Woodward, I have no clue what I would do without your support, your friendship and your wisdom. May the Ghost Bear never get you. Milicent's family, your kindness, patience and generosity are more deeply appreciated than I'll ever be able to express.

Matt Buck, goddamn. Your vision for a fucking excellent tattoo started this whole thing and your gorgeous cover for this book ended it. Thank you for all the tattoos and thank you for being a part of this. To Allan Amato, for taking all my favorite pictures of me.

My mermaid coven, my best friends, my lady bosses, my art queens, Lauren Panepinto and Allison Cimino. Your love, encouragement and inspiration not only made this book better, but made me better. Lauren, you've earned a million Last Words for all the help you gave every part of this book. I will happily spend the rest of my natural life shaking them up for you. Barbara and Joe—the Parentpintos—for all the hugs and support.

All the readers, booksellers, and librarians who embraced Milicent and supported this book. A thousand, thousand thanks to you. You made her story soar.

Finally, to all the women carrying on her legacy, my ever-lasting love. You're all heroes.

SOURCES

"Actor Is Found Dead in Auto." *The Independent Record*, 4 Sept. 1950.

Bell, Jack R. "Three Masquerade as Film 'Monsters' for Luncheon." *Kalamazoo Gazette*, Feb. 1954.

"Behind the Scenes in Hollywood." *The Vidette Messenger*, 8 Jul. 1960.

Boutelle, Sara Holmes. *Julia Morgan, Architect*. New York: Abbeville Press, 1995.

Carroll, Harrison. "Behind the Scenes in Hollywood." *Greensburg Daily News*, 24 Dec. 1956.

Carroll, Harrison. "Behind the Scenes in Hollywood." *The Index Journal*, 6 Oct. 1960.

Carroll, Harrison. "In Hollywood." *Lancester Eagle Gazette*, 16 Apr. 1959.

Carroll, Harrison. "In Hollywood." *New Castle News*, 27 Jan. 1969.

"Changes in Men's and Women's Labor Force Participation Rates." US Bureau of Labor Statistics. Accessed January 10, 2007. www.bls.gov.

Chouinard: A Living Legacy. California: Chouinard Foundation, 2001.

Coffman, Taylor. *The builders behind the castles: George Loorz & the F. C. Stolte Co.* San Luis Obispo County Historical Society, 1990.

Corby, Jane. "Science-Fictions Monster—Who Invents Them? A Girl!" *The Brooklyn Eagle*, 14 Feb. 1954.

"Career Nixes Title." *The Daily Notes*, 22 Nov. 1951.

"Earth Shakes for Astronauts." *Van Nuys Valley News*, 6 Apr. 1971.

"George Tobias Obituary." *The Des Moines Register*, 28 Feb. 1980.

"Graham Suicide Letter Interrupted by Friend." *Los Angeles Times*, 19 Sept. 1950.

Fate, Vincent Di. "The Fantastic Mystery of Milicent Patrick." TOR. Accessed October 27, 2011. Tor.com.

Hearst Castle Historian. "Milicent Patrick." 17 Aug. 1983.

Helmer, Vanessa. "A Quick History of Fashion Modeling." The Balance Careers. Accessed April 21, 2018. www.thebalancecareers.com.

Hill, Libby. "New Study Reveals Fewer Women Working Behind the Scenes in Hollywood." *Los Angeles Times*, 12 Jan. 2017.

Howie, William. "Baroness Wins Makeup Fame." *Los Angeles Examiner*, 13 Jul. 1952

Johnson, Mindy, et al. *Ink & Paint: The Women of Walt Disney's Animation*. California: Disney Editions, 2017.

Kastner, Victoria, and Stephen T. Hearst. *Hearst Ranch: Family, Land, and Legacy*. New York: Abrams, 2013.

Kastner, Victoria, and Victoria Garagliano. *Hearst Castle: The Biography of a Country House*. New York: Abrams, 2000.

Kay, Frances Russell. "Antans festival is 'gambol on green.'" *Van Nuys Valley News*, 21 Jul. 1977.

Kay, Frances Russell. "Friends luncheon all for Miss 'L.G.'" *Van Nuys Valley News*, 12 Jan. 1977.

Kay, Frances Russell. "Never Mind Reasons Just Send Invitations." *Van Nuys Valley News*, 10 Oct. 1974.

Kay, Frances Russell. "Partygoers Not Themselves When They Dress For Cause." *Van Nuys Valley News*, 2 Nov. 1967.

Kay, Frances Russell. "There's Good Looking For City's Art Lovers." *Van Nuys Valley News*, 28 Nov. 1972.

Kilday, Gregg. "Study: Women Held 18 Percent of Key Behind-the-Camera Roles in 2017's Top Movies." *The Hollywood Reporter*. Accessed January 10, 2018. www.hollywoodreporter.com.

Kilgallen, Dorothy. "Around New York." *News Journal*, 9 Dec. 1954.

Lamb, Dr. Frank W., et al. *San Simeon, A Brief History*. California: Poor Richard's Press, 1983.

Lauzen, Dr. Martha. "Still Too Few Women behind the Scenes in Hollywood." *Women's Media Center*. Accessed January 28, 2016. www.womensmedia-center.com.

Lewis, Oscar. *Fabulous San Simeon*. California: California Historical Society, 1958.

Loe, Nancy E. *Hearst Castle: An Interpretive History of W. R. Hearst's San Simeon estate*. Companion Press, 1994.

Luban, Milton. "Black Lagoon Diverting Science-Fiction Meller." *The Hollywood Reporter*, 9 Feb. 1954.

Maas, Virginia. "Photos for the News." *Van Nuys Valley News*, 24 Jun. 1971.

Mallory, Michael. *Universal Studios Monsters: A Legacy of Horror.* New York: Universe Publishing, 2009.

Marlowe, Peter. "A Brief History of Modelling." The Model Archives of Marlowe Press. Accessed November 2016. www.modelscomposites.com.

Melgarejo, A. "The Greatest Volcanoes of Mexico." *National Geographic,* Sept. 1910.

"Memorable Night at the Theater in Offing for ANTANS." *Van Nuys Valley News,* 11 Jan. 1970.

Morgan, Julia, et al. *San Simeon Revisited.* California: The Library Associates, California Polytechnic State University, 1987.

"Mrs. America: Women's Roles in the 1950s." Public Broadcasting Service. www.pbs.org.

Muscatine, Doris. *Old San Francisco: The Biography of a City from Early Days to the Earthquake.* New York: Putnam, 1975.

"Obituary, George Tobias, 78." *Asbury Park Press,* 28 Feb. 1980.

Perine, Robert. *Chouinard, an Art Vision Betrayed: The Story of the Chouinard Art Institute, 1921-1972.* California: Artra Publishing, 1985.

Phillips, Helen Charlot. *Pink and Blue Laughter.* Los Angeles: Hollywood House, 1944.

"Radio's Graham Commits Suicide." *The Independent,* 4 Sept. 1950.

"Radio Star Graham Commits Suicide." *Los Angeles Times,* 4 Sept. 1950.

Rubin, Joan Shelley, and Scott E. Casper. *The Oxford Encyclopedia of American Cultural and Intellectual History.* New York: Oxford University Press, 2013.

Skotak, Robert. "Queen of the Monster Makers." *Famous Monsters of Filmland,* July 1978.

Smith, Margarita Griggs. *The San Simeon Story: the Romantic Story of San Simeon, 1827-1958*. Minneapolis: Star-Reporter Pub. Co., 1958.

Taylor, Ethel M. "San Fernando Valley Living." *Van Nuys Valley News*, 26 Jan. 1967.

"The Beauty Who Loves the Beasts." *Mirror Magazine*. Feb. 1954.

Wadsworth, Ginger, and Julia Morgan. *Julia Morgan, Architect of Dreams*. Minneapolis: Lerner Publishing Group, 1990.

"WAIF Makes Waves on Benefit Cruise." *Van Nuys Valley News*, 15 Oct. 1970.

Weaver, Tom. *The Creature Chronicles: Exploring the Black Lagoon Trilogy*. North Carolina: McFarland, 2017.

Westmore, Frank, and Muriel Davidson. *The Westmores of Hollywood*. Philadelphia: Lippincott, 1976.

Winchester, Simon. *A Crack in the Edge of the World: America and the Great California Earthquake of 1906*. New York: HarperCollins Publishers, 2006.

Wolfe, Evelyn De. "Daughter Traces Builder's Role at Hearst Castle." *Los Angeles Times*, 12 Jan. 1986.

"Women in Animation: Numbers on the Rise." *Animation Career Review*. Accessed March 27, 2017, www.animationcareerreview.com.

"World Book Online Reference Center." *World Book*. www.worldbookonline.com.

INTERVIEWS

Gwen Ankers, June 2016
BJ Colangelo, March 2018
Mike Hill, June 2018
Kate Leth, May 2018
Eryn Krueger Mekash, May 2018
Karla Ortiz, June 2018
Chelsea Stardust, March 2018

INDEX

Page numbers in italics refer to photographs.

READER'S GUIDE

QUESTIONS FOR DISCUSSION

1. Would Milicent Patrick's life have been different if she had spent her formative years somewhere other than the Hearst Castle estate?

2. Who, among the adults in Milicent's adolescence, had the most influence on her?

3. How did Milicent's self-made Hollywood persona change her career? Would a persona affect your own career?

4. What kind of monster would you have liked to see Milicent design?

5. Why would you say it is important for women to be involved behind the scenes in films? What about horror films, in particular?

6. Do you think things would have turned out differently for Milicent if she'd confronted Bud Westmore and fought back?

7. Author Mallory O'Meara found many parallels between her life and Milicent's. Can you empathize with any part of Milicent's story?

8. What would you say Milicent's legacy is?

9. If you could ask Milicent one question, what would it be?